A Communicative Grammar

Interactions one

Third Edition

Elaine Kirn
West Los Angeles College

Darcy Jack
University of Phoenix
Tucson Unified School District

The McGraw-Hill Companies, Inc.

New York   St. Louis   San Francisco   Auckland   Bogotá   Caracas   Lisbon
London   Madrid   Mexico City   Milan   Montreal   New Delhi   San Juan
Singapore   Sydney   Tokyo   Toronto

This is an EDI book.

McGraw-Hill

*A Division of The **McGraw·Hill** Companies*

Interactions One
A Communicative Grammar

Copyright © 1996, 1990, 1985 by The McGraw-Hill Companies, Inc. All rights reserved.
Printed in the United States of America. Except as permitted under the United States Copyright
Act of 1976, no part of this publication may be reproduced or distributed in any form or by any
means, or stored in a data base or retrieval system, without the prior written permission of the
publisher.

4 5 6 7 8 9 0   DOC DOC   9 0 9

ISBN 0-07-034916-9
ISBN 0-07-114369-6

This book was set in Times Roman by Monotype Composition Company, Inc.

The editors were Tim Stookesberry, Bill Preston, Steve Vogel, and Caroline Jumper; the
designers were Lorna Lo, Suzanne Montazer, Francis Owens, and Elizabeth Williamson;
the production supervisors were Patricia Myers and Tanya Nigh; the index was prepared by
Jeanine Briggs; the cover was designed by Francis Owens; the cover illustrator was Susan
Pizzo; the photo researcher was Cindy Robinson, Seaside Publishing; illustrations were done by
Axelle Fortier, Sally Richardson, Wayne Clark, Rick Hackney, and David Bohn.

R. R. Donnelley & Sons Company, Crawfordsville, IN, was printer and binder.
Phoenix Color Corporation was cover separator and printer.

Library of Congress Catalog Card Number: 96-75138

Photo credits: *Page 1* © Walter Gilardetti; *29* © John Fung; *53* © Jim Harrison/Stock, Boston;
83 © Richard Hutchins/Photo Researchers, Inc.; *91* © Hiroyuki Matsumo/Black Star;
111 © John Coletti/Stock, Boston; *133* © John Fung; *155* © Bachman/Photo Researchers, Inc.;
179 Randy Taylor/Sygma; *205* © Walter Gilardetti; *215 (left)* © S. Shapiro/Sygma; *(center
and right)* © Sam Emerson/Sygma; *231* © David Austen/Stock, Boston; *259* © M. Greenlar/
The Image Works; *277* © John Fung.

Contents

CHAPTER **three**

Living to Eat or Eating to Live?   **53**

CHAPTER **four**

Getting Around the Community   **83**

Contents

CHAPTER **seven**

Health   **155**

CHAPTER **eight**

Entertainment and the Media   **179**

CHAPTER nine

Social Life

CHAPTER ten

Customs, Celebrations, and Holidays

CHAPTER **eleven**

Science and Technology 259

CHAPTER **twelve**

You, the Consumer 277

Preface
to the Third Edition

The Interactions One Program

The Interactions One Program consists of five texts and a variety of supplemental materials for high-beginning to low-intermediate students seeking to improve their English language skills. Each of the five texts in this program is carefully organized by chapter theme, vocabulary, grammar structures, and, where possible, language functions. As a result, information introduced in a chapter of any one of the Interactions One texts corresponds to and reinforces material taught in the same chapter of the other four books, creating a truly integrated, four-skills approach.

The Interactions One program is highly flexible. The texts in this series may be used together or separately, depending on students' needs and course goals. The books in this program include:

- **A Communicative Grammar Book.** Organized around grammatical topics, this book includes notional/functional material where appropriate. It presents all grammar in context and contains many types of communicative activities.
- **A Listening/Speaking Skills Book.** This book uses lively, natural language from various contexts, including dialogues, interviews, lectures, and announcements. Listening strategies emphasized include summarizing main ideas, making inferences, listening for stressed words, reductions and intonation. A variety of speaking skills complement the listening component.
- **A Reading Skills Book.** The reading selections contain sophisticated college-level material; however, vocabulary and grammar have been carefully controlled to be at students' level of comprehension. The text includes many vocabulary-building exercises and emphasizes reading strategies such as skimming, scanning, guessing meaning from context, understanding the structure and organization of a selection, increasing reading speed, and interpreting the author's point of view.
- **A Writing Process Book.** This book uses a process approach to writing, including many exercises on prewriting and revision. Exercises build skills in exploring and organizing ideas; developing vocabulary; using correct form and mechanics; using coherent structure, and editing, revising, and using feedback to create a final draft.
- **A Multi-Skills Activity Book.** New to this edition, this text gives students integrated practice in all four language skills. Among the communicative activities included in this text are exercises for the new video program that accompanies the Interactions One series.

Supplemental Materials

In addition to the five core texts outlined above, various supplemental materials are available to assist users of the third edition, including:

Instructor's Manual

Extensively revised for the new edition, this manual provides instructions and guidelines for using the five core texts separately or in various combinations to suit particular program needs. For each of the core texts, there is a separate section with answer keys, teaching tips, additional activities, and other suggestions. The testing materials have been greatly expanded in this edition.

Audio Program for Interactions One: A Listening/Speaking Skills Book

Completely rerecorded for the new edition, the audio program is designed to be used in conjunction with those exercises that are indicated with a cassette icon in the student text. Complete tapescripts are now included in the back of the student text.

Audio Program to Accompany Interactions One: A Reading Skills Book

This new optional audio program contains selected readings from the student text. These taped selections of poems, articles, stories, and speeches enable students to listen at their leisure to the natural oral discourse of native readers for intonation and modeling. Readings that are included in this program are indicated with a cassette icon in the student text.

Video

New to this edition, the video program for Interactions One contains authentic television segments that are coordinated with the twelve chapter themes in the five texts. Exercises and activities for this video are in the Multi-Skills Activity Book.

Interactions One: A Communicative Grammar, Third Edition

Rationale

Interactions One: A Communicative Grammar, third edition, is a challenging, fast-moving grammar book aimed at high-beginning to low-intermediate level academic students. Central to the Interactions One program, *Interactions One: A Communicative Grammar* follows the same content themes as the companion volumes, and it introduces, practices, and builds on the structures and vocabulary presented in those books. Although some previous exposure to English is assumed, the book requires no previous grammar mastery. Through precise, step-by-step sequencing, it guides students through the forms, meanings, and usage of eight basic verb tenses, modal auxiliaries, gerunds, and infinitives. Practice in troublesome areas such as articles, phrasal verbs, prepositions, and verb tense contrasts is also provided.

Contextualization

Interactions One: A Communicative Grammar teaches the patterns and rules of English grammar in context. It is based on the following principles:

- Information about *when* to use certain structures is as important as the forms and patterns themselves; the presentation and practice of grammar in situational contexts provides this information.
- The contextualization of grammar aids memory. Whereas isolated exercises might be forgotten as soon as they are completed, the association of rules with situations can help in learning. In addition, natural (and often humorous) contexts provide extra motivational interest of story lines.
- The presentation of grammar in context can provide extra motivation to learning: In addition to mastering grammar, students acquire useful vocabulary and information. Furthermore, contextualization stimulates thinking, offering students realistic opportunities for the expression of ideas, opinions, and feelings.
- For international students, contexts that take into account their cultural heritage and immediate surroundings are most meaningful. In *Interactions One: A Communicative Grammar,* students use grammatical structures to compare and contrast cultural characteristics of their native countries with those of the countries they may currently reside in.

Sequencing

Although grammar curricula necessarily differ with individual programs, the Interactions One program attempts to follow "typical" sequencing—i.e., earlier topics present generally simpler forms and patterns while later, more complex ones build on previously acquired knowledge. Steps to mastery are small: for example, in learning the present perfect continuous tense before the present perfect, students are not overburdened by new forms while they are concentrating on meanings. By the time they begin learning past participle forms for the present perfect, they have already learned the time concepts involved in the use of the tense.

Grammar points are consistently recycled. Every fourth chapter (Chapters Four, Eight, and Twelve) provides review and integrated practice of the major points of the previous three. Thus grammar mastery is cumulative, and students can acquire fairly sophisticated principles at an accelerated pace.

Exercises and activities proceed from controlled to creative. With each, students are expected to "do a little more"—i.e., to provide more of their own language. The least controlled activities in the **Using What You've Learned** sections at the end of each topic offer students the opportunity to use the target grammar for self-expression and communication.

Chapter Organization

Each chapter theme addresses three to five major topics that present and practice specific grammar structures. Each topic begins with an illustration to help contextualize the language that follows. **Setting the Context,** an introductory activity, can be a dialogue, reading, class discussion, brainstorm, prediction, or pair interview. The introductory activity highlights the structures to be taught in that section. New grammar points are then presented concisely in the form of easy-to-read charts. Exercises follow these presentations, providing controlled practice of the grammar points. Each topic culminates with less-structured, communicative activities in the **Using What You've Learned** section.

Chapters Seven through Twelve conclude with a **Focus on Testing** box. These new features include brief exercises designed to help students prepare for standardized tests like the TOEFL.

Suggestions for Use

The material in *Interations One: A Communicative Grammar* can be successfully presented in a variety of ways. Since most teachers have individual classroom styles that work for their particular groups and situations, no specific suggestions are presented here. There are, however, a variety of ideas for effective teaching techniques, including sample lesson plans, in the *Instructor's Manual* for the Interactions One program.

New to the Third Edition

1. **Streamlined Design.**   The new edition features an attractive two-color design and an extensively revised art program. These changes were initiated to make the books more appealing, up-to-date, and user-friendly. In addition, we made the books easier to use by simplifying complicated direction lines, numbering exercises and activities, and highlighting key information in shaded boxes and charts.
2. **New Chapter Theme on Science and Technology.**   The new edition features an entirely new theme for Chapter Eleven: Science and Technology. In addition, the themes for several other chapters have been broadened to include new content.
3. **Focus on Testing.**   These new boxed features, appearing in Chapters Seven through Twelve, are designed to help students prepare for standardized grammar and usage tests like the TOEFL.

4. **Variety of Introductory Activities.** In addition to opening dialogues, the new edition has a greater variety of introductory activities for grammar topics, including short readings, brainstorms, discussions, predictions, and pair interviews.

Acknowledgments

Our thanks to the following reviewers whose comments, both favorable and critical, were of great value in the development of the third edition of the Interactions/Mosaic series:

Jean Al-Sibai, University of North Carolina; Janet Alexander, Waterbury College; Roberta Alexander, San Diego City College; Julie Alpert, Santa Barbara City College; Anita Cook, Tidewater Community College; Anne Deal Beavers, Heald Business College; Larry Berking, Monroe Community College; Deborah Busch, Delaware County Community College; Patricia A. Card, Chaminade University of Honolulu; José A. Carmona, Hudson County Community College; Kathleen Carroll, Fontbonne College; Consuela Chase, Loyola University; Lee Chen, California State University; Karen Cheng, University of Malaya; Gaye Childress, University of North Texas; Maria Conforti, University of Colorado; Earsie A. de Feliz, Arkansas State University; Elizabeth Devlin-Foltz, Montgomery County Adult Education; Colleen Dick, San Francisco Institute of English; Marta Dmytrenko-Ahrabian, Wayne State University; Margo Duffy, Northeast Wisconsin Technical; Magali Duignan, Augusta College; Janet Dyar, Meridian Community College; Anne Ediger, San Diego City College; D. Frangie, Wayne State University; Robert Geryk, Wayne State University; Jeanne Gibson, American Language Academy; Kathleen Walsh Greene, Rhode Island College; Myra Harada, San Diego Mesa College; Kristin Hathhorn, Eastern Washington University; Mary Herbert, University of California-Davis; Joyce Homick, Houston Community College; Catherine Hutcheson, Texas Christian University; Suzie Johnston, Tyler Junior College; Donna Kauffman, Radford University; Emmie Lim, Cypress College; Patricia Mascarenas, Monte Vista Community School; Mark Mattison, Donnelly College; Diane Peak, Choate Rosemary Hall; James Pedersen, Irvine Valley College; Linda Quillan, Arkansas State University; Marnie Ramker, University of Illinois; Joan Roberts, The Doane Stuart School; Doralee Robertson, Jacksonville University; Ellen Rosen, Fullerton College; Jean Sawyer, American Language Academy; Frances Schulze, College of San Mateo; Sherrie R. Sellers, Brigham Young University; Tess M. Shafer, Edmonds Community College; Heinz F. Tengler, Lado International College; Sara Tipton, Wayne State University; Karen R. Vallejo, Brigham Young University; Susan Williams, University of Central Florida; Mary Shepard Wong, El Camino College; Cindy Yoder, Eastern Mennonite College; Cheryl L. Youtsey, Loyola University; Miriam Zahler, Wayne State University; Maria Zien, English Center, Miami; Yongmin Zhu, Los Medanos College; Norma Zorilla, Fresno Pacific College.

CHAPTER **one**

School Life

TOPIC **one**

The Verb be

Setting the Context

Conversation

CARLOS: Hi. I'm Carlos Torres.

HIROSHI: I'm glad to meet you, Carlos. My name is Hiroshi Watanabe.

CARLOS: Nice to meet you, Hiroshi. Are you a visa student?

HIROSHI: Yes, I am. I'm from Japan. How about you?

CARLOS: I'm from Mexico, but I'm a permanent resident. How are your classes?

HIROSHI: Great! How about your classes?

CARLOS: They're not too bad. The economics department is pretty good. Are you an undergraduate?

HIROSHI: Yes, I am. I'm a sophomore. And you?

CARLOS: I'm in my junior year. Is economics your major?

HIROSHI: Yes, it is. I'm interested in business.

CARLOS: I am too. Oh, here's the professor. Let's talk later.

exercise Answer *true* or *false* to these statements about the conversation.

1. The last names of the people are Carlos and Hiroshi.
2. The instructor isn't in the class at the beginning of the conversation.
3. Carlos and Hiroshi are citizens of the United States.
4. They're graduate students.
5. Carlos is Japanese and Hiroshi is Mexican.

A. Affirmative and Negative Statements; Contractions

The verb *be* has different forms after different subjects.

	examples	notes
Affirmative	**I am** from Japan.	Use *am* for the subject *I*.
	The students **are** late. You **are** twins!	Use *are* for a plural noun and these pronouns: *we, you, they, these,* or *those.*
	The teacher **is** over there.	Use *is* for a singular noun and these singular pronouns: *he, she, it, this,* or *that.*
Negative	**I am not** late. She **is not** in this class.	Use *not* after the verb *be* in negative sentences.

Contractions are short forms. They are used in conversation and informal writing. Full forms are used in more formal writing.

	full forms	contractions		
Affirmative	I am Mexican.	**I'm** Mexican.		
	She is a student.	**She's** a student.		
	It is Tuesday.	**It's** Tuesday.		
	We are permanent residents.	**We're** permanent residents.		
	You are good at science.	**You're** good at science.		
	They are in this class.	**They're** in this class.		
Negative	I am not interested.	**I'm not** interested.		*
	He is not in this department.	**He's not** in this department.		He **isn't** in this department.
	It is not here.	**It's not** here.		It **isn't** there.
	We are not visa students.	**We're not** visa students.	or	We **aren't** visa students.
	You are not married.	**You're not** married.		You **aren't** married.
	They are not friendly.	**They're not** friendly.		They **aren't** friendly.

*There is no contraction for am + not.

 **exercise 1**

Underline the verb *be* in statements in the conversation between Carlos and Hiroshi on page 2.

> **example:**   I'm Carlos Torres.

 **exercise 2**

Circle the correct words or word parts, as in the example.

DAVE: Hi. I [**'m** / 's] Dave.

MARY: Hello. We ['s / 're] Mary and Ellen Johnson.
                                    1

DAVE: Oh, you ['re / n't] twins!
                            2

MARY: No, we ['re not / isn't] twins. But we ['m / 're] sisters.
                            3   4

DAVE: But you ['s / 're] exactly alike!
                            5

ELLEN: No, I ['m / 's] nineteen years old, but
                        6

               Mary [isn't / aren't] even eighteen yet.
                                7

DAVE: Oh. Well, I ['m / are] glad to meet you!
                                8

               Mary and Ellen, this [is / He's] Carlos.
                                            9

MARY: Hi, Carlos.

ELLEN: Hello, Carlos.

CARLOS: Hello. (*to Dave*) They ['m / 're] twins!
                                        10

 **exercise 3**

Complete the sentences with forms of the verb *be*. Use contractions when possible. The first one is done as an example.

DAVE: (*to Carlos*) No, you *'re*_____ wrong. They _____ (not) twins.
                                                            1

               They _____ (not) alike at all—look again!
                        2

CARLOS: The instructor _____ (not) here yet. She _____ late.
                                3   4

4

Interactions I • Grammar

ELLEN: No, it _____ early. It _____ (not) even 9:45. My friends _____
5   6   7
(not) here yet either.

DAVE: Well, let's sit down. I _____ tired.
8

CARLOS: No. Let's have coffee first. The snack bar _____ open.
9

DAVE: No, thanks. I have to do homework. I _____ (not) ready for class
10
yet.

 **exercise 4**   Work in pairs. Describe the people. Use the words next to the pictures.

examples: Professor Winters **is** a good teacher.
He **isn't** a boring speaker.

Professor Winters

1. a good teacher
2. not a boring speaker
3. very funny
4. in the English department
5. tall and good-looking
6. not married

Doctor Silbert

7. a famous scientist
8. very busy
9. a hard worker
10. friendly
11. in the Chemistry Department
12. not bad-looking

These students

13. in my history class
14. not always interested in history
15. not awake during lectures
16. in their senior year
17. not very serious
18. always tired

Chapter One • School Life

B. Yes/No Questions and Short Answers

Yes/no questions ask for information that can be answered by *yes* or *no.* In a yes/no question, the verb comes before the subject.

	examples	possible answers	
		Affirmative	**Negative**
Affirmative Questions	**Am** I late?	Yes, you are.	No, you aren't.
	Are you from Japan?	Yes, I am.	No, I'm not.
	Is it cold?	Yes, it is.	No, it isn't.
Negative Questions	**Aren't** you early?	Yes, we are.	No, we aren't.
	Isn't that woman a professor?	Yes, she is.	No, she isn't.
	Aren't they twins?	Yes, they are.	No, they aren't.

The first box in the chart below gives more examples of affirmative yes/no questions. The second and third boxes give possible affirmative and negative short answers to these questions.

questions	affirmative answers	negative answers		
Am I early?	Yes, you are.*	No, you're not.		No, you aren't.†
Is he Japanese?	Yes, he is.	No, he's not.		No, he isn't.
Is she a scientist?	Yes, she is.	No, she's not.	or	No, she isn't
Is it late?	Yes, it is.	No, it's not.		No, it isn't.
Are you students?	Yes, we are.	No, we're not.		No, we aren't.
Are those boys twins?	Yes, they are.	No, they're not.		No, they aren't.

*Don't use contractions in affirmative short answers.
†Contractions are usually used in negative short answers.

 **exercise 5** In the conversation on page 2, put two lines under the verb *be* in yes/no questions and short answers.

> example: Is economics your major?
>   ==

 **exercise 6** Complete these sentences with affirmative or negative forms of the verb *be.* Use contractions when possible.

TONY: Hi. __Are__ you a new student?
          ₁

MING: Yes, I _____. My name _____ Liu Ming Ren.
          2   3

TONY: I _____ sorry. Please say that again.
        4
_____ your name Lou or Ron?
        5

MING: (*speaks slowly*) It _____ Liu Ming Ren.
                        6

TONY: Oh. Um . . . _____ Lou your first name?
                    7

MING: No, sorry it _____ . My first name _____
                   8   9
Ming Ren. Just call me Ming.

TONY: Well, OK . . . um . . . _____ this is your first
                             10
day here?

MING: Yes, it _____ .
              11

TONY: _____ you from China?
      12

MING: No, I _____ . I _____ from Vietnam. Wow! Look at that beautiful
            13   14
woman over there! _____ she a student in this class?
                  15

TONY: No, she _____ a student. She _____ the professor!
             16   17

exercise 7   Write the missing questions. Many different questions are possible.

example: A: Is Professor Winters a good teacher?

           B: Oh, yes. He's very interesting.

A: _____
                        1
B: Yes, his jokes are very good.

A: _____
                        2
B: No, he isn't. He's in the English Department.

A: _____
                        3
B: Yes, he is.

A: _____
                        4
B: No, she isn't. She's from New York.

A: _____
                        5
B: Yes, she is.

A: _____
                        6
B: No, I'm not.

exercise 8 Complete the conversation with statements and yes/no questions with *be*. Use the words in parentheses. Complete the short answers.

TONY: Ming, _____ this is Hiroshi _____.
(this / Hiroshi)

Hiroshi, Ming. _____.
1 (Ming / a new student in our history class)

HIROSHI: _____.
2 (I / glad to meet you)

MING: Happy to meet you too, Hiroshi.

_____?
3 (you / from Japan)

HIROSHI: Yes, I am. _____?
4 (your family / here)

MING: No, _____.
5 (I / alone)

HIROSHI: _____?
6 (your classes / good)

MING: Yes, _____!
7 (they / fantastic)

_____.
8 (our history teacher / beautiful)

HIROSHI: Ms. Stein?

TONY: Yeah, I think _____.
9 (I / in love)

HIROSHI: Forget it, Tony. _____.
10 (She / married)

Using What You've Learned

 Introduce yourself to a classmate and talk about school. Use sentences with *be*.

example: A: Hi, I'm Juan. I'm new here. Are you in this class?
B: Yes, I am.
A: Is the professor good?
B: I'm not sure. She's new here too.

activity 2

You can do this activity as a whole class or in groups of 8 to 10 people. Sit in a circle if possible. One student begins by making three statements about himself or herself using the present tense. The next student repeats the first student's information and then makes three statements about himself or herself. The third student repeats the first and second students' information, then makes three statements, and so on. If a student forgets some information, other group members can help.

example: A: **I'm** Elena. **I'm** from Russia. **I'm** a scientist.
B: **She's** Elena. **She's** from Russia. **She's** a scientist. **I'm** Leonid. **I'm** from Russia too. **I'm** a business major.
C: **They're** Elena and Leonid. They **aren't** from the Soviet Union anymore. **They're** from Russia. **She's** a scientist, and **he's** a business major. **I'm** . . .

activity 3

There are other ways to answer yes/no questions. Here are some examples of formal and informal affirmative and negative answers.

	FORMAL	INFORMAL
AFFIRMATIVE	Certainly.	Sure.
	Of course.	Yeah.
	I think so.	Uh-huh.
	I hope so.	Right.
NEGATIVE	Certainly not.	Nope.
	Of course not.	No way.
	I don't think so.	Uh-uh.
	I hope not.	Nah.
	I'm afraid not.	

Play this question and answer game quickly. Work in groups. Choose one student in each group to answer yes/no questions from the other group members. This student must tell the truth but must <u>not</u> use the words yes or no. If the student answers with yes or no, another student takes her or his place and continues the game.

example: A: Are you from Tokyo?
B: Of course.
C: So you're Japanese?
B: Certainly.
D: Is your family with you?
B: I'm afraid not.
A: Are you here alone?
B: Yes, I . . . Ooops!
(Another student continues.)

TOPIC **two**

The Simple Present Tense

Setting the Context

Conversation

BETTY: Hi, Ellen. Let's have coffee, okay?

ELLEN: Hi, Betty. Sure, that sounds great. Where do you want to go?

BETTY: Let's get a cup from the vending machine. The snack bar is too crowded.

ELLEN: Fine. Get a table, and I'll get the coffee. What do you take in your coffee?

BETTY: Cream and sugar, please. *(Betty sits at a table, and Ellen brings the coffee.)*

ELLEN: So, how do you like your classes this semester?

BETTY: I like them all, except for math. I don't like the instructor. He's terrible!

ELLEN: Why is he terrible?

BETTY: Well, he talks fast all the time, and he doesn't talk loud enough. He has terrible handwriting, and he makes mistakes on the board every day. And he never takes breaks.

ELLEN: Does he ever give homework?

BETTY: Sure he does. He gives an assignment every night, and it's really hard. We don't understand a thing, but he doesn't care. He also makes bad jokes in class!

ELLEN: Let's see . . . maybe you need to get a tutor. Don't wait until finals.

BETTY: That's a good idea. Who can I get?

ELLEN: I know someone. He never talks fast. He always speaks clearly. He says funny things all the time. He seldom gets angry. And he teaches math too!

BETTY: I like him already. Please tell me his name!

ELLEN: Mr. Michaels. He's my adviser.

BETTY: Mr. Michaels? He's my math teacher!

exercise Answer *true* or *false* to these statements about the conversation.

1. Betty and Ellen are students and they are friends.
2. Betty has a problem with her math class.
3. She thinks her math instructor is a very good teacher.
4. He never gives homework, and he explains things slowly and clearly.
5. Mr. Michaels is an adviser, a tutor, and a math teacher.

A. The Imperative Form: Instructions, Orders, and Suggestions

The imperative form uses the simple form of the verb.

	examples	notes
Affirmative	Come in.	To give instructions or orders, begin with a verb.
	Please sit down.	The subject *you* is understood. (It does not appear.)
	Be quiet, please.	Add the word *please* for politeness.
Negative	Don't talk. Please don't come in. Don't be late, please.	In the negative, *don't* comes before the verb.

For a first-person plural subject *(we)*, *let's* appears before the simple form of the verb.

	examples	notes
Affirmative	Let's have coffee.	An imperative with *let's* is a kind of suggestion.
Negative	Let's not wait.	

exercise  Circle the verbs for instructions and suggestions in the conversation between Betty and Ellen.

example: (Let's have) coffee, okay?

**exercise 2** What are the rules and customs of your English class? Give affirmative and negative instructions, orders, and suggestions using the imperative form. Use the phrases below and add examples of your own.

> **examples:** Don't be late to class.
> Please come in quietly.
> Let's ask questions in class.

1. be late to class
2. come in quietly
3. eat in class
4. drink coffee in class
5. work together on assignments
6. help your classmates
7. cheat on tests
8. be quiet in class
9. ask questions in class
10. talk loudly and clearly
11. get angry at the teacher
12. make mistakes
13. laugh at the mistakes of your classmates
14. say funny things in class
15. make bad jokes
16. sleep in class
17. speak your native language in class
18. take a long break
19. _____
20. _____

B. Affirmative and Negative Statements

The simple present tense is used to describe everyday activities. It is also used to express opinions and to make general statements of fact. With some verbs, the simple present shows an existing condition (something that is happening now). The chart below gives some examples.

	examples	**notes**
Everyday Activities	She **wears** jeans to class. Betty and Ellen often **study** together.	An object often follows the verb.
Opinions	I **don't like** the instructor. He **doesn't teach** math very well.	In negative statements, *do* or *does* comes before *not*. The main verb has no *-s* ending.
Statements of Fact	Lu **speaks** three languages. Mr. Michaels **teaches** math and **advises** students.	In third-person singular subjects, the verb ends in *-s*. (See Spelling Rules and Pronunciation Note.)
Existing Conditions	I **hear** music. He **doesn't understand** your question. We **need** a break.	Some other verbs that describe an existing condition: *like, want, seem, know, believe.*

Spelling Rules for -s Endings

For the third-person singular verb form, follow these spelling rules:

1. If the simple form of a verb ends in *-y* after a consonant, change the *y* to *i* and add *-es*.

   examples: carry / carries
   try / tries

2. If the simple form of a verb ends in *-s, -z, -sh, -ch, -x,* or *-o* (after a consonant), add *-es*.

   examples: teach / teaches
   pass / passes
   go / goes

3. There are two irregular verb forms.

   be / is
   have / has

4. In all other cases, add *-s* to the simple form.

   examples: wear / wears
   work / works
   pay / pays

Pronunciation Note

The *-s* ending is pronounced three ways, according to the ending of the verb:

1. */iz/* after *-ch, -sh, -s, -x,* and *-z* endings

   examples: teaches, washes, kisses, boxes, buzzes

2. */s/* after voiceless endings: *p, t, k,* or *f*

   examples: stops, hits, looks, laughs

3. */z/* after voiced consonant endings

   examples: calls, listens, plays, sounds, runs

 **exercise 3** In the conversation on pages 10 and 11, underline the simple present tense verbs in statements.

   example: Sure, that <u>sounds</u> great.

exercise 4 Use the phrases under the pictures to make present tense statements about the people in the pictures.

examples: Mr. Sommers is a teaching assistant.
He is not a professor.

Mr. Sommers

1. be a teaching assistant
2. not be a professor
3. help Mr. Michaels
4. teach three days a week
5. not give lectures

6. work with students in small groups
7. not wear a suit and a tie
8. like to wear jeans every day
9. not carry a briefcase
10. not have a board in his classroom

Ms. Wong and Mr. Garcia

1. (he) be a student adviser
2. (she) be a college administrator
3. (they) not teach classes
4. (they) not do classwork
5. (he) advise students on their classes
6. (she) often go to meetings

7. (she) not have an easy job
8. (he) help students with their problems
9. (they) not have enough time to do all their work
10. (they) not make a lot of money

C. Yes/No Questions and Short Answers

In simple present yes/no questions, a form of the verb *do* comes before the subject with verbs other than *be*. Use **does** with *he, she, it,* and **do** with *I, you, we, they.* The main verb has no **-s** ending. A form of *do* appears in short answers.

	examples	possible answers	
		Affirmative	**Negative**
Affirmative Questions	**Do I turn** here?	Yes, you do.	No, you don't.
	Does he do good work?*	Yes, he does.	No, he doesn't.
	Does she study a lot?	Yes, she does.	No, she doesn't.
	Does it work?	Yes, it does.	No, it doesn't.
	Do we need our umbrellas?	Yes, you do.	No, you don't.
	Do you have change for a dollar?	Yes, I do.	No, I don't.
	Do they know the address?	Yes, they do.	No, they don't.
Negative Questions	**Don't I need** a ticket?	Yes, you do.	No, you don't.
	Doesn't he teach English?	Yes, he does.	No, he doesn't.
	Doesn't she play the piano?	Yes, she does.	No, she doesn't.
	Doesn't it bite?	Yes, it does.	No, it doesn't.
	Don't we leave tonight?	Yes, we do.	No, we don't.
	Don't you do the homework?*	Yes, I do.	No, I don't.
	Don't they like pizza?	Yes, they do.	No, they don't.

*When *do* is the main verb, a form of *do* appears twice.

exercise 5

Work in pairs. Student A asks yes/no questions using the words below. Student B answers the questions with short answers. Add some questions of your own.

example: A: Do they have a cafeteria at this school?
B: Yes, they do. (or: No, they don't. They have a snack bar.)
A: Is the food good?
B: No, it isn't. It's terrible.

1. they have a cafeteria at this school
2. the food good
3. the place clean
4. it have comfortable chairs
5. students study there
6. it open late
7. anyone clean up
8. the place serve hamburgers
9. it have coffee
10. the prices high

exercise 6 Change roles. Now student B asks yes/no questions using these words. Student A gives short answers. Add some questions of your own.

1. you have an English class now
2. it meet in a new building
3. the classroom big
4. the instructor give lectures
5. you have homework assignments
6. your teacher late for class
7. you need help with your homework
8. the teacher talk too fast for you
9. you have a textbook
10. you study enough

exercise 7 Change partners. Write some yes/no questions about another person or place at your school (for example: your adviser, the library, and so on). Then take turns asking and answering each other's questions.

D. Information Questions and Answers

An information question begins with a question word. It cannot be answered by *yes* or *no*. When a form of *do* separates a question word from the subject, the main verb has no *-s* ending. This chart gives some examples.

question words	questions	possible answers	notes
who	**Who** is your adviser?	Mr. Michaels.	**Who** can be the subject of a question.
	Who are your teachers?	Mr. Sommers and Ms. Lee.	**Who** refers to people.
	Who helps you study?	Ellen and Betty.	**Who** usually takes a singular verb (except *be*).
whom	**Who** / **Whom** } do you ask?	My tutor.	**Who** (or **Whom**) is also used as an object.
			Whom is used only in formal questions.
			Who is used in informal speech.
what	**What** is in the bag?	My lunch.	**What** can be the subject of a question.
	What interests you?	Books and movies.	**What** refers to things.
	What do you want?	Some money.	**What** is also used as
	What does she teach?	History.	an object.

question words	questions	possible answers	notes
where	**Where** is the snack bar?	In the student center.	
	Where are your classes?	In the new science building.	
	Where does the class meet?	In Moore Hall.	**Where** refers to places.
	Where do we go now?	To English class.	
when	**When** is the final exam?	Next week.	
	When are our papers due?	On Wednesday.	
	When does class begin?	In five minutes.	**When** refers to time.
	When do you work?	On Mondays and Fridays.	
why	**Why** is the building closed?	It's a holiday.	
	Why aren't they home?	They're on vacation.	
	Why doesn't he study more?	He has a job after school.	**Why** refers to reasons.
	Why don't you see a doctor?	Because I'm not that sick.	
how	**How** is your math class?	Very hard.	**How** can refer to a degree (of something).
	How are you?	Pretty good.	**How** can refer to a state or condition (for example, health).
	How does she sing?	Beautifully.	**How** often refers to a way of doing something.
	How do you get to school?	By bus and subway.	

Note: Contractions for question words + *be* used in informal speech are: *who + is = who's; what + is =*

 **exercise 8**   In the conversation on pages 10 and 11, put two lines under the question words and the verbs.

example: <u>Where do</u> you want to <u>go</u>?

exercise 9

Study the answers below. Make information questions for each answer. Use the simple present tense and the question words *who, what, where, when, why* or *how*.

example: <u>How are you? or How do you feel</u>?

I'm sick.

1. _____?

She's my English teacher.

2. _____?

I walk to school.

3. _____?

He teaches math.

4. _____?

On Friday.

5. _____?

Because it's too expensive.

6. _____?

In the refrigerator.

7. _____?

It's blue.

8. _____?

It's too easy.

9. _____?

On the first floor.

10. _____?

Terribly.

**exercise 10**

Work in pairs. Student A makes information questions using the words below. Student B answers each of student A's questions with short answers. Add some questions of your own.

examples: How . . . your classes this term?

A: How are your classes this term?
B: They're boring.

Why . . . you like them?

A: Why don't you like them?
B: Because the courses are too easy.

1. Who . . . your English teacher?
2. How . . . you like him/her?
3. Why . . . you like him/her?
4. Where . . . your teacher from?
5. How . . . your teacher speak?
6. Who . . . you study with?
7. When . . . your English class?
8. Where . . . your English class meet?
9. What textbook . . . you use?
10. How . . . the textbook?

exercise 11 Change roles. Now student B makes information questions using these words. Student A answers student B's questions with short answers. Add some questions of your own.

1. What . . . you usually do in the morning?
2. When . . . you usually get to school?
3. Where . . . our ESL teacher's office?
4. What . . . the best place to study on campus?
5. Where . . . students meet between classes?
6. When . . . the school holidays this semester?
7. Where . . . you go for a cup of coffee?
8. How . . . you like the food in the cafeteria?
9. Why . . . you like it?
10. When . . . you usually go home?

E. Frequency Adverbs

Frequency adverbs modify verbs or adjectives. They describe how many times or what percentage of time something happens. Here are the meanings of some frequency adverbs in approximate percentages of time:

always	=	100%
usually	=	90%
often	=	70%
sometimes	=	50%
occasionally	=	20%
seldom	=	10%
never	=	0%

The charts on page 20 give some examples of frequency adverbs in affirmative and negative statements and questions. Notice where the frequency adverbs appear in the statements and questions.

	examples	notes
Affirmative	Students are **always** busy. He's **often** hungry. She **sometimes** gets sick. Students **occasionally** meet. They're **seldom** together.	In statements, one-word frequency adverbs usually come after the verb *be* but before other verbs.
Negative	I'm **not often** tired. Kim **isn't always** here. Tony **is never** late. She **doesn't often** rest. We **don't ever** want to go there again.* They **don't usually** study.	

	examples	possible answers		notes
		Affirmative	**Negative**	
Affirmative Questions	Are you **often** homesick? Does the teacher **ever** give quizzes?* Do they **always** eat pizza for lunch?	Yes, always. often. sometimes. occasionally.	No, not often. seldom. never.	In questions, one-word frequency adverbs usually come after the subject.
Negative Questions	**Don't** you **ever** get homesick?* **Doesn't** he **often** come to class late? **Don't** we **always** enjoy the weekend?			

*Use *ever* only in negative statements and in questions (*not ever = never*).

A frequency phrase usually follows the verb phrase.

examples	notes
He teaches **three times a week.** We have a test **every month.** Do you relax **now and then**?	Here are examples of frequency phrases: *every day, every other week, every two hours, once a year, now and then.*

exercise 12   Put a box around the frequency adverbs and phrases in the conversation on pages 10 and 11.

> examples: Well, he talks fast all the time.

exercise 13   Complete the conversation. Put the words under the lines in correct order to make sentences as in the example. When you finish, practice the conversation with a partner.

TONY: _____ You often look tired _____ , Hiroshi.
(tired / look / You / often)

_____?
1 (get / eight hours of sleep / you / usually / Don't)

HIROSHI: No. _____.
2 (I / five days a week / eight o'clock classes / have)

But _____.
3 (rarely / before 2:00 A.M. / get to bed / I)

TONY: Why, Hiroshi? _____?
4 (Do / go out / every night / you)

HIROSHI: Oh, no. _____.
5 (never / during the week / I / go out)

_____.
6 (My roommate and I / every night / study together)

_____.
7 (before 1:00 in the morning / usually / don't / finish / We)

In fact, _____.
8 (seldom / goes to bed / my roommate / before 3:00)

TONY: That sounds terrible. _____?
9 (work so hard / always / you / Do)

HIROSHI: Yes, because _____.
10 (always / worried about grades / we're)

TONY: Well, you graduate soon, right? What do you plan to do then?

HIROSHI: Sleep!

exercise 14   Work in pairs. Take turns using the phrases below to ask and answer present tense questions. Add frequency adverbs to your questions and answers.

examples: A: Do you **often** eat hamburgers for dinner?
B: No, not **often.** I **occasionally** eat hamburgers for dinner.

(Change roles.)
B: Are you **ever** tired in class?
A: Yes, I am. I'm **sometimes** tired in class.

1. stay up all night
2. need to cram for a test
3. get eight hours of sleep
4. ask questions in class
5. be worried about school
6. not understand the teacher
7. not do your homework
8. study with friends
9. get help from a tutor
10. ask for advice
11. be satisfied with your grades
12. get perfect grades

Using What You've Learned

activity 1

Interview three of your classmates. Write ten different questions to ask each person. Write some:

- yes/no questions with *be*.
- yes/no questions with *do* + verb in the simple present tense.
- information questions with question words.
- questions with frequency adverbs.

examples:	STUDENT 1	STUDENT 2	STUDENT 3
1. What is your name?	_____	_____	_____
2. Where are you from?	_____	_____	_____
3. Are you married?	_____	_____	_____
4. Do you live on campus?	_____	_____	_____
5. Do you like American food?	_____	_____	_____
6. Do you ever eat hamburgers?	_____	_____	_____

Ask your questions. Take notes on your classmates' answers. Keep your notes for Activity 2.

activity 2

Use the notes from your interviews in Activity 1. Introduce one of the classmates you interviewed to the class. Use information from your interview. Make some affirmative and negative statements about the person you introduce.

examples: A: This is Sam Chen. He's from Taiwan. He's married. He likes American food, but he doesn't like cheese.

   B: I'd like to introduce Linda Hernandez. She's from Mexico City. She isn't married. She lives in an apartment off campus. She walks to school.

activity 3

1. Cut a piece of paper into eight or more pieces.
2. Write one noun, adjective, or adverb on each piece. Turn your pieces over, so no one can see your words.
3. Choose a partner. Sit facing each other.
4. Turn over one of your pieces. Your partner looks at your word and makes a question. The question must have your word for its answer.
5. Answer your partner's question with a statement.
6. Now your partner turns over one of his or her pieces. You make a question. Your question must have his or her word for its answer.
7. Your partner answer's your question.
8. Play until you make questions and answers for all the words.

example: A: (Turns over piece with the word *black.*)
B: What color is my hair?
A: It's black.
B: (Turns over piece with the word *Wednesday.*)
A: When do we have English class?
B: On Wednesday.
A: (Turns over piece with the word *fast.*)
B: How does our teacher speak?
A: He speaks *fast.*

TOPIC **three**

Personal Pronouns, Possessive Adjectives, and Pronouns

Setting the Context
Conversation

CARLOS: Hi, Dave. You look tired!

DAVE: Tired? I'm exhausted.

CARLOS: Okay, you look exhausted! Why?

DAVE: Well, Monday through Friday I get up at 6:00 in the morning. On Tuesdays and Thursdays, Ruth—she's my wife—needs our car for work. We don't have a second car. Her sister and brother-in-law live across the street. They have a car, but they need theirs every day, so I can't use it. So I take the bus to school. It takes about thirty minutes and stops near the campus. Then I have to hurry to my first class in Moore Hall. It's across the campus, about a five-minute walk. Our math instructor is Mr. Michaels. He begins his class at exactly 8:00, but some students—like me—are usually late. Of course, he doesn't always finish his lecture on time, so then I have to run across the campus again to my English class. It's in Shriver Hall. The instructor is really good, but she talks fast, and I don't like to miss any of her lecture. And now I have to run to my next class . . .

CARLOS: I know—it's across the campus! Now *I'm* exhausted!

DAVE: Right! See you later, Carlos!

CARLOS: See you, Dave!

exercise   Answer *true* or *false* to these statements about the conversation.

1. Dave has an easy schedule this semester, so he's relaxed.
2. His wife, her sister, and their brother-in-law need their cars for work, so he takes the bus to school.
3. The bus takes him to Moore Hall.
4. Moore Hall is across the campus from Shriver Hall.
5. Dave has other classes in other places on campus.

A. Personal Pronouns

A pronoun replaces a noun. Study the examples in the chart. The nouns are underlined in the first sentences. Notice how the pronouns replace the nouns.

	examples
Singular Pronouns	"This is <u>Jack Thomas</u> speaking. **I** am lost. Who can help **me**?"
	"<u>Dave</u>, **you** look sick. Why don't **you** see a doctor?"
	<u>Carlos</u> is from Mexico. **He** is a new student. Please give **him** a textbook.
	<u>Ms. Sanchez</u> is the teacher. **She** teaches Spanish. Go to **her** class.
	Here's <u>the computer</u>. **It** is heavy. Take **it**. Be careful with **it**.
Plural Pronouns	"It's <u>Ellen and Betty</u>. **We** are downstairs. Please let **us** in."
	"<u>Carlos and Hiroshi</u>, **you** look tired. Can I take **you** home?"
	"<u>Ellen and Betty</u> are here. **They** want to come in. Please let **them** in."

A personal pronoun can be the subject or object of a sentence. An object pronoun comes after a verb or a preposition.

	forms	examples
Subject Pronouns	I	**I** need help.
	you	**You** look sick.
	he	**He** studies hard.
	she	**She** is an excellent teacher.
	it	**It** is very heavy.
	we	**We** are in the cafeteria.
	you	**You** are very busy today.
	they	**They** are thirsty.
Object Pronouns	me	Who can help **me**?
	you	Can the doctor see **you** today?
	him	The teacher gave **him** a good grade.
	her	I want to study English with **her**.
	it	Please put **it** over there.
	us	Please meet **us** for lunch.
	you	Can I see **you** tomorrow?
	them	Give **them** something to drink.

exercise 1  Underline the nouns in the sentences below. Circle the pronouns that replace the nouns. Draw arrows to show which pronouns replace which nouns.

examples: Dave and Carlos are students. They go to the same school. They like it.

1. Dave is exhausted. He is very busy all the time.

2. Dave and Ruth have a car, but they both need to use it.

3. Ruth is Dave's wife. She needs the car on Tuesdays and Thursdays. He can't use it on those days.

4. Ruth's sister and brother-in-law have a car, but they need it. Dave wants to take their car to school, but they can't let him use it.

5. When Dave can't take the car to school, he takes the bus. It stops near the campus.

6. Dave's first class is in Moore Hall. It is about a five-minute walk.

7. Mr. Michaels is Dave's math instructor. He always begins class on time. It starts exactly at 8:00.

8. Dave's second class is English. It's in Shriver Hall. It is across the campus.

9. The English instructor talks fast, but she is a good teacher.

10. Dave doesn't like to be late for the English lecture. He doesn't want to miss any of it.

B. Possessive Adjectives and Pronouns

A possessive adjective comes before a noun. A possessive pronoun does not come before a noun. This chart gives some examples.

	forms	examples
Possessive Adjectives	my	That isn't **my** pen.
	your	**Your** class is in Moore Hall.
	his	It's **his** problem.
	her	It's **her** car.
	its	**Its** name is French.
	our	**Our** seats are here.
	your	Are these **your** shoes?
	their	**Their** socks are over there.
Possessive Pronouns	mine	That pen isn't **mine**.
	his	The problem is **his**.
	hers	The car is **hers**.
	ours	Please take **ours**.
	yours	These shoes are **yours**.
	theirs	These socks are **theirs**.

In the conversation between Carlos and Dave on pages 23 and 24,

- underline the subject pronouns
- put two lines under the object pronouns
- circle the possessive adjectives
- put a box around the possessive pronouns

example: My wife needs our car for work. We don't have a second car. Her sister and brother-in-law live across the street. They have a car, but they need theirs every day, so I can't use it.

exercise 3   Read the conversation between Carlos and Hiroshi in Topic One on page 2. Circle the personal pronouns and possessive adjectives.

exercise 4   Read the three paragraphs. Fill in the correct personal pronouns, possessive adjectives, and pronouns as in the examples.

       _____Our_____ English teacher is Ms. Young. _____ name
           1   2

sounds Korean, but _____ isn't Korean. _____'s
                       3   4

American. _____I_____ like _____ teaching style, and
                5   6

_____ speaks slowly. _____ handwriting is clear, so
   7   8

_____ can read _____ on the board easily.
   9   10

      This school has many academic counselors. Sometimes _____they_____
                                               11

speak to _____us_____ in class. _____ tell _____
           12   13   14

about school facilities, rules, and customs. Students go to _____
                                             15

offices all the time and make appointments with _____.
                                       16

_____ talk about _____ courses and problems. Mr.
   17   18

Michaels is _____ favorite counselor, so I see only _____.
            19   20

      College textbooks are expensive, but _____ aren't available
                                       21

to students in the library, so students have to buy _____ at
                                       22

the bookstore. Of course, this grammar book isn't expensive, and

_____ has good information in _____ . Most students
   23   24

have all of _____ books for this semester, but _____I_____
            25   26

don't have _____ yet. _____ don't have enough money
                 27   28

to buy _____.
          29

Using What You've Learned

activity 1

1. Work in small groups. Each student chooses a person or place from the list below. (You can add your own examples.)

        the school library   your English teacher or another professor
        the cafeteria or snack bar   a teaching assistant
        the ESL department   a counselor or tutor
        your classroom   a friend

2. Take turns talking about your person or place for one minute. (Look at the example on page 28.) How many personal pronouns, possessive adjectives, and pronouns can you use?

3. The other group members will listen carefully so they can count them.

4. Who used the most pronouns and possessives?

example: The library on this campus is in the Learning Resource Building. **It** has many books in **it,** but **I** don't usually read **them. I** prefer the magazines. **They**'re on the second floor. **You** can't take **them** home, but **you** can read **them** in the library. The head librarian is Ms. Frohloff. **She**'s nice. **My** sister and **I** like to ask **her** questions. *(Total = 14)*

activity 2

1. Write for ten minutes about your school life. Use only the simple present tense.

   example: I go to West Los Angeles College. I live in Hollywood, so I drive to school. It takes about forty minutes.

2. When you finish, exchange papers with another student. Write questions to find out more information about your partner's statements.

   example: Why do you go to this school? Where do you live in Hollywood? (What is your address?) How do you drive to school? (What freeway do you take?)

3. Exchange your papers again. In a conversation, answer each other's questions.

4. Join another pair of students. Take turns. Talk about your partner for one minute. Then ask and answer questions to continue the conversation.

CHAPTER two

Experiencing Nature

in this chapter

there is/are

Setting the Context

Conversation

HIROSHI: Are there big hills on this hike to Emerald Lake?

CARLOS: No, there aren't.

JULIE: Don't worry, Hiroshi. There are meadows and grass on the way. There aren't any rocks on the trail. And there's no hurry.

HIROSHI: Are there forests? Is there a river?

JULIE: Yes, there's a big forest.

CARLOS: And there's a beautiful river too.

ELLEN: Is there water in that canteen?

CARLOS: Yes, there's fresh water in it.

HIROSHI: Who has all the food? There isn't any food in my backpack.

JULIE: There is food in mine. But there isn't any insect repellent.

CARLOS: That's okay. Let's go. This is a great hike. And there's not a cloud in the sky.

Answer these questions about the conversation.

1. Where are Carlos, Julie, Hiroshi, and Ellen going to hike?
2. What do they have with them?
3. What don't they have?
4. Describe the hiking trail. Use statements with *There is . . .* or *There are. . . .*

there is/are

There is (singular) and *there are* (plural) appear before the subject of a sentence. They indicate that something exists. Sentences with *there is/are* usually have a place expression. The place expressions are underlined in the examples in the charts below.

	examples	notes
Affirmative Statements	**There's** water <u>in my canteen</u>. **There are** meadows <u>on the way</u>.	*There is = There's*
Negative Statements	**There's no** hurry. **There aren't** any rocks <u>on the trail</u>.	*There's no = There isn't any* *There aren't any = There are no*

	examples	possible short answers	
		Affirmative	**Negative**
Affirmative Questions	**Is there** a river <u>near the trail</u>?	Yes, **there is.**	No, **there isn't.**/ No, **there's not.**
	Are there any sleeping bags?	Yes, **there are.**	No, **there aren't.**
Negative Questions	**Isn't there** a map <u>of the park</u>?	Yes, **there is.**	No, **there isn't.**/ No, **there's not.**
	Aren't there hills <u>on the hike</u>?	Yes, **there are.**	No, **there aren't.**

exercise 1 Underline the verb phrases with *there is/are* in the conversation on page 30.

example: <u>Are there</u> big hills on this hike to Emerald Lake?

exercise 2

Complete the sentences with one or more of these words: *there, there's, is, isn't, are, aren't.*

HAROLD: Maude, ___there's___ nothing to do in the city. Let's go camping!

MAUDE: Camping? But _____ any people our age in the mountains.

1

HAROLD: Sure _____. And _____ camping equipment in

2   3

the garage. Let's see . . . I think _____ a tent, and

4

_____ two sleeping bags.

5

MAUDE: But _____ a camp stove?

6

HAROLD: Yes, _____. But _____ no backpacks, and

7   8

_____ any hiking boots.

9

MAUDE: That's okay. _____ bathrooms and showers at the campgrounds?

10

HAROLD: Of course _____. And _____ beautiful green

11   12

meadows and flowers.

MAUDE: Oh? Then _____ mosquitoes in the mountains?

13

HAROLD: Maybe _____. But they

14

bite only young people.

MAUDE: Well, then . . . let's go—next year.

HAROLD: What? But _____ no time

15

like the present!

exercise 3

Describe the picture below. Use sentences beginning with *there is/are.*

examples: There is a deer standing in the meadow.

There are two people by the river.

Interactions I • Grammar

Using What You've Learned

activity 1

Work in pairs. Student A looks at the picture below for one minute and then closes the book. Student B asks student A questions with *there is/are* about the picture. (Student B keeps the book open but doesn't let student A see the picture.) Student A tries to answer student B's questions from memory.

example: B: Is there a river?
A: No, there's not. But there's a nice lake. There are two sailboats on the lake.
B: Are there any animals?
A: Yes, there are. There are three deer.

activity 2

Repeat Activity 1 with a nature picture from a magazine or calendar. This time, student B looks at the picture and student A asks questions.

activity 3

Close your eyes and relax. Think about your favorite place in nature. Choose a partner. Student A describes the place. Student B draws a simple picture of the place. Then change roles; student B describes a place and student A draws.

TOPIC **two**

Questions with whose and Possessive Nouns

Setting the Context

Conversation

ELLEN: This is a great lunch! I'm really hungry from today's hike.

HIROSHI: Me, too. Whose apples are these? They're delicious!

ELLEN: They're Julie's. They're from her parents' farm.

HIROSHI: They're really good. I'm thirsty. Do you have any water?

ELLEN: No, but there's some in Carlos's canteen. Save some for the hike back to Paradise Cove.

HIROSHI: Sure. Where is Carlos, anyway?

ELLEN: He's sleeping under that tree over there. Let's wake him up. It's time to start back to the campground.

HIROSHI: O.K., I'll wake him. What about Julie?

ELLEN: She's reading a book. I'll get her.

Answer these questions about the conversation.

1. Why are Ellen and Hiroshi hungry?
2. Whose apples does Hiroshi like?
3. Where are the apples from?
4. Whose canteen has water?
5. What does Ellen want to do now?

Questions with *whose*

examples	possible answers	notes
Whose tent is this? **Whose canteen** is that?	**Hiroshi's** (It's) **Carlos's.** **Carlos'.**	**Whose** is used to ask questions about possession. Use *this/these* for thing(s) close to you.
Whose farm is it?	(It's) **Julie's parents'** (farm).	
Whose apples are these? **Whose backpacks** are those?	(They're) **Julie's.** **Ellen's and Julie's.**	Use *that/those* for thing(s) not close to you.

Possessive Nouns

		possessive forms	notes
Singular Nouns	Carlos Hiroshi tomorrow the boy the student the lady the child the man	**Carlos's** or **Carlos'** (car) **Hiroshi's** (boots) **tomorrow's** (weather) **the boy's** (pencil) **the student's** (book) **the lady's** (ring) **the child's** (toy) **the man's** (watch)	If a singular noun ends in -s, add 's or ' for the possessive form. If a singular noun does not end in -s, add 's.
Plural Nouns	the boys the students the ladies the Smiths the men the children people	**the boys'** (bicycles) **the students'** (tent) **the ladies'** (coats) **the Smiths'** (house) **the men's** (team) **the children's** (toys) **the people's** (choice)	If a plural noun ends in -s, add '. The Smiths = the Smith family If a plural noun does not end in -s, add 's.

exercise 1 Circle the possessive nouns in the conversation on page 34.

example: I'm really hungry from (today's) hike.

 **exercise 2**   Write questions and answers about the pictures as in the examples.

examples:

book / Ellen

Q: Whose book is this   ?

A: It's Ellen's   .

clothes / the girls

Q: Whose clothes are these   ?

A: They're the girls'   .

1. sandwich / Francis

Q: _____?

A: _____.

2. garbage / other people

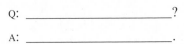

Q: _____?

A: _____.

3. sailboat / brother

Q: _____?

A: _____.

4. backpacks / children

Q: _____?

A: _____.

Interactions I • Grammar

5. bicycles / those boys

Q: _____?

A: _____.

6. sleeping bags / my parents

Q: _____?

A: _____.

exercise **3**  Complete the sentences below. Use the possessive forms of the nouns in parentheses. The first one is done as an example.

1. (Mr. Jones)   That's ____Mr. Jones'____ canteen by the tent.

2. (today)   _____ weather is going to be hot and sunny.

3. (Julie's parents)   _____ house is on a farm in the country.

4. (women)   There's a nice _____ clothing store on 5th Avenue.

5. (boyfriend)   I don't have a backpack, but you can use my _____.

6. (brothers)   His _____ names are John and Jeff.

7. (campers)   The _____ tents are falling down in the storm.

8. (wife)   My _____ sister is a doctor.

9. (weeks)   I have two _____ vacation in August; I'm going to hike in England.

10. (advisers)   The _____ offices are on the second floor.

Using What You've Learned

activity   Each student shows an object, names it, and puts in on a desk or table. (*Example:* This is my ski jacket.) Then the instructor points to each object, and the class asks and answers questions about it.

example: (*Instructor points to the ski jacket.*)
   A: Whose ski jacket is that?
   B: It's Dennis's.

The Present Continuous Tense

Setting the Context

Conversation

HIROSHI: Oh, thank goodness. There's Paradise Cove at last.

JULIE: Oh, my back is killing me. I have to rest again.

ELLEN: That backpack is very heavy. Carlos, please carry Julie's pack back to camp. She's really having trouble.

CARLOS: Sure.

JULIE: Oh, thank you, Carlos. Aren't you getting tired, too?

CARLOS: Well, yes, I *am* a little tired. But we're getting close now.

ELLEN: Hey! Look at the campground! What's going on down there?

JULIE: Hiroshi's tent is falling down.

HIROSHI: Oh, no! *(He sits down on a big rock.)*

ELLEN: Hiroshi, don't stop now. We're almost there!

HIROSHI: These aren't my boots, and they're killing me. Jim's feet are so small. I'm going barefoot the rest of the way.

CARLOS: Look at the river! There's a book floating away! It's Anita's. She's sleeping!

JULIE: Oh, dear. Let's hurry. Everything is going wrong!

Answer these questions according to the conversation.

1. What is Julie's problem?
2. What are Hiroshi's problems?
3. What is Anita's problem?

The Present Continuous Tense

To make the present continuous tense, use a form of the verb *be* before the *-ing* form of a main verb. Use the present continuous to describe an action that is in progress* or happening now. It also describes a period of time that includes the present: an action started in the past, is continuing now (in the present), and will end in the future. The charts below give some examples.

Statements

	examples	notes
Affirmative	My feet **are killing** me. Julie **is having** trouble.	In examples 1 and 2, the action is happening now. See **Spelling Rules for *-ing* Verbs** on page 40.
	There**'s** a bear **eating** our food!	With *there is/are*, use an *-ing* verb after the subject.
	We**'re enjoying** nature this spring.	In this example, the action is happening over a period of time that includes the present (this spring).
Negative	Hiroshi **isn't wearing** boots. They **aren't going** on the hike. We **aren't joking**.	Use contractions with forms of *be* and *not*.

Yes/No Questions

	examples	possible answers	
		Affirmative	**Negative**
Affirmative	**Is** Carlos **carrying** her backpack?	Yes, he is.	No, he isn't.
	Are there any hikers **walking** on the trail?	Yes, there are.	No, there aren't.
Negative	**Isn't** he **wearing** boots?	Yes, he is.	No, he isn't.
	Aren't you **getting** tired?	Yes, I am.	No, I'm not.

*The present continuous is also called the present progressive.

Information Questions

	examples	possible answers
Affirmative	**What's going on*** down there? **Why are** you **sneezing**?	Hiroshi's tent **is falling down.*** I**'m getting** a cold.
Negative	**Who isn't hiking** to Emerald Lake? **Why aren't** they **wearing** shoes?	Anita and Paul **aren't going.** Their feet **are killing** them.

*Some verbs can appear with a preposition. The verb and the preposition form a *phrasal verb.*

Spelling Rules for *-ing* Verbs

1. If the simple form ends in silent *-e* after a consonant, drop the *-e* and add *-ing*.

   examples: have / having   sneeze / sneezing

2. If the simple form ends in *-ie,* change the *-ie* to *y* and add *-ing*.

   examples: die / dying   untie / untying

3. If the simple form has one syllable and ends in one consonant after one vowel, double the last consonant (except *x*) and add *-ing*.

   examples: get / getting   run / running

   Note: The letters *w* and *y* at the end of a word are considered vowels, not consonants.

   examples: row / rowing   play / playing

4. If the simple form ends in an accented (stressed) syllable, follow the rule above for one final consonant after one vowel.

   example: begín / beginning

   Note: If the last syllable is not accented, just add *-ing*.

   example: háppen / happening

5. For all other verbs add *-ing* to the simple form.

   examples: walk / walking   eat / eating   carry / carrying

 **exercise** Underline the present continuous verb phrases in the conversation on page 38.

   example: Oh, my back <u>is killing</u> me.

Fill in the blanks with the present continuous forms of the verbs in parentheses. The first one is done as an example.

PAUL: Ah-choo! Ah-choo!

ANITA: Paul! Why _____are_____ you _____sneezing_____?
                          1 (sneeze)
_____ you _____ _____?
                          2 (get sick)

PAUL: Maybe. The water in the river is really cold.

ANITA: You _____ _____!
                          3 (shiver)
Why _____ you _____
                          4 (not wear)
a shirt and pants?

PAUL: You're right. I _____ _____.
                          5 (freeze)

ANITA: Where's my book?

PAUL: Let's see . . . Oh, it's in the water!

It _____ _____ down the
                 6 (float)
river. Ow! *(He hits his back.)*

ANITA: What's the matter?

PAUL: I think there _____ something
                          7 (bite)
_____ me.

ANITA: Let me see. Oh, Paul! There are mosquitoes all
over your back!

PAUL: Anita, look! The hikers _____
                          8 (come)
_____ back.

ANITA: Where? I don't see them.

PAUL: They _____ _____ down the trail.
                 9 (walk)

ANITA: Oh, yeah. Now I see them. But they

_____ _____. They
       10 (not, walk)
_____ _____. Why
       11 (run)
_____ they _____ so fast?
                 12 (go)

PAUL: I don't know.

ANITA: There _____ something _____
                          13 (move)
behind them. What is it? Is that a deer?

PAUL: No, it's a *bear*! They _____
                          14 (run)
_____ away from a bear.

Describe the action in the pictures in the present continuous. Write two sentences for each picture using the cue words. The first one is done as an example.

1.

- Julie / give / her backpack / to Carlos
- Her back / kill her

Julie is giving her backpack to Carlos.

Her back is killing her.

2.

- Paul / get dressed
- Mosquitoes / bite him

3.

- The tents / fall down
- Anita / fix them

4.

- Julie / make lunch
- The hamburgers / burn

5.

- Ellen / sit on a rock

- A snake / come toward her

6.

- Hiroshi / throw Jim's boots in the river
- They / float away

_____

_____

7.

- Carlos / make noise
- The bear / run away

8.

- Ellen and Hiroshi / have lunch
- They eat / apples

_____

_____

 **exercise 4**

Work in pairs. Look at the pictures on page 38. Student A asks present continuous questions with the cue words. Student B answers the questions.

example: Who / run / with no backpack?

A: Who is running with no backpack?
B: Julie is running with no backpack.

1. the sky / get cloudy?
2. Who / sleep?
3. What / the bear / do?
4. What / Paul / wear?
5. the hikers / have trouble?
6. What / the deer / do?
7. What / happen / to the tents?
8. What / Hiroshi / do?

 **exercise 5**

Change roles. Now student B asks present continuous questions with the new cue words, and student A answers.

1. the weather / change?
2. What / the hikers / do?
3. Who / carry / Julie's backpack?
4. What / Paul / do?
5. people / swim?
6. Where / Anita's book / go?
7. Why / Hiroshi / carry / the boots?
8. What / Anita / do?

Using What You've Learned

 **activity**

Work in small groups. Take turns choosing one item from each list. Pretend you are in that place, at that time. Imagine the activities of the people there and describe them to the group. Other group members guess the scene.

example: A: There are many people here. People are swimming. One man is fishing. Children are playing in the sand.
B: You're at the beach in summer.

PLACES	TIMES
in the mountains	in winter
in the desert	in summer
on a river	in spring
at the beach	in fall
at a lake	
at a park	
in a forest	

Impersonal it

Setting the Context

Conversation

ELLEN: Oh, no! It's starting to rain.

PAUL: That can't be. It's August! It never rains in the mountains in August.

JULIE: Uh-oh. I can feel it too.

HIROSHI: Me, too. We're getting all wet. Can we run to that tree?

ELLEN: No, there might be lightning.

PAUL: There isn't any lightning. Let's go! *(They run to the tree.)*

ANITA: Whew! Not a minute too soon. Will you look at that? It's pouring!

ELLEN: I can't believe this.

CARLOS: The storm may not last long.

HIROSHI: Look. Now, it's hailing! What will happen to our tents?

ANITA: Can we pack up and go back to the cars?

CARLOS: It's too late for that. It's ten miles to the cars. It's almost dark.

ELLEN: Can't we do anything?

HIROSHI: Don't worry. The rain will stop.

ALL: But when?

HIROSHI: Oh, maybe next week?

 **exercise** Answer these questions about the picture and the conversation.

1. Describe the changes in the weather.
2. Describe the condition of the campground.
3. What will happen next?

Impersonal *it*

Impersonal *it* is used in statements and questions to talk about time, distance, and the weather. This chart gives some examples.

	statements	questions	notes
Time	It's getting late. It's 12:30. It's night. It's Wednesday, May 2. It's winter.	Is **it** late? What time is **it**? When is **it**? What day is **it**? Is **it** summer in Australia?	Use impersonal *it* with clock time, time of day, days of the week, months, dates, and seasons.
Distance	It's two miles to the lake.* It's too far to walk. It isn't very far.	Is **it** far? How far is **it** to the car? Is **it** a long way?	Use impersonal *it* with feet, yards, miles, kilometers, and the word *far*. *a long way* = *far*
Weather	It's very cold today. It's pouring outside. It isn't raining very hard.	Is **it** cold in the forest? What's **it** like out? What's **it** doing outside?	Use impersonal *it* before adjectives (*cold, sunny,* and so on) and verbs (*rain, snow,* and so on) about the weather.

*The word *far* is not used in statements when a specific distance is given; for example:
   CORRECT: It's two miles.
   INCORRECT: It's two miles far.

 **exercise 1** Circle the uses of impersonal *it* in the conversation on page 45.

exercise 2 Write sentences about time, weather, and distance in pictures 1 to 4. Use impersonal *it*. Write as many sentences as you can for each picture. When you finish, work with another classmate. Read each other's sentences. Who wrote the most sentences?

    example: It's raining. It's warm. It's not far to Paradise Cove.

46

1.

2.

3.

4.

Using What You've Learned

activity

Work with a partner. Role play this situation. Student A invites student B to do something. Student B doesn't want to go and gives his or her reasons. Student A tries to persuade student B to go. Use sentences with impersonal *it*. Practice your conversation, then perform your role-play for the class.

example:

A: Let's go to a movie.

B: I don't want to. It's late.

A: It's only 9:00. Come on! It will be fun!

B: No. It's too far to the movie theater.

A: Don't worry about it. It's not that far. I'll drive.

B: I don't think so. It's cold outside.

A: It's not very cold. You can wear a coat. Come on!

B: Oh, all right. (*or* No, thanks. Maybe some other time.)

Modal Verbs: **can, may, might, will**

Setting the Context

Conversation

Read the conversation on page 45 again. Notice the uses of the words *can, may, might,* and *will.*

exercise ▼   Answer these questions about the conversation.

1. What can Julie feel?
2. What does Ellen think there might be?
3. What can they do to get out of the rain?
4. What can't Ellen believe?
5. What does Carlos think about the storm?
6. Why can't they go back to the cars?
7. What does Hiroshi think will happen?
8. What do you think they will do now?

A. Forms and Patterns

Can, may, might, and *will* are four modal verbs. These charts give some examples of their position in statements and questions.

Statements

	examples	notes
Affirmative	I **can** feel it. It **may** stop soon. The tents **might** fall down. We**'ll** call you tonight.	In a statement, a modal comes before the simple form of the verb. Don't use *to* before the verb. Contractions with *will: I will = I'll; he will = he'll; she will = she'll; we will = we'll; you will = you'll; they will = they'll*
Negative	I **can't** swim. He **may not** go with us. The streets **might not** be safe. It **won't** be crowded.	Negative contractions: *cannot = can't* and *will not = won't*

Yes/No Questions

	examples	possible answers		notes
		Affirmative	**Negative**	
Affirmative	**Can** you go with us?	Yes, I **can.**	No, I **can't**	In a yes/no question, a modal comes before the subject.
	Might it rain tonight?	Yes, it **might.**	No, it **won't.**	
	Will we get there late?	Yes, we **will.**	No, we **won't.**	
Negative	**Can't** the children swim?	Yes, they **can.**	No, they **can't.**	
	Won't it be hot in August?	Yes, it **will.**	No, it **won't.**	

Information Questions

	examples	possible answers	notes
Affirmative	What **can** we do?	We **can** run to that tree.	In an information question, a modal comes after the question word.
	Who **may** visit us?	Carlos **may** visit.	
	What **might** happen?	You **might** get sick.	
	Where **will** they go?	They**'ll** stay home.	
Negative	What **can't** he eat?	He **can't** eat meat.	
	Who **may not** play?	Hiroshi. His feet hurt.	
	Who **might not** go?	Ellen and Julie.	
	Why **won't** Anita visit?	She's too busy.	

B. Meanings

Modals have more than one meaning or use. This chart gives some examples of their meanings in this chapter.

modals	meaning	examples
can	ability	I **can** speak English. He **can't** swim. **Can** you dance?
may **might**	future possibility	It **may** rain. (= Maybe it will rain; maybe it won't.) I **might** not go. (= Maybe I won't go; maybe I will.)
will	future plans predictions	I'**ll** see you tomorrow. (= I plan to see you tomorrow.) The movie **won't** be crowded. (= I predict the movie won't be crowded.) **Will** we get there on time?

 **exercise 1** Underline the modals in the conversation on page 45. Tell the meaning of each.

example: I <u>can</u> feel it too. = ability

 **exercise 2** Write about your plans for the next semester or term break (vacation). Describe what you may or might do, what you can do, and what you will do. Write as many sentences as you can. When you finish, work with another classmate. Read each other's sentences. Who wrote the most sentences?

example: Next vacation, I'll take it easy. I may take a trip with some friends. We might camp or hike in the country. Or we might stay in the city.

exercise 3 Circle the correct words in 1 to 22. The first one is done as an example.

There are some clouds, but it [willn't rain / (won't rain)] today. At least I don't think it [will rain / 'ill rains]. It [will being / will be] a beautiful day. I [might to catch / might catch] some fish. They [can might be / might be] big fish. Uh-oh. There's water coming into the boat. There [might be / will to be] a leak. How [can / can't] I [find / finding] it? I [not / can't] [see / to

see] the bottom of the boat under all the water. Help! Help! Who [can / do]
[help / helped] me? What [can / cans] anyone [do / will do]? What's that
12   13   14
noise? It ['ll / might] [is / be] a waterfall. Oh, no! It *is* a waterfall! Well, I
15   16
[mayn't / might not] [will save / save] the boat, but I [can / 'll] [be / do]
17   18   19   20
able to save my life. I [can / cann't] [swim / swimming]!
21   22

Using What You've Learned

Work in pairs. Have a conversation using modals. Talk about your abilities, future
plans, and so on. Use the words below and your own words.

swim	row a boat	cook over a campfire
sail	build a fire	read a map
hike	ride a horse	set up a tent

example: A: I can't swim. Can you?
B: Yes, I can swim well. Can you sail?
A: No, I can't. But my friend can sail. I might go sailing with her
soon.
B: Where will you go?

Work in small groups. Take turns making statements with modals about each of the situations in 1 to 5. Tell what might (or might not) or will (or won't) happen in each situation.

example: You're driving on an icy mountain road. You go around a curve in the road. A deer suddenly jumps out in front of your car. What might happen?

A: I will hit the deer.
B: I might have an accident.
C: The car might slide on the ice.
D: I will try to stop.

1. Carlos, Hiroshi, Paul, Julie, Anita, and Ellen are standing under a big tree. It's raining hard and there is thunder and lightning.

2. You and your friends return to your campground late in the evening after a long hike. There is a bear eating your food.

3. Some hikers are on the top of a high mountain. It's very windy, and there are a lot of dark clouds in the sky.

4. Some campers want to start a fire for dinner. Their matches are wet from the rain last night.

5. Some students are hiking on a new trail. It's almost dark and they're lost.

Work in small groups. Take turns talking about yourself and your hometown or country. One student at a time answers questions from other group members. Use the questions below. Add other questions if you like.

1. How far is it from here to your hometown or country?
2. What time is it there now? (Is it early or late in the day?)
3. What season is it? How is the weather now? What are people doing outdoors?
4. What is your favorite season in your country or hometown? Why? What can you do in that season? How might the weather be?
5. How far is it from your hometown to the capital? How far is it to the mountains? To the ocean? To a lake? How can people get to these places?
6. What other outdoor activities might people enjoy in your hometown or country? Describe them.
7. When will you probably go back to your hometown or country? What will you do for fun outdoors?
8. Think about a friend or family member in your hometown or country. What is he or she probably doing right now?

CHAPTER three

Living to Eat or Eating to Live?

in this chapter

Nouns and Expressions of Quantity

1.

2.

3.

Setting the Context
Reading

The Changing American Diet

What are some examples of "typical" American meals? On the weekend, a typical breakfast may consist of two or three eggs, some pancakes with butter and syrup, and several pieces of bacon. During the week, some people have only toast or a sweet roll and some juice or coffee for breakfast. Or they might eat a bowl of cold cereal with some milk. For lunch, many people eat junk food. For example, they may stop at a fastfood place for a cheeseburger or a hot dog with a little catsup or mustard and some relish, some french fries, a milkshake or a soft drink, and a few cookies. A typical American dinner consists of meat, a baked potato, several slices of white bread or a few rolls, and maybe a little salad. And dinner often ends with dessert—typically, pie and ice cream or cake.

Nutritionalists don't believe that the typical American diet is very healthy. Many kinds of American food are high in sugar, salt, fat, caffeine, or cholesterol. These food substances may cause disease. In general, Americans don't eat much whole-grain food, fish, vegetables, and fruit, which contain important vitamins, protein, and fiber.

However, some Americans are becoming more interested in good health, and they are changing their eating habits. They are eating more whole-grain bread and cereal, and less white bread and sugar cereal. They are eating more chicken and fish, and less red meat. Many people are eating more fresh vegetables, and fewer frozen or canned vegetables. They are drinking less coffee (high in caffeine) and soda (high in sugar), and more decaffeinated coffee, herbal tea, and fruit juice.

4.

exercise Answer these questions about the reading.

1. What does a "typical" American breakfast consist of?
2. What might an American have for lunch at a fast-food place?
3. Describe a typical American dinner.
4. How are some Americans changing their eating habits? What kinds of food are they eating?
5. Do you think the meals in the pictures on page 54 are good for the health? Why or why not?

A. Count and Noncount Nouns

	examples		notes
	Singular	**Plural**	
Count Nouns	a **meal** an **egg** one **roll** a **drink** a **potato**	three **meals** some **eggs** a few **rolls** many **drinks** **potatoes**	Singular count nouns often have *a, an,* or *one* before them. Plural count nouns can have numbers or expressions of quantity* before them. Most plural count nouns have *-s* or *-es* endings.
Noncount Nouns	butter some **juice** a lot of **salt** a little **sugar** much **food** **health** a cup of **coffee** a piece of **bacon** a bowl of **cereal**		Some expressions of quantity can be used before noncount nouns but <u>not</u> *a, an,* or numbers. Noncount counts have no plural forms; they do not take *-s* or *-es* endings. In English, most noncount nouns describe whole things (or groups of things) made up of smaller or different parts, such as *meat, salt, food, juice,* etc.[†] Some noncount nouns describe abstract things, such as *health, information, work, time,* and so on.

*Some expressions of quantity are: *some, a few, a lot of, a little, much, many.* (See subtopics B, C, and E.)

[†]To describe a particular or smaller quantity of some noncount nouns, use unit expressions, such as *a cup of (tea), a piece of (toast), a glass of (milk), a slice of (bread), a grain of (rice), a bowl of (soup).*

exercise 1 Underline the singular count nouns in the reading on page 55. Put two lines under the plural nouns. Circle the noncount nouns.

> **example:** What are some <u>examples</u> of "typical" American <u>meals</u>? On the <u>weekend</u>, a typical <u>breakfast</u> may consist of two or three <u>eggs</u>, some <u>pancakes</u> with (butter) and (syrup,) and several pieces of (bacon.)

exercise 2 Work with a partner. Take turns describing the pictures on pages 54 and 55. (Student A describes pictures 1 and 3; student B describes pictures 2 and 4.) Make sentences beginning with *there is/are* and using singular, plural, and noncount nouns.

> **example:** STUDENT A: There are two plates in the first picture. On one plate, there are two eggs and some bacon.

exercise 3 Look around the classroom. For five minutes, write as many sentences as you can about different singular, plural, and noncount nouns. When you finish, work with another classmate. Read each other's sentences. Whose sentences have the most nouns of different kinds?

> **example:** There's a clock on the wall. There are books on the shelf. There's some paper on the teacher's desk.

B. *some* and *any*

Some and *any* may appear before noncount and plural count nouns. This chart gives some examples.

	examples	notes
some	There are **some** eggs in the refrigerator. Please eat **some** vegetables. There's **some** milk in that cup. Do you want **some** ice cream? Would you like **some** fruit?	*Some* is used in affirmative statements and questions.
any	I **don't** use **any** salt. There **aren't any*** hot dogs. There **isn't any*** sugar in this soda. Do you have **any** bananas? **Isn't** there **any** rice?	*Any* is used in negative statements. *Any* is used in affirmative and negative questions.

*Not any before noncount and plural count nouns means *no;* for example:
   There aren't any hot dogs. = There are <u>no</u> hot dogs. There isn't any sugar. = There is <u>no</u> sugar.
Don't use two negatives; for example:
   CORRECT: There isn't any food. Or: There is no food.
   INCORRECT: There isn't <u>no</u> food.

exercise **4**   Complete the sentences below. Use *some* or *any* as in the examples. More than one answer might be correct.

1. Mary always eats __some__ fruit for breakfast.

2. I'm a vegetarian; I don't eat __any__ meat.

3. Is there _____ milk in the refrigerator?

4. I want _____ coffee, but there isn't _____ decaffeinated coffee left.

5. Do you want _____ lemon in your tea?

6. I need to buy _____ food; I don't have _____ fruit or vegetables.

7. Would you like _____ salt or catsup on your french fries?

8. Do you have _____ mineral water?

9. I'd like _____ onions and _____ mushrooms on my pizza.

10. John doesn't eat _____ red meat, but he may eat _____ fish.

11. Fred wants _____ chocolate ice cream, and Linda wants _____ apple pie.

12. I don't want _____ ice cream, but I'd like to try _____ frozen yogurt.

13. Is there _____ sugar in that soda?

14. I'd like _____ eggs, but I don't want _____ bacon.

15. I'm going to the supermarket. Do we need _____ bread?

   Work with a partner. Take turns asking and answering questions about the food in the pictures on pages 54 and 55. Use *some* or *any* in your questions and answers.

example: A: Is there any juice in the breakfast picture?
           B: There isn't any juice, but there is some coffee.

   Look at the picture below. It shows different things you can use to make an ice cream sundae. Describe your favorite ice cream sundae. Write sentences using *some* or *any*. An example is on the next page.

example: My sundae has some vanilla and chocolate ice cream, but it doesn't have any strawberry ice cream. It has some nuts and whipped cream.

When you finish, work with another classmate. Take turns describing your favorite sundae.

example: A: What's your favorite sundae?
B: It has some vanilla and chocolate ice cream.

C. *a lot of / many / much*

These expressions are used to show a large quantity of something. *A lot of* may appear before noncount and plural count nouns. *Many* may appear only before plural count nouns. *Much* may appear only before noncount nouns. This chart gives some examples.

	examples	notes
a lot of	There is **a lot of** salt in this soup. She doesn't eat **a lot of** hamburgers. Is there **a lot of** fresh fruit in the market? Don't you eat **a lot of** vegetables?	*A lot of* is used in affirmative and negative statements and questions.
many	**Many** fast-food restaurants serve hot dogs. I don't like **many** kinds of vegetables. Are **many** Americans changing their diet? Aren't there **many** eggs in the refrigerator?	*Many* is used in affirmative and negative statements and questions.
much	They don't eat **much** red meat. We don't drink **much** tea or coffee. Does chicken have **much** cholesterol? Don't they eat **much** fish?	*Much* is used mainly in negative statements and affirmative and negative questions. *Much* usually isn't used in affirmative statements; use *a lot of* instead.

 **exercise 7** Describe the pictures. Write sentences using *a lot of, many,* or *much* as in the examples.

ICE CREAM

1. There is a lot of ice cream.

COOKIES

2. There aren't many cookies.

There aren't a lot of cookies.

MILK

3. _____

APPLES

4. _____

PIZZA

5. _____

RICE

6. _____

PANCAKES

7. _____

SPAGHETTI

8. _____

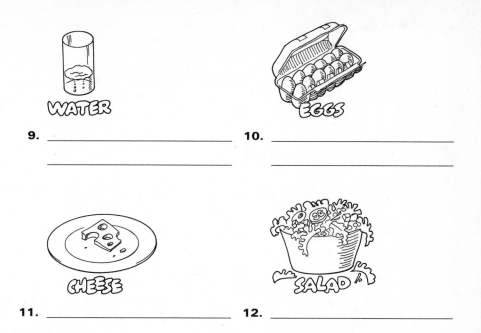

9. _____

10. _____

11. _____

12. _____

D. Asking Questions with *how many / how much*

	questions	possible answers	notes
how many	**How many** eggs do you want? **How many** cakes are you making? **How many** vegetables do I get?	Two. Only one. Three.	Use *how many* in questions before plural count nouns.
how much	**How much** coffee* does he drink? **How much** rice do we need? **How much** pizza* can you eat?	Three cups. Ten pounds. Two slices.	Use *how much* in questions before noncount nouns.

*You can also ask: *How many cups of coffee does he drink?* (Answer: Three.) and *How many slices of pizza can you eat?* (Answer: Two.)

exercise 8   Work with a partner. Take turns asking and answering questions about the pictures on pages 60 and 61. Use *how many* or *how much*.

example: A: How much ice cream is in the bowl?
           B: There's a lot of ice cream. How many cookies are on the plate?
           A: Two. (*or* There aren't many.)

E.   *a few / a little*

A few and *a little* are used to show a small quantity of something. *A few* appears only before plural count nouns. *A little* appears only before noncount nouns.

	examples	notes
a few	There are **a few** eggs in the refrigerator. She only likes **a few** vegetables. Would you like **a few** potatoes? Aren't there **a few** cookies in the box?	*A few* and *a little* are used in affirmative statements and in affirmative and negative questions.
a little	I'd like **a little** salt on my french fries. There's **a little** ice cream in the freezer. Is there **a little** sugar in that bowl? Don't you want **a little** milk in your tea?	

exercise 9   Complete the sentences below. Use *a few* or *a little*. The first one is done as an example.

1. I need ____a little____ sugar to make a cake.

2. Do they want _____ catsup on their french fries?

3. Can you get me _____ apples and _____ orange juice?

4. I'd like tea with _____ cream and sugar, please.

5. Does your brother want _____ pieces of bacon with his eggs?

6. Would you like _____ vegetable soup?

7. There are _____ hot dogs, but there aren't any hamburgers.

8. They're having _____ cups of coffee with their dessert.

9. They need _____ rolls at that table.

10. We have _____ vanilla ice cream, but there isn't any chocolate.

Using What You've Learned

activity 1

You can do this activity as a whole class or in groups. Sit in a circle if possible. One student begins by completing the sentence

I need _____ from the store.

with a quantity expression and a noun. The next student repeats the first item and adds a new item. The next student repeats the first two items and adds one more, and so on. If a student forgets some information, other students can help him or her.

example: A: I need a lot of milk from the store.
B: I need a lot of milk and some bananas from the store.
C: I need a lot of milk, some bananas, and a little butter from the store.

Variation: The first student names an item that begins with the letter "a"; the second student, an item that begins with "b"; the third student, an item that begins with "c"; and so on.

activity 2

If possible, get a menu from a restaurant that you go to or know about. (If you can't get a real menu, think about the kinds of food you can eat at the restaurant.) Write a paragraph describing the kinds of food at this restaurant. Use count and noncount nouns and expressions of quantity.

example: Pongsri is a good Thai restaurant. You can eat a lot of delicious Thai food there. They have many chicken, beef, and pork dishes. Many dishes come with rice or noodles. They also serve a lot of fish and other seafood. They have a few salads and some soup.

When you finish, work with another classmate. Read each other's descriptions. Are your count and noncount nouns used with the right expressions of quantity? (If you aren't sure, ask your teacher.) Do you want to go to your partner's restaurant? Why or why not?

If you like, read some other classmates' descriptions. Make a restaurant guide for your class by collecting and copying all your descriptions.

activity 3

Think of some food you like to eat or make yourself, such as a salad, a sandwich, a pizza, or a dish from your home country. Write a brief description of your favorite salad, sandwich, and so on. Use as many expressions of quantity as you can. (If you don't know the English words for some items, ask your teacher or classmates.)

example: My favorite salad has a lot of lettuce and tomatoes. It has some carrots and a few mushrooms.

When you finish, form small groups. Take turns describing your favorite dishes. Which dishes do you want to try?

activity 4 Write about your eating habits for ten minutes. Use as many count and noncount nouns and expressions of quantity as possible.

> **example:** I usually eat healthy food. For breakfast, I usually have a bowl of cereal with fruit and low-fat milk. I drink only decaffeinated coffee with a little milk and without any sugar. Later in the morning, I have a snack—usually a piece of fruit. For lunch, I have a bowl of soup and some salad.

When you finish writing, work with another classmate. Take turns reading each other's papers. Then write some questions with *how much* or *how many* to ask your partner for more information.

> **example:** How many snacks do you eat every day?
> How much coffee do you usually drink?

Return your papers and read each other's questions. Discuss the answers with your partner. How are your partner's eating habits similar to yours? How are they different?

TOPIC **two**
Comparisons

Setting the Context

Conversation

DOLORES: Diane! Hello, there!

DIANE: Oh, hello, Dolores.

DOLORES: My goodness! You certainly have a lot of things in your cart!

DIANE: Yes, well, you know we have five children.

DOLORES: Are you buying Pearly White Dishwashing Liquid? There are cheaper brands.

DIANE: It's more expensive than other brands, but I think it lasts longer.

DOLORES: Why are you buying that huge package of spaghetti? There are smaller sizes . . .

DIANE: The larger size is always cheaper. Well, nice seeing you again . . .

DOLORES: Those cherries look nicer than the strawberries in my cart! May I taste one? *(She takes a cherry.)* Oh, my. They're much tastier than the cherries last year.

DIANE: Dolores, I have to get home as soon as possible.

DOLORES: Do you really like brown rice better than white rice? It cooks more slowly.

DIANE: Brown rice tastes just as good as white rice, and it's more nutritious.

DOLORES: You know, the sign says this market is cheaper, but I think it's just as expensive as the others. It's farther too. What do you think?

DIANE: I think one market is as good as any other. Well, I'll let you go now, Dolores. I know you're as busy as I am.

 exercise Answer these questions about the conversation.

1. What is Dolores asking Diane questions about?
2. Why does Diane buy Pearly White Dishwashing Liquid?
3. Why does Diane buy the larger size package of spaghetti?
4. What does Dolores think about the cherries in Diane's cart?
5. Why does Diane buy brown rice?
6. What do Dolores and Diane think about Save-A-Lot Market?
7. Is Diane enjoying the conversation? How do you know?

A. Comparisons with *as ... as* and *less ... than*

Use the phrase *as* + adjective or adverb + *as* to compare two or more people or things in affirmative and negative statements and questions. You can use the pattern *less* + adjective or adverb + *than* in some negative comparisons. This chart gives some examples.

examples	notes
This market is **as expensive as** the others. You're **as busy as** I am. Are the cherries **as nice as** the strawberries?	Affirmative sentences compare things that are the same in some way. (All the markets are expensive. You and I are both busy.)
Pearly White isn't **as cheap** (**as** other brands). Brown rice doesn't cook **as quickly** (**as** white rice). Aren't the cherries **as good as** (the cherries) last year?	Negative sentences compare things that are different in some way. You can leave out the words in parentheses if they are understood by the reader or listener.
White rice is **less nutritious** (**than** brown rice). White rice isn't **as nutritious** (**as** brown rice). I'm **less busy than** you are. I'm not **as busy as** you are.	*Less* is the opposite of *more*. The two sentences in each pair have the same meaning. You can use *less* with many adjectives that have two or more syllables; *less* is usually not used with one-syllable adjectives.

 **exercise 1** Underline the phrases with *as . . . as* in the conversation on page 65.

 **exercise 2** Compare the items below. Write affirmative or negative sentences using *as . . . as* and the adjectives under the pictures. If possible, write sentences using *less . . . than*. (Use the notes in the chart to help you.) The first two are done as examples.

1. expensive

Pie is as expensive as cake.

_____

2. cheap

Milk isn't as expensive as cream.

Milk is less expensive than cream.

3. delicious

_____

_____

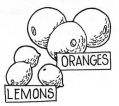

4. sweet

_____

_____

5. nutritious

_____

_____

5. cook quickly

_____

_____

7. healthy

_____

_____

8. fresh

_____

_____

B. Comparisons with ... *-er than* and *more ... than*

Use the pattern adjective or adverb + *-er than* or *more* + adjective or adverb + *than* to compare two or more people or things that are different. The chart on page 68 gives some examples.

	examples	notes
One-Syllable Adjectives and Adverbs	These cherries are **sweeter than** those. This market is **cheaper than** the others. Brown rice cooks **slower than** white rice. These eggs are **bigger than** those.	Add *-er* to most one-syllable adjectives and adverbs. If a word ends in one vowel and one consonant, double the last consonant and add *-er*. *Example:* big / bigger
Two-Syllable Adjectives Ending in -y	This fish is **tastier than** that. Thai food is **spicier than** American food. Fruit is **healthier than** ice cream.	If a word ends in *-y*, change the *y* to *i* and add *-er*.
Adjectives and Adverbs with Two or More Syllables	It's **more expensive than** the other brands. It's **more nutritious than** white rice. Fresh vegetables are **more delicious than** frozen ones.	Use *more* with most adjectives that have two or more syllables.
Irregular Forms	Cream tastes **better than** milk. Coffee is **worse** for your health **than** tea. The health food store is **farther** (or **further**) **than** the supermarket.	The comparative forms of *good, bad,* and *far* are irregular: *good / better* *bad / worse* *far / farther (further)*

exercise 3   Circle the comparisons with *. . . -er than* and *more . . . than* and the irregular comparative forms in the conversation on page 65.

exercise 4   Work with a partner. Take turns comparing the two food items in each picture on page 69. Use words from the following list, and add other words of your own. Make as many sentences as you can for each picture using *as . . . as, less . . . than, -er than,* or *more . . . than.* Several answers may be correct for each picture.

expensive	tasty	spicy
healthy	(taste) good	easy (to make)
delicious	bad	(cook) fast
nutritious	sweet	

    examples: A: Ice cream isn't as healthy as frozen yogurt.
                  B: Ice cream tastes better than frozen yogurt.
                  A: Ice cream is sweeter than frozen yogurt.
                  B: Ice cream is as expensive as frozen yogurt.
                  A: I don't know about that. I think frozen yogurt is more expensive.

Variation: Write your sentences first. Then work with a partner and compare your sentences.

1.

2.

3.

4.

5.

6.

7.

8.

9.

Compare American food to food in your native country.

10.

Compare food from two other countries.

C. More Comparisons: *as much/many ... as* and *more/less/fewer ... than*

Use *as much/many ... as* and *more/less/fewer ... than* to compare numbers or amounts of count or noncount nouns. This chart gives some examples.

examples	notes
Does frozen yogurt have **as many calories as** ice cream?	Use *as many ... as* with plural count nouns.
Fruit juice doesn't have **as much sugar as** soda.	Use *as much ... as* with noncount nouns.
I eat **more apples than** oranges.	Use *more* before plural count and noncount nouns.
She drinks **more tea than** coffee.	
There is **less sugar than** salt in this sauce.	Use *less* only before noncount nouns.
Canned food has **fewer vitamins than** frozen food.	Use *fewer* only before plural count nouns.

exercise 5   Compare the food items in the pictures. Use the words under the pictures to make sentences with *as much/many ... as* or *more/less/fewer ... than*. The first item is done as an example.

steak / chicken / market

1. _____ There's more steak than chicken at the market. _____

_____ There's less chicken than steak at the market. _____

peaches / bananas / bowl

2. _____

_____

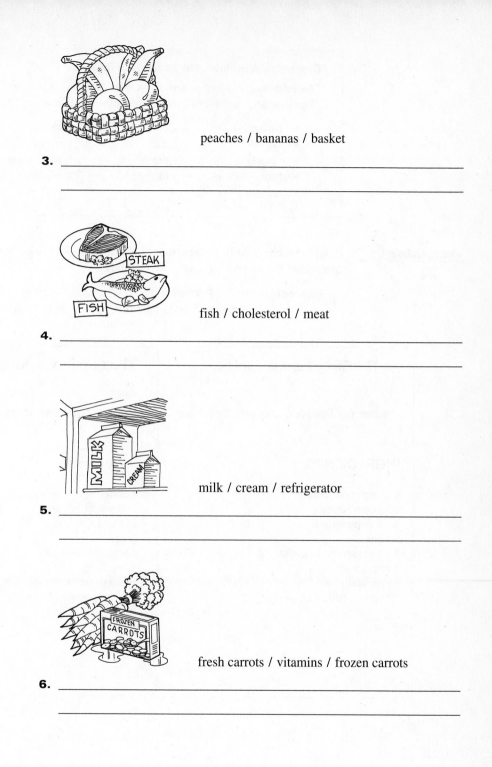

peaches / bananas / basket

3. _____

_____

fish / cholesterol / meat

4. _____

_____

milk / cream / refrigerator

5. _____

_____

fresh carrots / vitamins / frozen carrots

6. _____

_____

Describing Amounts of Ingredients in Recipes

The following measures are commonly used for ingredients in recipes. The measures are listed from largest (pound) to smallest (teaspoon):

- pound(s)   1 pound   =   16 ounces
- cup(s)   1 cup   =   8 ounces
- ounce(s)   1 ounce   =   2 tablespoons
- tablespoon(s)   1 tablespoon   =   3 teaspoons
- teaspoon(s)

 **exercise 6**   Read the recipes for brownies from two different cookbooks. Write sentences comparing the ingredients in the two recipes.

example: The first recipe uses more chocolate than the second. The first recipe uses as much butter as the second.

The Fancy Farmer Cookbook	**The Fun of Cooking Cookbook**
Recipe for Double Chocolate Brownies	**Recipe for Peanut Butter Brownies**
INGREDIENTS	Ingredients:
5 ounces chocolate 1/2 pound butter 1 3/4 cups sugar 5 eggs 1 1/2 teaspoons vanilla 1 cup flour 1 cup walnuts 1 cup chocolate chips	4 ounces chocolate 1/2 pound butter 2 cups sugar 4 eggs 1 teaspoon vanilla 1 cup flour 1 cup peanuts 1/2 cup peanut butter

1.

2.

Using What You've Learned

For ten minutes, write about the typical diet of people from your home country. Use as many count and noncount nouns and expressions of quantity as you can.

> **example:** People from Mexico often eat a lot of rice and beans. Mexican dishes can contain many kinds of meat and seafood: beef, pork, chicken, fish, shrimp, and so on. Mexicans use many spices, such as chili peppers, garlic, onions, and cilantro (also called coriander). They usually eat some tortillas (a kind of flat bread) with each meal.

When you finish writing, work with a partner from another country. Tell your partner about the typical diet of people from your country. Listen to your partner's information. Together, write sentences to compare the food from your two countries.

> **example:** Typical Mexican food is spicier than typical German food. Mexicans eat a lot more rice and beans than Germans, and Germans eat a lot more bread and potatoes.

Then work with another pair of students. Discuss your sentences comparing the different foods.

activity 2

Work with a partner. Together, choose one of the food dishes from the following list, or another dish that you both know how to make. Separately, make a list of the ingredients from your favorite recipe for that dish.

an omelette	cookies
a fish dish	a kind of soup
pancakes	another kind of dessert
a cake	a meat dish
spaghetti	a vegetable dish

When you finish, compare your lists of ingredients. Make sentences comparing your recipes.

example recipes:

Afredo's omelette
1. 2 eggs
2. 1/2 cup grated cheese
3. 1 chopped sausage
4. 1 small onion, chopped
5. 1 clove chopped garlic
6. 1 teaspoon chili sauce

Anna's omelette
1. 3 eggs
2. 3/4 cup grated cheese
3. 6 sliced mushrooms
4. 1/2 green pepper, chopped

example sentences:

ANNA: My recipe has more eggs than yours. Your omelette has more ingredients than mine.

ALFREDO: My omelette is spicier than yours.

Modal Verbs: Requests, Offers, and Permission

Setting the Context

Conversation

WAITER: Good evening, folks. How may I help you?

HIROSHI: Can you tell us what the specials are?

WAITER: Sure. There are two specials tonight. One is chicken in wine sauce. The other is broiled swordfish.

ELLEN: The fish sounds delicious. Could I have it with a baked potato?

WAITER: Yes, of course.

CARLOS: I'll have a steak. Would you cook it medium rare, please?

WAITER: Certainly. Would you like a baked potato too?

CARLOS: No, I'll have french fries.

WAITER: All right. *(to Hiroshi)* How about you?

HIROSHI: I'd like the chicken with wine sauce and a baked potato.

WAITER: Very good. Can I get you something to drink?

ELLEN: Just water for me, thanks.

HIROSHI: Me too.

CARLOS: I'd like some iced tea, please.

WAITER: Two waters and an iced tea. Anything else?

HIROSHI: Uh, yes. Waiter, can we smoke here?

WAITER: No, you can't. This is the nonsmoking section.

HIROSHI: I thought so. Will you please ask that man over there to put out his cigarette? The smoke is bothering me.

WAITER: Yes, certainly.

Answer these questions about the conversation.

1. Who orders the specials?
2. What does Ellen request with her fish?
3. How does Carlos like his steak cooked? What does he request?
4. What does Hiroshi ask the waiter permission to do?
5. What does Hiroshi ask the waiter to do?

Modal Verbs

Requests

The modals *may, can, could, will,* or *would* can be used with the simple form of a verb in questions to make polite requests.

questions	possible answers	notes
May I (we) **have** the check?	Here you are.	*May* is not used in questions with *you*.
Could you please **bring** a fork?	Of course.	Adding the word *please* makes a
Will you **pass** the salt, please?	Certainly.	request more polite.
Would you **suggest** a dessert?	I'd be glad to.	
Can we **get** a menu, please?	Sure.	*Can* is more informal.

Offers

The modals *may* and *can* are used with the simple form of a verb to make polite offers.

questions	possible answers
May I **help** you?	Yes. Can I get a menu?
Can I **get** you something to drink?	No, thanks.

Permission

May, could, and *can* are used with the simple form of a verb to ask permission.

examples	possible answers	notes
May we **join** you?	Sure. Please sit down.	*May* and *could* are con-
Could I **borrow** some money?	Sorry, I don't have any.	sidered more polite.
Can I **use** a credit card?	Yes, of course.	*Can* is more informal.
Customers **may use** credit cards. You **can pay** by check. You **can't smoke** here.		You can also use *may* or *can* in statements about permission.

Underline the modal verb phrases in the conversation on page 74. Next to each phrase, put an R if it is a request, an O if it is an offer, and a P if it is a request for permission.

example: How <u>may</u> I <u>help</u> you? O

Circle the correct words in 1 to 14. The first one is done as an example.

HIROSHI: [May /(Would)] you please [pass / to pass] the hot sauce, Ellen?
1

ELLEN: Sure. You really like spicy food! [Will / Can] I [have / having] the
2 3

tartar sauce, Carlos?

CARLOS: [May / Will] I [ask / to ask] you something? Why do you put tartar
4 5

sauce on your fish? Yuk!

ELLEN: *(laughing)* [Will / Might] you [be / are] quiet, Carlos?
6 7

CARLOS: Sorry, but I need more butter. [Can / Are] you [call / to call] the
8 9

waiter, Hiroshi?

HIROSHI: *(snaps his fingers)* Waiter! [Can / Could] you [bring / brings] us
10 11

more butter, please?

ELLEN: Shh . . . [May / Could] you talk more softly? And [may / would] I
12 13

[make / to make] a suggestion? Please don't snap your fingers in a
14

restaurant. It isn't polite.

Complete the following conversation. Use these modals: *will, would, may, can, could,* and the pronouns: *I, you,* or *we.* More than one answer may be correct. The first two are done as examples.

CARLOS: Psssst! Waiter!

ELLEN: Carlos, _____may_____ _____I_____ make a request? Please don't hiss
1 2

at the waiter. It's not considered polite in the United States.

CARLOS: Oh, I didn't know that. _____ _____ wave at him?
3 4

ELLEN: Sure, that's fine.

WAITER: Yes, _____ _____ get you something else?
5 6

CARLOS: _____ _____ get a cup of coffee, please?
　　　　　 7 　　　　 8

WAITER: Sure.

ELLEN: _____ _____ have the check too, please?
　　　　 9 　　　　 10

WAITER: Right away.

ELLEN: _____ _____ pay by credit card?
　　　　 11 　　　　 12

WAITER: Yes, you can.

Using What You've Learned

activity　Work with a partner. Write a dialogue for one of the following situations, or make up a situation of your own. In your dialogue, try to use comparisons and modal verbs to make requests, offers, and requests for permission. Practice your dialogue and perform it for the class.

1. A mother and child are in a supermarket. The child wants some candy or other sweet things, but the mother wants to buy more healthy food.

example:　A: Can I have a candy bar?
　　　　　 B: How about some fruit? It's much better for you.
　　　　　 A: Candy tastes sweeter than fruit. Can we buy a cake?

2. Two students are having dinner at a restaurant. One has a lot of money. The other doesn't have much money.

example:　A: May I recommend the steak?
　　　　　 B: A hamburger costs a lot less than a steak.
　　　　　 A: Yes, but it isn't as tasty.

3. Two roommates are cooking together. One student loves American food. The other likes only food from his or her country.

example:　A: Can you give me the chili pepper?
　　　　　 B: Please don't put much chili pepper in the sauce.
　　　　　 A: But food in my country is spicier than American food. American food is very bland.

The Future: going to

Setting the Context
Conversation

CARLOS: It's finally Friday! What are we going to do this weekend?

ANITA: Well, we're going to have a picnic tomorrow, right? Aren't we going to meet at the park?

ELLEN: Oh, I'm sorry. I can't make it. My family is having a backyard barbecue. I'm going to help my mother and father.

CARLOS: You mean, you're going to cook? Are your parents going to invite us?

ELLEN: Well, uh . . .

ANITA: It's too bad you can't go, Ellen. How about you, Hiroshi? You're going to go to the picnic, right?

HIROSHI: Well, who's going to make the food?

ANITA: Uh . . .

HIROSHI: I can't cook, you know. Why don't we all meet in a nice restaurant?

CARLOS: Are you going to pay, Hiroshi?

exercise Answer these questions about the conversation.

1. What is Ellen going to do tomorrow?
2. What does Anita think they're all going to do?
3. What does Hiroshi want?
4. How do you think the conversation is going to end?

The Future: going to

You can use a phrase with a form of *be* + *going to* + a simple form of a verb to talk about future plans. These charts give some examples.

Statements

	examples	notes
Affirmative	Some friends **are going to have** a picnic. We**'re going to meet** at the park. There**'s going to be** a barbecue on Saturday. Ellen **is going to help** her parents.	In quick, informal speech, *going to* sounds like *gonna*. Do not use *gonna* in writing.
Negative	Hiroshi **isn't going to cook**. There **aren't going to be** many people. The friends **aren't going to agree**. I**'m not going to go**.	

Yes/No Questions

	examples	possible answers	
		Affirmative	**Negative**
Affirmative	**Is** Hiroshi **going to cook**?	Yes, he is.	No, he isn't.
	Is the barbecue **going to be** on Saturday?	Yes, it is.	No, it isn't.
	Are Ellen's friends **going to go**?	Yes, they are.	No, they aren't.
Negative	**Isn't** Ellen **going to come** to the picnic?	Yes, she is.	No, she isn't.
	Isn't it **going to rain** on Saturday?	Yes, it is.	No, it isn't.
	Aren't they **going to cook** food?	Yes, they are.	No, they aren't.

Information Questions

	examples	possible answers
Affirmative	**What is** Carlos **going to make**?	Guacamole.
	Where are you **going to meet**?	In the park.
	When is the barbecue **going to start**?	At five o'clock.
Negative	**Why aren't** you **going to come**?	I have to work.
	Who isn't going to be** there?	Ellen.

 **exercise 1** Underline the verb phrases with *going to* in the conversation on page 78.

> **example:** What <u>are</u> we <u>going to</u> do this weekend?

exercise 2 Write the missing forms of the verb *be* and *going to* in the blanks. The first one is done as an example.

HIROSHI: I can't pay for everybody's dinner! I'm_____ not even
                                                                    1

___*going to*___ bring much money.

CARLOS: Then we'_____ not _____ meet at a restaurant!
                                2

ANITA: Well, _____ we _____ have a picnic tomorrow?
                                3

CARLOS: Yes, we _____.
                                4

ELLEN: No, we _____.
                                5

CARLOS: Who'_____ cook? _____ you _____
                                6   7

make the food, Anita?

ANITA: Who, me? I can make a few dishes, but who _____ buy the
                                                                          8

ingredients? Who _____ help? Where _____ we
                                9   10

_____ prepare the food? When _____ we
                                                                  11

_____ get together?

ELLEN: I'_____ have time on Sunday. Why don't we have the picnic
                        12

Sunday afternoon?

CARLOS: That's fine with me.

HIROSHI: Me too. But what _____ we _____ do about food?
                                            13

ANITA: We'_____ all _____ work together! Carlos, what
                        14

_____ you _____ make?
                15

CARLOS: I can make guacamole.

HIROSHI: What's *that*?

CARLOS: You'_____ find out on Sunday!
                        16

ELLEN: I'_____ make potato salad.
                17

ANITA: Great! Hiroshi, you and I _____ cook hot dogs and ham-
                                        18

burgers. I'_____ show you how.
                    19

ALL: This _____ be fun!
             20

 **exercise 3**

To make their dishes for the picnic on Sunday, Carlos and Ellen are going to use these recipes. Read each recipe. Then write sentences describing the steps Carlos and Ellen are going to follow to make his or her dish. Use *be + going to* and the following sequence words to describe the steps: *First, Next, Then, After that, Finally.*

example: First, Carlos is going to put two tablespoons of lemon juice into a bowl. Next, he's going to cut two avocados in half and remove the seeds and skin. Then, . . .

Carlos's Guacamole	Ellen's Potato Salad
INGREDIENTS:	**INGREDIENTS:**
• 2 tablespoons lemon juice	• 6 medium red potatoes
• 2 medium ripe avocados	• 1/4 cup chopped onion
• 1 or 2 garlic cloves	• 1/4 cup chopped celery
• 1/2 teaspoon salt	• 1/4 cup chopped pickles
• 1 small onion, chopped	• 1/4 cup water or chicken broth
• 1/2 teaspoon hot sauce (Tabasco sauce or salsa)	• 1/2 teaspoon sugar
	• 1/2 teaspoon salt
	• 1/8 teaspoon paprika
Put the lemon juice in a mixing bowl. Cut the avocados in half. Remove the seeds and skin. Mash the avocados in a bowl with the lemon juice. Chop the garlic and onions and put them in the bowl. Add the salt and hot sauce. Mix the ingredients well. Serve the guacamole with tortilla chips.	Boil the potatoes. Then peel and slice them. Sauté the potatoes in oil. Chop the onion, celery, and pickles. Add them to the potatoes. Sauté them until brown. Add the chicken broth, sugar, salt, and paprika. Mix the ingredients well. Serve the potato salad warm.

1.   **2.**

Using What You've Learned

activity **1** Work with a partner. Talk about your future plans. Ask and answer questions about what you are going to do after class, tomorrow, on the weekend, next week, next month, next year, in five years, and so on. Then join another pair. Take turns telling the other group members three of your partner's plans for the future.

activity **2** Work in small groups. Choose one of these topics, or another topic related to food:

- a dinner party
- picnics
- shopping for food
- taking someone out for dinner

How are customs related to these topics different in your home country from customs in North America?

example: A: In this country, supermarkets stay open later than in my
                country.
            B: Here, you can buy a lot of food in large packages.
            C: We go shopping more often in my country, but we seldom go
                to supermarkets.

CHAPTER four

Getting Around the Community

in this chapter

TOPIC ONE

Reviewing the Simple Present Tense, the Present Continuous Tense, and the Future: going to

Setting the Context

Look at the scene above. Study the different places, people, and activities. Then do the exercises below.

Answer *true* or *false* to these statements about the scene. Correct the false statements. The first one is done as an example.

    1. <u>False</u>   Two travelers with backpacks are ~~entering~~ ^{leaving} the bus station. The

        woman is ^{looking at a map} ~~taking a picture~~, and the man is carrying a ^{camera} ~~map~~.

2. _____ It's morning, and it's time for breakfast.

3. _____ An office clerk is going to mail some letters and packages.

4. _____ Businesspeople often go out to lunch together. Three bank employees are talking about where to eat.

5. _____ It's a cloudy day, and it's getting cooler. It's probably not going to snow.

6. _____ Some gas stations are self service. Customers get their own gas and pay the cashier.

7. _____ Paramedics often take sick or injured people to an emergency room by ambulance.

8. _____ An optometrist takes care of people's feet. In the medical building, an optometrist is examining a patient.

9. _____ Some musicians are playing guitars in the park. There are no people listening or giving money.

10. _____ A soldier and a waitress are using the telephone.

 Answer these questions about the scene.

1. There are two street vendors in the picture. What kind of food do they sell?
2. There's a woman in a business suit with her briefcase. Why is she running?
3. A man is running to his parked car. What is going to happen next?
4. What time of day is it? How do you know?
5. Do you think this is the weekend? Why or why not?
6. Describe the weather. Do you think the weather is going to change soon?
7. Who is your favorite person in the picture? Why?
8. Imagine yourself in the scene. What are you doing? What are you going to do next?

exercise 3 Write five more questions about the scene. When you finish, choose a partner. Take turns asking and answering your questions.

The Simple Present Tense Versus the Present Continuous Tense

	examples	notes
Simple Present	She **takes** the train to work every day. Businesspeople often **eat** lunch together. Most cities **have** a downtown area. This restaurant **makes** the best pizza. **Does** food **cost** a lot in this city? That bus **doesn't look** very crowded. **Do** you **know** the subway system well?	Use the simple present tense to show repeated action in the present. You can also use the simple present to make statements of fact and to express opinions. With some verbs, the simple present shows an existing condition—something that is happening now.*
Present Continuous	She**'s running** for the bus. I**'m not using** the computer right now. Who**'s selling** hot dogs this afternoon? He **is playing** music in the park today. **Are** they **going** out to dinner tonight?	Use the present continuous tense to show action in progress (happening now). The present continuous also shows action happening over a period of time that includes the present and future.

*Some other verbs that describe an existing condition: *like, want, need, seem, believe, understand, remember, hear, sound, love, hate.* These verbs are not used in the present continuous tense.

The Present Continuous Tense (Future Meaning) and the Future: *going to*

	examples	notes
Present Continuous (Future Meaning)	A vendor **is selling** hot dogs this afternoon. The tourists **are staying** in a hotel tonight. The musician **isn't leaving** for a while. When **are** we **eating** dinner? **Aren't** you **going** downtown this weekend?	The present continuous tense may have future meaning when it describes a planned event. This future meaning is often indicated by time expressions: today, this evening, tomorrow, soon, later, and so on.
The Future *going to*	The bus **is going to leave** on time. They**'re going to have** a good lunch. **Isn't** it **going to rain** this weekend? The tourists **are** probably **going to take** a lot of pictures.	Use *be* + *going to* + simple form of verb to talk about future activity, plans, or predictions.

> *Note:* You can also use ***will + simple form of verb*** to talk about the future. Sometimes *will* and *be + going to* have basically the same meaning. For example:
>   The bus **will leave** on time. = The bus **is going to leave** on time.
>   The tourists **will** probably **take** a lot of pictures. = The tourists **are** probably **going to take** a lot of pictures.
> However, *will* (not *be + going to*) is usually needed to make future plans and predictions. (See Summary of Modal Verbs on page 94 of this chapter.)

**exercise 4**   Circle the simple present tense verbs in the statements and questions in Exercises 1 and 2 on pages 84 and 85. Underline the present continuous verb phrases. Put two lines under verb phrases with *going to*.

   examples: Two travelers with backpacks <u>are entering</u> the bus station.

   It(')s morning, and it(')s time for breakfast.

   An office clerk is <u>going to mail</u> some letters and packages.

**exercise 5**   Answer the questions in the box below about the people in the pictures on pages 87–89. Use the words next to the pictures and add other words of your own. Use correct verb endings.

What	does	a street vendor an optometrist	usually do?
	do	tourists	

   examples: A street vendor often sells food.

   He always works outside.

   He sometimes moves from place to place.

   Tourists travel to many interesting places.

   They usually take pictures.

   Tourists often buy souvenirs.

1. office clerk
   • work in an office
   • take mail to the post office
   • file information

2. businesspeople

- use the telephone a lot
- write reports
- go to meetings

_____

_____

_____

3. mail carrier

- drive a mail truck
- walk every day
- work outside

_____

_____

_____

4. service-station attendant

- collect money from customers
- pump gas
- wash windshields for customers

_____

_____

_____

5. paramedics

- rescue people from accidents
- ride in an ambulance
- take sick people to the hospital

_____

_____

_____

6. dentist

- examine people's teeth
- fill cavities and clean teeth
- take X-rays

_____

_____

_____

7. cook

- prepare food
- clean the kitchen
- take out garbage

_____

_____

_____

8. Choose another job and describe it.

_____

_____

_____

 **6** For the pictures in Exercise 5, answer the questions in the box below. Use your own words. You can make both affirmative and negative statements.

What	is are	the . . . doing now?

example: The office clerk is working in an office now. He isn't taking mail
to the post office. He is filing some information.

Work with a partner. Look at the scene on page 84. Take turns asking and answering the questions below about these people:

1. musician
2. hot dog vendor
3. soldier
4. delivery person

5. business people
6. waitress
7. police officer
8. ice cream vendor

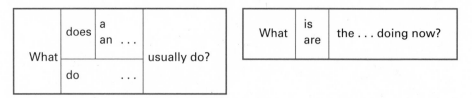

examples: A: What does a musician usually do?
B: A musician usually studies and plays music. What is the musician doing now?
A: He's playing music in the park. (He's playing a saxophone. He's playing jazz.)

exercise

Look at the scene on page 84 again. Write an affirmative and negative answer to the question below about each of these people. The first one is done as an example:

> What is probably going to happen next?

1. tourists outside bus station

   The tourists are probably going to get lost.

   They aren't going to take any pictures.

2. woman running for bus

   _____

   _____

3. office clerk outside post office

   _____

   _____

4. young man running to his car

   _____

   _____

5. cook outside pizza restaurant

   _____

   _____

6. children walking with parents

   _____

   _____

Using What You've Learned

 **activity 1**

Make a postcard of your city or town. Use an index card or piece of paper. Paste or draw a picture of an interesting place in your city on the front of the postcard. Then turn it over and write to a friend or family member. Tell them something about your city. Describe the picture on the card. Then tell what you are doing now. Tell them something you are going to do in the future.

When you finish, share your postcards in small groups. Do any of the postcards show the same place? Which pictures are most interesting? If you like, mail your postcards. Here is an example.

Dear Raúl,

Greetings from Fort Lee, New Jersey! The picture on the front shows the George Washington Bridge. It goes from Fort Lee to New York City. You can take a bus across the bridge, or you can walk across. The view from the bridge is great!

I'm going to school in New York City, but I'm living with my uncle here in Fort Lee. It takes about half an hour to get to school by bus and subway.

I love New York City! This weekend, I'm going to go to a Broadway play.

How are you? Please write. Take care,

Juan

 **activity 2**

Work with a partner. Look at different parts of the entertainment section of your local newspaper. For example, student A looks at musical events, student B looks at new movies. Take turns talking about activities that are happening now in your city or town. Ask and answer questions like the following and others of your own.

- *What teams are playing sports?*
- *When and where are they playing?*
- *What musicians or groups are playing? When and where?*
- *Are you going to go to any concerts?*

- *What movies are opening?*
- *What actors are starring in them?*
- *What museums are having exhibits?*
- *Are you going to see any exhibits?*

 **activity 3**

Bring in newspapers, magazines, or books that have pictures showing lots of activities happening at once. Work in small groups. Take turns describing what is happening, what's going to happen next, and what usually happens in the situations.

Reviewing Modal Verbs;
Phrasal Verbs

Setting the Context
Conversations

exercise 1   Match the conversations on page 93 with the pictures below. Write the number of each picture in the box next to the matching conversation.

A: May I help you?

B: Yes, please. I'd like a one-way ticket for the 8:30 bus to Chicago. Will the bus leave on time?

A: It might leave a little late. Right now, that bus is fifteen minutes late. But the driver may make up the time and get in before 8:30.

B: Well, that's okay. How much is it?

A: That is $89. You can get a special rate for two people. Is your friend going with you?

B: No, he can't go. He needs to get back to school.

A: Here's your ticket and change. Your bus leaves from platform 12. Have a good trip.

B: Thanks. By the way, can we smoke in here?

A: No, you can't. You'll have to go outside. Don't go far. The bus may show up soon.

C: Will you fill up the tank, please?

D: Sure. Can I check the oil for you?

C: No, thanks. That won't be necessary, but could you please clean off the windshield?

D: No problem.

C: And would you give me directions to Highway 10?

D: Sure. You can go straight on this road. Make a left at the third traffic light. Then watch out for signs for Highway 10.

C: Make a left at the third light?

D: Yes. Look out for a shopping mall there. You can't miss it. Make the left turn there.

C: Thanks. (She starts to drive away.)

D: Hey, don't take off! That's $11.50 for the gas.

E: What can I do for you today?

F: Will this package get to New York by Friday?

E: We can't get it there that fast by regular first class mail. You could send it express mail.

F: No, that's too expensive. First class will be all right. Will it get there by Monday?

E: It could arrive on Monday, but it will probably get there on Tuesday.

F: Okay. How much is it?

E: $4.90. Would you like to insure it? Do you need a return receipt.

F: I don't want to insure it, but I would like a return receipt.

E: Please fill out this form.

G: Can I take out $200 from my savings account, please?

H: Of course. May I have your withdrawal slip and your passbook, please?

G: Here you are.

H: How would you like that?

G: Excuse me? What do you mean?

H: How do you want the money?

G: Uh . . . I don't understand.

H: Would you like fifty-dollar bills? Twenties? Tens?

G: Oh, I see. Twenties will be fine, thanks.

 **exercise 2**   Answer these questions about the conversations.

1. How would the bank customer like the $200?
2. What are two ways you can send a small package from the U.S. Postal Service?
3. What will the traveler at the bus station probably do next?
4. The driver is going to leave the gas station. What might happen next?

Summary of Modal Verbs

Modals have more than one meaning. This chart summarizes some of their meanings.

modals	meaning	examples	notes
can	ability	You **can go** straight on this road. We **can't get** it there that fast. **Can** you **speak** Spanish?	When another verb follows a modal, it is always in the simple form.
can **may** **would**	offers	**Can** I **check** the oil for you? **May** I **help** you? **Would** you **like** fifty-dollar bills?	
can, could **may**	permission	**Can** we **smoke** in here? You **may smoke** outside the building.	
can, could **will, would** **may**	requests	**Can** I **take out** $200 from my account? **Could** you **clean off** the windshield? **Will** you **fill up** the tank, please? **Would** you **give** me directions? **May** I **have** your passbook, please?	*Can* is more informal. *May* is not used in questions with *you*.
may **might** **could**	future possibility	The driver **may get in** before 8:30. The bus **might leave** a little late. The package **could arrive** on Monday.	
will	future plans predictions	**Will** the package **get** there by Monday? It **will** probably **get** there on Tuesday.	

exercise 3 Underline the modal verb phrases in the conversations on page 93. Tell the meaning of each phrase.

example: <u>May</u> I <u>help</u> you? = *offer*

exercise 4 In the four conversations here and on page 96, complete the sentences with modal verbs. More than one answer may be correct. The first one is done as an example.

1. A: I want to deposit these checks in my savings account, please.

B: Of course. _____Would_____ you please write your name on the back?

1
_____ you fill out a deposit slip? And _____ I

2   3
have your passbook?

A: Sure. And _____ you also check my balance?

4

B: Certainly.

2. A: _____ I help you?

5

B: Yes. _____ you tell me the departure time for the next bus

6
to Houston?

A: That bus usually leaves at 6:15. But they're having a little trouble with

it. It _____ pull out late.

7

B: That _____ (not) be a problem. I _____ take one

8   9
ticket please, round-trip.

A: That _____ be $68.00. You _____ check your bag

10   11
or take it with you on the bus. Is that your dog?

B: Yes.

A: I'm sorry, but you _____ (not) take him along on the bus.

12

3. A: What _____ I do for you today?

13

B: I have a delivery notice from the post office. _____ I pick up

14

this package here?

A: Yes, you _____.

15

B: And _____ I send out a registered letter?

16

A: Of course you _____. _____ you please fill out

17   18
this form? Don't leave out any information.

4. A: Fill it up?

B: No, I don't need gas today. But my car is making a strange noise.

_____ you take a look at it?

19

A: Sure.

(He looks at the engine. Steam is coming out.)

A: You _____ have a problem with the cooling system. It
         20
_____ be a leak. Or it _____ be the water pump.
      21   22

B: _____ you fix it?
      23

A: I _____ (not) do it right this minute. _____ you
         24   25
wait a while? I _____ have some time in about half an hour.
                      26

B: Okay. I _____ wait. _____ I use your phone?
                 27   28

Phrasal Verbs

A phrasal verb is a verb + one or more adverbs or prepositions that usually has
a special meaning. Many phrasal verbs have different meanings in different
contexts. Two examples: *take + off* can mean *leave (place)* or *remove (clothes),*
and *get + out + of* can mean *leave (a car, a bed,* and so on) or *avoid (doing
something that you don't like).* Some phrasal verbs can be separated by noun or
pronoun objects. Other phrasal verbs cannot be separated. This chart gives
some examples from this chapter.

phrasal verbs		examples
Can Be Separated	make up	He may **make up** the time. He may **make** the time **up.** He may **make** it **up.***
	fill out	Please **fill out** this form. Please **fill** this form **out.** Please **fill** it **out.**
	clean off	**Clean off** your shoes. **Clean** your shoes **off.** **Clean** them **off.**
Cannot Be Separated	show up	Is John going to **show up?** Will he **show up?**
	look out for	**Look out** for the gas station. **Look out** for it.
	get in	The train might **get in** before 1:00. It might **get in** before 1:00.

*For phrasal verbs that can be separated:
    You can put the noun either between the verb and the preposition or after the preposition.
    You can put the pronoun only between the verb and the preposition.
      CORRECT: He may make it up.
      INCORRECT: He may make up it.

exercise 5   Put two lines under the phrasal verbs in the conversations on page 93.

   example: But the driver may <u><u>make up</u></u> the time and <u><u>get in</u></u> before 8:30.

exercise 6   Study the following phrasal verbs and their meanings. Then fill in each blank 1 to 18 with one of the phrasal verbs. (Try to use each phrasal verb only once.) The first one is done as an example.

call up	= telephone
catch up on	= get back on schedule
check in	= register at a hotel
drop by	= visit
get away from	= leave
get on	= enter (a bus, etc.)
gets in	= arrives
get up	= wake up
go back	= return
going on	= happening
go out of	= leave (a building)
go to	= attend
pick up	= get, buy
show up	= appear, come
sit down	= sit
stay up	= stay awake
take in	= go to, see
walk around	= take a walk

Jean and Laura _____*go to*_____ a college in a small town.
₁
Sometimes on the weekend they like to _____ campus and
₂
visit the city. On Friday they _____ a hotel to reserve a
₃
room for Saturday.

On Saturday morning, Jean and Laura _____ early to

get a bus to the city. When the bus _____ the city, they

_____ at their hotel. Then they _____ a

copy of the local newspaper. The newspaper tells what is _____

in the city.

Jean and Laura like to _____ the downtown area.

For lunch, they _____ at a table outside a cafe. After lunch

they go shopping, then they _____ to the hotel for a rest.

In the evening, they _____ the hotel and have dinner

in a nice restaurant. Then they _____ a movie. After that,

they _____ a dance club. They _____

very late!

On Sunday afternoon, Jean and Laura _____ a bus back

to town. They _____ their homework on Sunday night.

They want to be ready for school when they _____ for class

on Monday morning.

 **exercise 7**

Read the questions below. Work with a partner. Take turns asking and answering the questions. When you ask a question, substitute a phrasal verb for the under-lined word(s). When you answer, use the phrasal verb and your own words. The first one is done as an example.

example: **1.** Where do you <u>attend</u> school?

    A: Where do you go to school?

    B: I go to the University of Hawaii.

1. Where do you <u>attend</u> school?

2. How often do you <u>telephone</u> your family?

3. Where can I <u>get</u> today's newspaper?

4. Are you going to <u>return to</u> this school next year?

5. Do you plan to <u>see</u> a movie this weekend?

6. How do you learn about what's <u>happening</u> in the world?

7. Are you planning to <u>visit</u> the library this weekend?

8. Is it safe to <u>take a walk in</u> this campus at night?

9. Do you usually <u>leave</u> campus on weekends?

10. How late do you usually <u>stay awake</u> on Saturday night?

Using What You've Learned

Work with a partner. Write a dialogue about two of the situations below. (You can choose another situation of your own.) Use the phrasal verbs listed for each situation and as many modal verbs as you can. When you finish, practice your dialogues. Perform one of them for the class.

1. You are two roommates studying in a dormitory. One of you wants to listen to the stereo. The other doesn't want to—you can't study with music playing. Use some of these phrasal verbs (and others of your own):

   turn on   = start (a machine)
   turn off   = stop (a machine)
   turn down = decrease (lower) the sound
   turn up   = increase the sound

   example: A: Please don't turn on the stereo. I'm trying to study.
              B: Music helps me study.
              A: I can't study with loud music. Could you turn it down?
              B: Sure. Is that better?
              A: No, I can still hear it. Would you turn it off?

2. You are a customer and salesperson in a clothing store. You want to buy a sweater, but you aren't sure of the size. The salesperson asks you to try on some sweaters. You don't know what color to buy, and you ask the salesperson to choose one. Use some of these phrasal verbs (and others of your own):

   put on   = put clothing on
   take off = remove clothing
   try on   = put clothing on to see if it is the right size
   pick out = choose

3. You are a student and a librarian. You want to find out some information about a famous writer, artist, scientist—you choose the person. You ask the librarian for help. Ask the librarian how to check out a book, magazine, video, and so on about this famous person. Use some of these phrasal verbs (and others of your own):

   find out   = discover or learn information about
   look up   = look for information in a reference book, data base, and so on
   check out = borrow from the library
   fill out   = complete a form

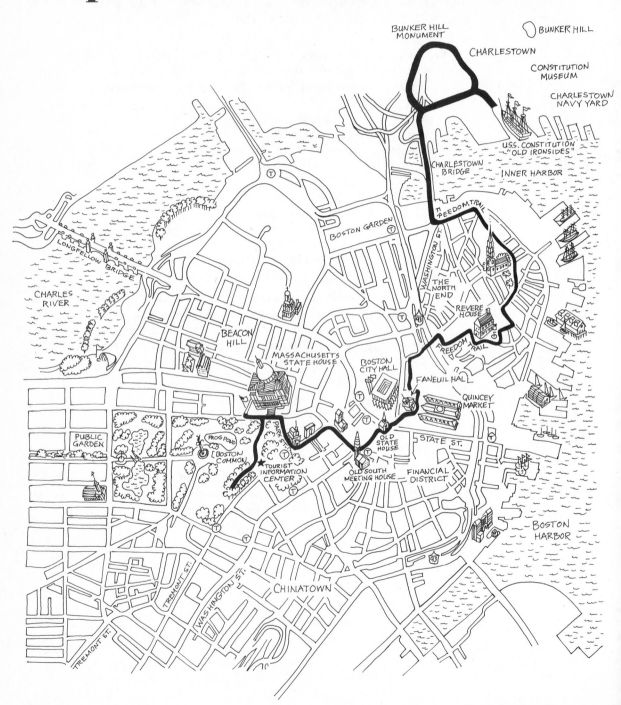

Setting the Context

Reading

Boston's Historic Freedom Trail

A great way to see old downtown Boston during the day is to walk the Freedom Trail. The trail is three miles long, and it takes you by many famous, historic places from the time of the American Revolution (1775–1783). The trail starts at an information booth in Boston Common, a large park next to Boston's
5 Public Gardens. The booth is on Tremont Street between the Park Street and Tremont Street subway stations. You can get tour information and a trail map at the booth. Here are some of the interesting stops on the trail.

One important stop is the Old State House at Washington and State Streets. Built in 1712, it now has a museum with exhibits on Boston history. From the
10 Old State House, you can walk through Faneuil Hall and Quincy Market. These old, historic buildings are now a busy center for shopping, dining, and entertainment. Many stores in Quincy Market stay open until 9:00 P.M. After dinner, you can come back here to shop in the evening.

When you leave Quincy Market, you can walk under the expressway (Interstate 93) to Boston's North End. This part of Boston has many wonderful
15 Italian shops, cafes, and restaurants. Also in the North End is the Revere House, another important stop on the Freedom Trail. It is the home of Paul Revere (1735–1818), patriot of the American Revolution. Built in 1676, it is the oldest standing building in Boston.

20 The *U.S.S. Constitution*, a famous warship built in 1797, is across the Inner Harbor in the Charlestown Navy Yard. You can walk over the Charlestown Bridge to get there. The *U.S.S. Constitution,* also known as "Old Ironsides," is the oldest American warship afloat today. The *U.S.S. Constitution* Museum is near the ship. You can visit the ship for free, but you have to pay to visit the
25 museum.

Near the Charlestown Navy Yard is the Bunker Hill Monument, the last stop on the Freedom Trail. The monument commemorates the Battle of Bunker Hill fought on June 17, 1775. You can visit the monument for free.

exercise Answer these questions about the Freedom Trail.

1. What kinds of places can you visit along the Freedom Trail?
2. Where is the information booth in Boston Common?
3. How can you get from Quincy Market to the North End?
4. What can you do in the North End?
5. How can you get from the North End to the Charlestown Navy Yard?

Prepositions of Place

Place phrases usually begin with prepositions. You can use the verb *be* + a prepositional phrase to talk about place or location. Some prepositions show location and direction (movement). You can use them after verbs of motion such as *go, walk, run, drive.* This chart gives examples of some common prepositions of place.

	examples	notes
in	There are many Italian restaurants **in the North End.** The Freedom trail is **in Boston.** Boston is a city **in Massachusetts.** Massachusetts is **in the United States.** Québec is a province **in Canada.** The United States and Canada are **in North America.**	Use *in* before towns, cities, states, provinces, countries, continents.
on	There is a subway station **on Park Street.** The Boston Museum of Fine Arts is **on Huntington Avenue.**	Use *on* before streets.
at	The Old State House is **at Washington and State Streets.** The Boston International Hostel is **at 12 Hemenway Street.**	Use *at* with street addresses.
between	The information booth is **between two subway stations.**	
near	The museum is **near the ship.**	
next to	Boston Common is **next to the Public Gardens.**	
across	Can we walk **across the Charlestown Bridge**?	
under	You can walk **under the expressway** to the North End.	Two or more prepositional phrases may be used together.

	examples	
over	Go **over the Charlestown Bridge** to the Navy Yard.	
from . . . to	Let's walk **from Faneuil Hall to the North End.**	
through	I sometimes run **through Boston Common** on weekends.	

Prepositions of Time

Time phrases also usually begin with prepositions. The noun part of the phrase names a time: *morning, noon, night, spring, summer, May, Monday,* and so on. This chart gives examples of some common prepositions of time.

	examples	notes
in	Built **in 1797**, "Old Ironsides" is a famous warship. Boston is especially beautiful **in autumn**. The weather in Boston is usually very cold **in January**. Quincy Market is a good place to shop **in the evening**.	Use *in* before years, seasons, months, and parts of the day.
on	Some stores and museums are closed **on Sunday**. The Battle of Bunker Hill was fought **on June 17, 1775**. Most stores in the United States close **on December 25**.	Use *on* before days of the week and dates.
at	The Revere House closes **at 4:15**. Let's meet for lunch **at noon** in Quincy Market. It's fun to walk around the North End **at night**. The train gets in **at midnight**.	Use *at* before a specific time of day and with the nouns *noon, night, midnight*.

examples	
from . . . to	The Revere House is open **from 9:30 A.M. to 5:15 P.M.** during the summer.
during	We're going to walk the Freedom Trail **during the afternoon.**
until	Many stores in Quincy Market are open **until 9:00 P.M.**
before	I want to visit the Revere House **before dinner.**
after	Let's walk around the North End **after lunch.**

 **exercise 1**

Circle the prepositions of place and time in the reading on page 101. Next to each one, put a P if it is a preposition of place and a T if it is a preposition of time.

> example: A great way to see old downtown Boston (during) the day is to walk the Freedom Trail.

exercise 2

Complete the sentences with prepositions from the list below. The first one is done as an example.

at   in   on   from   to   during   until   after   under

1. Boston is _____in_____ Massachusetts, a state _____in_____ the

    northeastern part of the United States.

2. The Freedom Trail starts _____ an information booth

    _____ Tremont Street _____ Boston Common.

3. The Old State House is open _____ 9:30 A.M. _____

    5:00 P.M. _____ the summer.

4. Harvard University, _____ Cambridge, Massachusetts, is the

    oldest university _____ the United States.

5. The Lucky Dragon restaurant is _____ 45 Beach Street

    _____ Chinatown.

6. To go _____ Quincy Market _____ the North End,

walk _____ Interstate 93.

7. The Boston Children's Museum is _____ Congress Street. It is

open _____ Friday evenings _____ 9:00 P.M.

8. Many fine stores _____ Boston are _____

Newbury Street. The Victor Hugo Bookshop is _____

339 Newbury Street.

9. Quincy Market is a good place to shop _____ the evening

_____ dinner because many shops are open _____

9:00 P.M.

10. La Piccola Venezia is a good Italian restaurant _____ 63 Salem

Street _____ the North End.

Using What You've Learned

activity 1

Work with a partner. Take turns asking and answering questions about the
locations of people and things in the classroom. Use prepositions of place in
your answers. Use prepositions from the chart on pages 102 and 103 and others
you may know.

> **example:** A: Where are the desks?
> B: On the floor. Where are the chairs?
> A: Under the desks. Where is Nobu?
> B: He's sitting near the door. Where . . . ?

activity 2

Make a list of things you plan to do this week, including the weekend. List both
fun activities (for example, going to the movies) and work (studying in the library,
cleaning your room, and so on). When you finish your list, choose a partner.
Exchange your lists. Then take turns asking questions about the activities on your
lists. Use prepositions of place and time in your answers.

> **example:** A: What day are you going to the movies?
> B: On Saturday.
> A: What time on Saturday?
> B: At 7:30 in the evening.
> A: Where is the movie playing?
> B: At the Multiplex Cinema on Main Street. When are you going
> to do the laundry?

TOPIC four

Indefinite and Definite Nouns

Setting the Context

Reading

Read "Boston's Historic Freedom Trail" on page 101 again. Notice the use of the words *a, an, the,* and *some.*

exercise

Answer these questions about the Freedom Trail.

1. Where does the trail start?
2. What does the Old State House have?
3. What part of Boston has many Italian restaurants?
4. What is the oldest standing building in Boston?
5. Where is the *U.S.S. Constitution*?
6. What battle was fought on June 17, 1775?

Indefinite Nouns

Indefinite nouns identify general or unspecific things. You can use indefinite nouns to talk about things in general or about any one (or some) of a group of things. You can use the indefinite articles *a* and *an* (or no article) or expressions of quantity such as *some* and *any* with different singular and plural count or noncount indefinite nouns. This chart gives some examples.

	examples	notes
Singular Count Nouns	Boston has **an aquarium.**	Use *a/an** when you first mention something.
	Boston Common is **a** beautiful **park.**	Use *a/an* to talk about one of a group of things.
	"Old Ironsides" is **a** famous **warship.**	
Plural Count Nouns	There are **some** great **restaurants** in Chinatown.	You can often use *some* with plural count and noncount indefinite nouns.
	She's writing **postcards** to her friends.	
	Are there **any** cheap **hotels** in Boston?	Use *any* in questions.

*Use *a* with words that begin with consonant sounds. Use *an* with words that begin with vowel sounds.

	examples	notes
Noncount Nouns	I want **some information** about sightseeing tours. Do we have **time** to visit Quincy Market?	Don't use *a/an* before indefinite plural or noncount nouns.

Definite Nouns

Definite nouns identify specific, special, or unique things. You can use the definite article *the* (or no article) with singular and plural count or noncount definite nouns. This chart gives some examples.

	examples	notes
Singular Count Nouns	Boston has **an aquarium. The aquarium** is on Central Wharf. It's **the New England Aquarium.** The oldest standing **building** in Boston is **the Revere House.** Do you want to take **the subway** or **the bus**? We're going to **the city** this weekend. **The teacher** isn't here today.	Use *the* when you mention an indefinite noun again. Use *the* to talk about something specific, special, or unique. Use *the* when you and your listener both know the thing or person you are talking about.
Plural Count Nouns	The booth is between **the** Park Street and Tremont Street subway **stations.** **The restaurants** in **the North End** are wonderful.	
Noncount Nouns	Is this **the information** you want? **The time** is now 9:30 A.M. I like going to **museums.** You can get **information** at the booth. **Chinese food** is delicious.	Don't use *the* with plural count nouns or noncount nouns when you are talking about things in general.

Using *the* with Names

There are many different rules for the use of *the* with names. Here are a few.

	examples	notes
People	President Kennedy Queen Elizabeth	Don't use *the* with titles and names of specific people.
Places	Washington Street New York City California Vancouver Japan	Don't use *the* with names of streets, cities, states, provinces, and most countries. There are some exceptions, for example: The Hague, the United States, the Netherlands.
Buildings	the Revere House the Old State House the Park Plaza Hotel	Usually, use *the* with names of buildings.
Historical Events	the American Revolution the Battle of Bunker Hill	Use *the* with names of historical events.

exercise 1

Underline the indefinite articles and nouns in the reading on page 101. Put two lines under the definite articles and nouns.

example: A great <u>way</u> to see old downtown Boston during <u>the day</u> is to walk <u>the Freedom Trail</u>.

exercise 2

Fill in the blanks with *a, an, the,* X (for no article), *some* or *any,* as in the examples. In some blanks, more than one answer might be correct.

Where can we stay in ___the___ city of ___X___ Boston? _____ Hotel
      1   2   3
Meridian is expensive, but maybe we can find _____ smaller hotel in _____
                                             4   5
area further from _____ downtown area.
                   6

_____ President John F. Kennedy was from _____ Massachusetts. There's
  7   8
_____ important building with his name—_____ JFK Building— on _____
  9   10   11
New Sudbury Street.

I like _____ aquariums. There's _____ interesting aquarium at _____
       12   13   14
Boston Harbor. Do they ever have _____ new exhibits? If we go there, we
                                 15
can learn about _____ sea animals and _____ plant life.
                16   17

Only a few cities in _____ United States have _____ subway systems.
18   19

Boston has _____ subway system and also _____ trolley. _____ Tourists
20   21   22

can get on and off _____ trolley at _____ twelve different places.
23   24

Do you like _____ historic ships and _____ monuments? _____ "Old
25   26   27

Ironsides" was _____ warship during _____ War of 1812. You can learn
28   29

about _____ Battle of Bunker Hill at _____ Bunker Hill Pavilion, which has
30   31

_____ multimedia program about this famous battle.
32

Using What You've Learned

activity 1

How well do you know your own city or town? What is your favorite place or activity in your city or town? Write for fifteen minutes on one of the topics below. Be sure to explain why the place or activity is your favorite. Pay special attention to your use of prepositions and nouns.

1. your favorite restaurant or eating place
2. your favorite shopping area or store
3. your favorite cultural place (a museum, a concert hall, a theater, and so on)
4. your favorite recreational place (an amusement park, a place for sports, an area in nature, and so on)

When you finish writing, exchange papers with another student. Read each other's descriptions. Underline any words or parts of your partner's description that aren't clear. Write a question next to any part(s) that you would like to know more about.

Return your papers. Read your partner's comments about your description. Discuss any questions you may have with your partner. Rewrite your description, making any necessary changes.

If you like, make a class book about your city and visit some of your class-mates' favorite places.

activity 2

Jean and Laura are taking a three-day trip to New York City. Where might they go? What might they see and do? First, look at the list of places and activities here and on the next page. You can also add ideas of your own. Circle the places and activities that you think Jean and Laura would enjoy.

- Ellis Island
- Statue of Liberty
- Empire State Building
- Rockefeller Center
- Central Park
- World Trade Center
- Metropolitan Museum of Art

- Chinatown
- Little Italy
- Greenwich Village
- Harlem
- Fifth Avenue
- 42nd Street
- Times Square
- department stores
- Museum of Modern Art

- a concert
- Madison Square Garden
- a sports event
- art galleries
- bookstores
- Museum of Natural History
- South Street Seaport

• St. Patrick's Cathedral	• theater district	• ethnic restaurants
• United Nations	• a play	• _____
	• Carnegie Hall	• _____

Form groups of three. Work together to plan Jean and Laura's three-day trip. Discuss the different places and activities that you circled. Agree on *fifteen* places or activities. Decide which places Jean and Laura will visit and what activities they will do on *each* of the three days.

Each group member takes one day of their trip and writes a plan for that day. When you write your day's plan, pay special attention to the use of prepositions and nouns. When you finish, take turns telling each other your plans.

Then share your three-day plans with the class. How were your choices similar and different?

example: On the first day, Jean and Laura will visit the Empire State Building in the morning. Then they will walk on Fifth Avenue to Rockefeller Center. After they walk around Rockefeller Center, Jean and Laura can walk to Central Park. They can buy some hot dogs for lunch from a street vendor and eat them in the park. After lunch, they can rent bicycles and ride through the park.

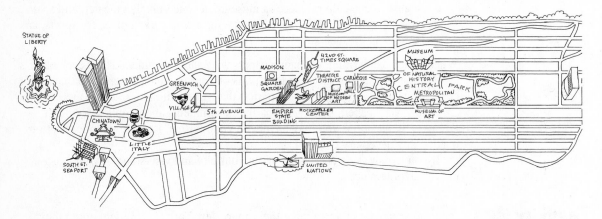

activity **3**

Get some tourist maps of your city or town, or other cities in the United States or Canada. Work in small groups. Each group works with a different map. Plan a tour of your city and write a description of it. In your description, answer these questions:

1. What places are you going to visit? Why? (What can you do and see there?)
2. What will your route be? How will you get from one place to another?
3. When are you going to start? How long will you stay at each place?
4. When will you get back? What will you bring with you?

Show your map and present your tour to the class. The class chooses the best place to visit.

Interactions I • Grammar

Home

in this chapter

The Simple Past Tense (Regular Verbs)

Setting the Context

Conversation

FATHER: Did I ever talk to you kids about the good old days?

JASON: The good old days?

FATHER: Yeah . . . when your mother and I were your age. We worked hard in the 1950s, but we enjoyed life.

JASON: You didn't have many machines, right? Your family didn't own a computer, or a VCR, or a compact disk player, or a stereo system, or . . .

JESSICA: What? You mean TV didn't exist?

FATHER: Oh, television existed, but in black and white—not in color. Anyway, we didn't own a set. My father decided we didn't need television.

JESSICA: What did you do for fun? Did you use to go to the movies every night?

FATHER: No, we didn't use to go to the movies. We stayed home and entertained ourselves.

JASON: How did you live without a big-screen TV, and video games, and CDs? What happened in the evening?

FATHER: Well, the children played games—like checkers and chess and Monopoly. My sister used to play rock and roll records on her record player, and we used to dance. We listened to the radio and discussed current events. My mother and father used to talk a lot—or they argued.

MOTHER: Not my family. My parents didn't use to talk much. My father liked to read a lot. My mother knitted and sewed. She used to cook every day. I usually helped in the kitchen.

JESSICA: Really? Why did you cook every day? Why didn't you order pizza from a restaurant?

MOTHER: Because my father wanted home-cooked meals. Of course, we didn't have a microwave oven or a food processor or a dishwasher or . . . .

JESSICA: What? No dishwasher? Who used to wash the dishes?

MOTHER: I used to wash them in the sink, and my sister used to dry them.

JESSICA: Didn't your brother do any housework? Didn't your father help?

MOTHER: No, I'm afraid not. Only the women worked in the house in those days.

FATHER: Yes, those *were* the good old days.

exercise ▼▼▼ Answer these questions about the conversation.

1. What are the children talking about with their parents?
2. What machines did the father's family own in the 1950s? What didn't they have?
3. What did the father's family use to do for fun in the evening?
4. How was the mother's family different from the father's family in those days?
5. Who did the housework in the mother's family? Why?

A. Statements with Regular Verbs

Use the simple past tense to talk about completed past events and activities. The chart below gives some examples.

	examples	notes
Affirmative	I usually **helped** in the kitchen. My mother **knitted** and **sewed**. We **listened** to music and **discussed** current events. The children **played** games.	
Negative	My father decided we **didn't need** television. We **didn't order** pizza from a restaurant. Your family **didn't own** a computer. My parents **didn't talk** much.	For negative past tense verbs, use *didn't* before the simple form of the main verb.

Spelling Rules for *-ed* Endings

1. If the simple form of a verb ends in *-y* after a consonant, change the *-y* to *i* and add *-ed.*

   examples: try / tried   carry / carried   knit / knitted

2. If the simple form of a verb of one syllable ends in one consonant after a vowel, double the last consonant (except *x*) and add *-ed.*

   examples: plan / planned   stop / stopped

   Note: The letters *w* and *y* at the end of words are vowels, not consonants.

   examples: row / rowed   play / played

3. If the simple form of a verb ends in an accented (stressed) syllable, follow the rule above for one final consonant after one vowel.

   examples: permit / permitted   prefer / preferred

4. If the simple form of a verb ends in *-e,* add only *-d.*

   examples: tie / tied   change / changed

5. Add *-ed* to the simple form of all other regular verbs.

   examples: want / wanted   ask / asked   belong / belonged

Pronunciation Note

The *-ed* ending is pronounced three ways, according to the end of the verb:

- /ed/ after *d,* and *t* endings

  examples: existed, knitted, needed, wanted

- /t/ after voiceless endings

  examples: cooked, helped, talked, washed, watched

- /d/ after voiced endings

  examples: argued, danced, listened, lived, played, sewed

 **exercise 1**   In the conversation on pages 112 and 113, circle the regular past tense verbs in affirmative statements. Put a box around the negative past tense verbs.

examples: We worked hard in the 1950s, but we enjoyed life.
Your family didn't own a computer or a VCR.

 **exercise 2**   Fill in the blanks with the correct simple past tense forms of the regular verbs in parentheses. The first one is done as an example.

In my childhood, we _____didn't watch_____ much TV inside the house
                        1 (not watch)

in hot weather. We _____ an air conditioner, so on warm
                          2 (not own)

summer evenings, we _____ outside on the porch for hours.
                            3 (stay)

We children _____ games or _____ at
                  4 (play)   5 (look)

comic books. My dad _____ back and forth in his rocking
                            6 (rock)

chair. Sometimes he _____ his pipe or _____
                            7 (smoke)   8 (try)

to do a crossword puzzle in the newspaper. Occasionally some neighbors

_____ us on the porch. Then dad _____
            9 (visit)   10 (stop)

reading the newspaper and _____ current events with them.
                                  11 (discuss)

Together they _____ about the future of the United States.
                      12 (argue)

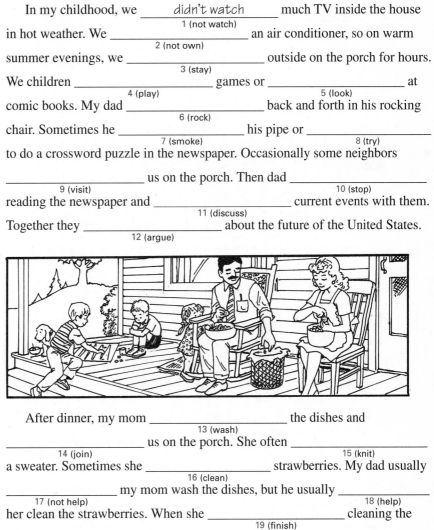

After dinner, my mom _____ the dishes and
                            13 (wash)

_____ us on the porch. She often _____
          14 (join)   15 (knit)

a sweater. Sometimes she _____ strawberries. My dad usually
                                16 (clean)

_____ my mom wash the dishes, but he usually _____
          17 (not help)   18 (help)

her clean the strawberries. When she _____ cleaning the
                                              19 (finish)

strawberries, she _____ them into the kitchen. She
                          20 (carry)

_____ a few minutes later with big bowls of strawberries
          21 (return)

and cream. My family always _____ those summer
                                    22 (enjoy)

evenings on the porch.

exercise 3 Think about your childhood. Write an affirmative or negative past tense statement about your childhood using each of the verb phrases in 1 to 20. You can tell about yourself and other family members. If you like, write more sentences using your own ideas.

examples: My parents talked about the "good old days."
             We children didn't listen to our parents very well.

1. talk about the "good old days"
2. listen to our parents
3. work hard
4. enjoy life
5. own many modern machines
6. need a lot of money
7. stay home after dinner
8. entertain ourselves
9. play games
10. dance to music from records

11. discuss current events
12. argue and disagree
13. visit neighbors or friends
14. knit or sew
15. cook or bake
16. help in the kitchen
17. order food from restaurants
18. wash dishes in the sink
19. dry dishes with a towel
20. work in the house

B. Yes/No Questions

The yes/no question form of the simple past tense often includes *did(n't)* before the subject (singular and plural). Note that the main verb in the question is in the simple form: There is no final *-ed* ending.

	examples	possible answers	
		Affirmative	**Negative**
Affirmative Questions	**Did** I ever **talk** to you about the 1950s?	Yes, you **did.**	No, you **didn't.**
	Did your family **cook** with a microwave?	Yes, we **did.**	No, we **didn't.**
	Did the neighbors often **visit** you?	Yes, they **did.**	No, they **didn't.**
Negative Questions	**Didn't** your father **help** with the housework?	Yes, he **did.**	No, he **didn't.**
	Didn't you **own** a TV set?	Yes, we **did.**	No, we **didn't.**
	Didn't your parents **argue** a lot?	Yes, they **did.**	No, they **didn't.**

exercise 4 Underline the yes/no question past tense verb forms in the conversation on pages 112 and 113.

example: Did I ever <u>talk</u> to you kids about the good old days?

exercise 5 What did you do last weekend? Work with a partner. Student A asks simple past tense questions using the cue words in 1 to 16. Student B answers. Then change roles (student B asks the questions, and student A answers). When you give a yes answer to a question, explain what you did in a simple past tense sentence.

examples: A: Did you clean your room last weekend?
B: No, I didn't.

A: Did you play any sports last weekend?
B: Yes, I did. I played tennis on Saturday afternoon.

1. clean your room?
2. play any sports?
3. listen to the radio?
4. watch TV?
5. look at a newspaper?
6. telephone your family?
7. visit your friends?
8. shop for clothing?
9. study at home?
10. finish your homework?
11. receive any letters or packages?
12. mail any letters or packages?
13. wash your clothes?
14. cook dinner?
15. stay up late?
16. enjoy yourself?

When you finish, join with another pair of students. Take turns telling the group five things that your partner did (or didn't do) last weekend.

C. Information Questions

Many information questions use *did* before the subject (singular and plural); a few information questions use *didn't* before the subject. Note that when *who* or *what* is the subject of the sentence, the main verb is in the simple past tense and *did* or *didn't* is not used before the subject. The chart below gives some examples.

examples	possible answers	notes
How did you **live** without a big-screen TV?	We entertained ourselves.	In information questions with *did* and *didn't*, the main verb is in the simple form. There is no final -ed ending.
Where did your relatives **stay**?	In the bedroom upstairs.	
When did your relatives **visit**?	They visited on holidays.	
Why did you **cook** every day?	My father liked to eat at home.	
Why didn't you **order** pizza from a restaurant?	We wanted home-cooked meals.	
What happened in the evening?	We stayed home.	When *who* or *what* is the subject, use the simple past tense in the main verb.
Who danced in the evening?	My sister and I.	
Who argued a lot?	My parents.	

 **exercise 6**   Put two lines under the information question forms (the question words and past tense verbs) in the conversation on pages 112 and 113.

  example: What did you do for fun?

exercise 7   The following ten information questions have no question words. Fill in the blanks with question words from the list. Then think about your past life. In the space under each question, write an answer in the simple past tense.

  What   Where   When   Who   How   Why

  1. _____ machines or electronic equipment did your family own?

  _____

  2. _____ cooked food for your family?

  _____

  3. _____ shopped for food?

  _____

  4. _____ did you travel around your city or town?

  _____

  5. _____ did you play with?

  _____

  6. _____ games or sports did you play?

  _____

  7. _____ did you start school?

  _____

  8. _____ television programs did you watch?

  _____

  9. _____ did you want to study English?

  _____

  10. _____ did you decide to study at this school?

  _____

When you finish, choose a partner. Take turns asking and answering the ten information questions. How are your answers similar? How are they different?

D. *used to + Verb*

Used to + a simple form of a verb expresses a habit or activity that existed in the past but is no longer happening in the present.

	examples	notes
Statements	We **used to dance.** She **used to cook** every day. My parents **didn't use to talk** much.	With *did(n't)* in questions and negative statements, there is no *-d* past-tense ending on *use.*
Questions	Who **used to wash** the dishes? **Did** your mother and father **use to argue** a lot? **Didn't** she **use to live** in New York?	

exercise 8 Put three lines under the verb phrases with *use(d) to* in the conversation on pages 112 and 113.

> **example:** <u>Did</u> you <u>use to go</u> to the movies every night?

exercise 9 Work with a partner. Take turns asking and answering questions about your life before you came here to study. Use verb phrases with *use(d) to* and the cue words in 1 to 8 below.

> **example:**   A: Where did you use to live?
> B: I used to live in a house in a small town.

1. Where / you / live?
2. Who / you / live with?
3. What kind / food / you / cook?
4. How / you / travel / to school?
5. How often / you / visit your friends?
6. How / you / entertain yourself?
7. What kind / music / you / listen to?
8. How often / you / clean your room?

Using What You've Learned

activity 1 Work in small groups. Think about the questions you discussed in Exercises 7 and 9. Take turns discussing the differences between your present life and your life before you came here to study. Use verb phrases with *use(d) to* to talk about the past.

> **example:**   A: I used to live with my family. We lived in a house in a small city. Now I live in a dorm with a roommate.
> B: My mother used to cook meals for my family. Now I usually eat in the cafeteria or in a restaurant.

How are your group members' experiences similiar? How are they different?

activity 2

Bring in to class photographs from books, newspapers, magazines, or other sources that show home and family scenes from the past. Work in small groups. Each group looks at one old photograph. Make as many past-tense sentences as you can about your picture. Try to use regular verbs only (if you use irregular verbs, use *use(d) to*). If the book, magazine, newspaper, and so on doesn't tell you, guess the time and place of the picture. Give reasons for your guesses. One student in each group writes down the group's sentences about the picture.

Each group chooses a person to tell the class about their picture. (Other group members may help.) After each group finishes, other groups can ask questions or make guesses about the picture.

As a class, discuss these questions for each picture:

- What does the picture show about the home or family life of people at that time?
- Does the picture show typical or average people of that time? Why or why not?

TOPIC two

The Simple Past Tense (Irregular Verbs)

Setting the Context

Conversation

JILL: I met a new neighbor the day before yesterday. He and I had a long talk last night.

KAREN: Oh, that's interesting! Tell me all about him.

JILL: His name is Yutaka. He's a student from Japan.

KAREN: Where's he going to study?

JILL: He applied for admission to UCLA last winter and got his letter of acceptance on May 10.

KAREN: That was only a few weeks ago. How did his family feel?

JILL: They felt very proud. Four days after he got the letter, his mother bought him a plane ticket and some clothes for his trip to the United States.

KAREN: What about his friends in Japan? Did they give him a going-away party?

JILL: Yes, they did. The night before he left Japan, his friends gave him a big going-away party. Then his family took him to the airport the next day. That was May 17.

KAREN: Did he get to Los Angeles the next day?

JILL: Actually, he got here the same day, on May 17. There's a one-day time difference between Japan and California.

KAREN: Oh, right. Where did he stay after that?

JILL: For his first two weeks here, Yutaka had to stay in a hotel. He spent a week trying to find an apartment.

KAREN: And he found one—right here in our building!

JILL: Yeah. He moved in several days ago, on June 1.

KAREN: That's great! Well, I can't wait to meet him.

Answer these questions about the pictures and the conversation.

1. Who met Yutaka last night? How do you think they met?
2. When did Yutaka apply for admission to UCLA? When did he get his letter of acceptance? How long ago did he get his letter of acceptance?
3. How long did the preparations for his trip take? What did Yutaka's mother buy him? What did his friends do the night before his trip?
4. When did Yutaka leave Japan? How did he get to Los Angeles?
5. What did Yutaka have to go through when he got to the airport in Los Angeles?
6. Where did Yutaka stay during his first two weeks in Los Angeles? How did he get there?
7. What did he look for the next day? How much time did he spend trying to find an apartment? When did he move into his new apartment?

A. Irregular Past Tense Verbs

Many common verbs have irregular past tense forms. These forms do not end in -ed. Charts A, B, and C list some common irregular verbs alphabetically in groups.

examples		notes
Simple Form	**Past Tense**	
cost	cost	
cut	cut	The simple and past forms of these verbs are the same.
let	let	
put	put	
lend	lent	
send	sent	In some verbs, the simple form ends in -d and the past form ends in -t.
spend	spent	
have	had	
make	made	Some verbs have other consonant changes in the past tense.
pay	paid	

B. More Irregular Past Tense Verbs

examples notes

Simple Form	Past Tense	Simple Form	Past Tense	notes
begin	began	meet	met	
drink	drank	read	read	
drive	drove	ring	rang	
eat	ate	run	ran	Many verbs have vowel changes in the past tense.
find	found	see	saw	
get	got	sing	sang	
give	gave	take	took	
know	knew	tear	tore	

C. Other Irregular Past Tense Verbs

Simple Form	Past Tense	Simple Form	Past Tense	notes
be	was / were	leave	left	
bring	brought	lose	lost	
buy	bought	say	said	
catch	caught	sell	sold	
do	did	sleep	slept	Many verbs have consonant and vowel changes in the past tense.
feel	felt	teach	taught	
go	went	tell	told	
hear	heard	think	thought	
keep	kept			

Expressions of Past Time

Here are some examples of expressions for past time:

yesterday	in April 1982	next
the day before yesterday	in 1993	the next day
last night	a few minutes ago	after that
last Monday evening	a year ago	a week later
last year	a long time ago	
on May 1	then	

exercise 1   Circle the irregular past tense verbs in the conversation on page 121. Underline all the expressions of past time.

> **example:**   I met a new neighbor the day before yesterday.

exercise 2   In the story below, Yutaka describes his last week in Japan and his first two weeks in the United States. Fill in the blanks with past tense forms of appropriate verbs from charts A, B, and C on pages 122 and 123. The first three are done as examples. *Notes:*

- The letter in parentheses next to each number tells you which chart has an appropriate verb for that blank. You can also use the context of the sentences to help choose the verbs.
- You can use some verbs more than once.
- More than one verb might be correct for a few blanks.
- You will not use all the verbs in the charts.

UCLA ___sent___ me the letter of acceptance on May 10.
1 (A)

I ___let___ my father read the letter first. Then he ___read___ it
2 (A)   3 (B)

aloud to the whole family. I know he _____ proud. I was really
4 (C)

excited. I _____ badly that night. The next day, I _____
5 (C)   6 (B)

my father downtown. We _____ dinner in a nice restaurant. Two
7 (B)

days later, I _____ shopping for some new clothes with my mother.
8 (C)

The clothes _____ a lot of money, but my mother proudly
9 (A)

_____ the money.
10 (A)

My going-away party was great! My friends and I stayed up late and

_____ songs. The alarm clock _____ the next morning,
11 (B)   12 (B)

but I didn't hear it. We had to hurry. My parents quickly _____ me
13 (B)

to the airport, and I _____
14 (C)

the plane just in time. That

_____ me a lesson: Next
15 (C)

time I'll get up earlier. On the

airplane, I _____ about
16 (C)

my wonderful family and friends,

and I _____ to get a little
17 (B)

homesick!

We _____ to Los Angeles eleven hours later. After going
 18 (B)
through immigration and customs, I _____ a taxi to a hotel. Then I
 19 (B)
_____ a newspaper and a map of the city at a shop near the hotel.
 20 (C)
I _____ that I had to find an apartment soon, so I _____
 21 (B)   22 (B)
the classified ads.

I _____ a lot of telephone calls the first few days, but I didn't
 23 (A)
have any luck. Someone _____ me that I had to look for For Rent
 24 (C)
signs. I walked around the city, but after a few days I _____ tired. So
 25 (C)
I _____ to an apartment rental agency. I _____ the agency
 26 (C)   27 (A)
a fee, and they _____ me
 28 (B)
a list of apartments. A week later, I

_____ a one-bedroom
 29 (B)
apartment in a really nice building.

The day before yesterday, I

_____ a young woman
 30 (B)
named Jill.

Using What You've Learned

Work in small groups. Continue the story in Exercise 2. What do you think happened to Yutaka next? Each person in the group adds one past tense statement. Use expressions of past time if possible. How many sentences can your group make?

example: A: Yutaka liked Jill.
          B: He asked Jill for a date the next day.
          C: Jill said yes.
          D: They went to the movies a week later.

Work with a partner. Take turns telling each other about your first trip to or arrival in this city. Use the simple past tense and expressions of past time. Ask each other questions to get more information about any part(s) of your stories.

example: A: I left my country by boat on June 14. I traveled for eight days.
             Then I arrived in San Francisco.
          B: Why didn't you fly?
          A: I had a lot of time, and I wanted to go by boat.

Then write down your partner's story. When you finish, join another pair of students. Take turns telling your partners' stories to the group. Ask and answer questions about your stories.

activity 3

Choose twenty verbs. Include regular and irregular verbs. You can use any of the verbs from this chapter or choose others from the list of most common irregular verbs on pages 122 and 123.

1. Make a set of twenty flash cards for your verbs. You can use index cards, or cut paper into twenty pieces.
2. Write the present form of the verb on one side of each card and the past tense on the other side. When you finish, shuffle your cards so that the simple and past forms of the verbs are mixed up. Put your pile of cards on the desk in front of you.
3. Work with a partner. Sit side by side so you can see each other's cards.
4. Look at your partner's top (first) card. Read the verb, then give the other form of the verb. If you give the correct form, take your partner's card. If you make a mistake, your partner keeps the card and puts it at the bottom of his or her pile.
5. Now your partner reads your top card and gives the other verb form. If your partner gives the correct form, he or she gets the card. If not, put the card at the bottom of your pile.
6. Play until one person gets all of the other player's cards.

example:

A: *(Looks at B's top card.)*	Teach. Taught.	*(Correct: A takes B's card.)*
B: *(Looks at A's top card.)*	Keep. Keeped.	*(Incorrect: B keeps card and puts at bottom of pile.)*
A: *(Looks at B's next card.)*	Went. Go.	*(Correct: A takes B's card.)*
B: *(Looks at A's next card.)*	Cut. Cut.	*(Correct: B takes A's card.)*

To make the game more difficult:

- Each student must also make a sentence with the correct form of the verb.
- The sentence must show the meaning of the verb and include a time expression.

Keep your verb flash cards. You will use them in another activity later in this chapter.

TOPIC **three**
Connecting Sentences

Setting the Context
Conversation

JEAN-PAUL: I'm homesick.

CARMEN: I'm usually very happy here, but sometimes I get homesick. When I think about my family, my friends, and my home, I start to feel sad.

JEAN-PAUL: I know. It gets lonely here because people don't spend time together. They're always in a hurry, so they don't talk to each other.

DENISE: Sure they do. We talked at the party last Saturday, and after it ended, we all went out for ice cream. Remember?

JEAN-PAUL: Of course, but we only do those things on weekends. In France, as soon as my classes ended every day, I used to meet my friends. We visited people, or we sat in a café.

CARMEN: Before I came here, I always used to talk to my family at home. We used to spend two hours at dinner every day, and the food was wonderful. We put candles on the table, and there was an elegant atmosphere. We certainly didn't use to eat fast food or TV dinners.

DENISE: How did you use to have time for long meals? Didn't you have to study?

CARMEN: Of course I did, but . . . I'm homesick.

JEAN-PAUL: Me, too.

Answer these questions about the conversation on page 127.

1. How are Jean-Paul and Carmen feeling?
2. Do they understand each other's feelings?
3. Does Denise understand their feelings?
4. Why are they feeling that way?
5. What does Jean-Paul miss? What does Carmen miss?

A. Connecting Sentences with *and, but, or,* and *so*

And, but, or, and *so* may be used to connect two or more independent clauses. Independent clauses are complete sentences. There is usually a comma before these connecting words. (In very short sentences the comma is sometimes left out.)

	examples	notes
and	Americans usually go out on Saturday nights, **and** they stay home on Sundays.	*And* means "in addition." It connects similar ideas or adds information.
but	I don't really like fast foods, **but** I eat them anyway.	*But* means "by contrast." It connects opposing ideas.
or	Did you use to drink tea, **or** did you prefer coffee in your country?	*Or* expresses an alternative or a choice.
so	She doesn't cook very well, **so** she eats TV dinners.	*So* introduces a result.

exercise 1

Circle the connecting words in the conversation on page 127.

example: I'm usually happy here, but sometimes I get homesick.

exercise 2

Combine the sentences 1 to 14 below with *and, but, or,* or *so*. There might be more than one correct answer for some sentences.

example: In my country, many relatives used to live together, so we had to have a big house.

1. In my country, many relatives used to live together. We had to have a big house.
2. My parents' house was in the country. We used to have a lot of farm animals.

3. I liked to feed the cows. I didn't like to feed the chickens.
4. I shared a room with two brothers. It was crowded.
5. The men in the family worked outside the house. The women usually worked inside.
6. My sister and I cleaned the house. My mother took care of the baby.
7. My grandmother used to have a vegetable garden. We grew some of our own food.
8. The men often went out in the evening. The women usually stayed at home.
9. The young children used to play games. The teenagers used to dance to music.
10. We didn't have CDs then. We listened to records instead.
11. Our friends used to visit us every Saturday. We would meet them in town.
12. We had a big lunch on Sunday. The food was always delicious. We ate a lot.
13. Our relatives visited us on holidays. We ate and drank. We danced and sang.
14. We didn't have a lot of modern appliances. We had to work hard. We always enjoyed life there.

B. Adverb Clauses with *because, before, after, as soon as,* and *when*

Because, before, after, as soon as, and *when* are used to introduce adverb clauses. An adverb clause is not a complete sentence. It must be connected to an independent clause (a complete sentence). The chart below gives some examples. Notice that no comma is used when the adverb clause comes after an independent clause. When the adverb clause comes before an independent clause, a comma is used to separate the two clauses.

	examples	notes
because	I felt homesick **because I missed my family.** **Because I missed my family,** I felt homesick.	An adverb clause with *because* shows cause and effect.
before	I lived with my family **before I came to Toronto.** **Before I came to Toronto,** I lived with my family.	Adverb clauses with *before, after, as soon as,* and *when* show time relationships.
after	I found a roommate **after I rented the apartment.** **After I rented the apartment,** I found a roommate.	

	examples	notes
as soon as	We became friends **as soon as he moved in.** **As soon as he moved in,** we became friends.	*As soon as* means "immediately after."
when	Did you clean the house **when you lived at home?** **When you lived at home,** did you clean the house?	*When* means "at the time that."

 **exercise 3** Underline the adverb clauses in the conversation on page 127. Notice which clauses have commas and which do not.

> **example:** <u>When I think about my family, my friends, and my home,</u> I start to feel sad.

exercise 4 Change each present tense verb in the sentences below to the past tense. Then connect each pair of sentences with *because, before, after, as soon as,* or *when.* There might be more than one correct answer for some sentences.

> **example:** I started to feel homesick after I said good-bye to my family and friends.

  1. I start to feel homesick. I say good-bye to my family and friends.
  2. I call my family from the airport. I go through customs.
  3. I don't understand the people at the airport. They talk very quickly.
  4. I start to look for housing. I arrive in this city.
  5. I find a nice room. I look for several weeks.
  6. I am lonely. I don't know anyone here.
  7. It is difficult to understand Americans. They talk to me on the street.
  8. I begin to feel better. I meet some students in my classes.
  9. We do some activities together. We become friends.
  10. I visit their homes. They introduce me to more people.

 **exercise 5** Write the past tense form of each verb in parentheses. Then connect the two sentences in each item with the word in brackets.

> **example:** When I <u>arrived</u> in Canada a few years ago, I <u>didn't have</u> a place to live.

  1. I _____*arrived*_____ in Canada a few years ago. I
  1 (arrive)
  _____*didn't have*_____ a place to live. [When]
  2 (not have)

2. I _____ how to find housing. I _____
   <small>3 (not know)</small>   <small>4 (stay)</small>
with friends for a while. [so]

3. On my first day, I _____ a city map. It
   <small>5 (buy)</small>
_____ me find an apartment. [but]
   <small>6 (not help)</small>

4. Then I _____ a newspaper. I _____
   <small>7 (get)</small>   <small>8 (study)</small>
the apartment ads. [and]

5. I _____ them. I _____ the
   <small>9 (not understand)</small>   <small>10 (not know)</small>
abbreviations. [because]

6. A friend _____ the abbreviations to me. I
   <small>11 (explain)</small>
_____ out several interesting ads. [After]
   <small>12 (pick)</small>

7. I _____ a large apartment with a swimming pool, tennis
   <small>13 (want)</small>
courts, modern furniture, and air conditioning. I _____
                                                <small>14 (notice)</small>
the prices. [before]

8. I _____ about the housing market. I _____
   <small>15 (learn)</small>   <small>16 (begin)</small>
to look for apartments in less expensive areas. [As soon as]

9. The one-bedroom apartments _____ affordable. Some
                                   <small>17 (seem)</small>
of them _____ with furniture. [and]
        <small>18 (come)</small>

10. I _____ a lot of places. I finally _____
   <small>19 (call)</small>   <small>20 (find)</small>
a nice apartment. [but]

Using What You've Learned

Complete these past tense sentences, using information about yourself.

1. I decided to come to this country (city, school) because _____

_____

2. I _____ before I came here.

3. I felt _____ when _____

4. _____ after I arrived here.

5. I found a _____ as soon as _____

6. My English was _____, so _____

7. I didn't _____, but _____

8. Because _____, I _____

Work in small groups. Take turns reading one of your sentences. The rest of the group asks questions. Continue to read and discuss your other sentences.

example: A: I decided to come to this country because I wanted to get married.

B: Did you want to marry someone from your country or someone from here?

Then each student tells the class one thing about each classmate from your group.

activity 2

Choose a topic from the list below. Prepare a short speech (not more than two minutes) on the topic. Use the past tense. If possible, use some connecting words and adverb clauses in your speech.

- My Favorite Childhood Memories
- My Trip to the United States or Canada
- My First Day in This Country (or City)
- Life with My Roommate(s)
- A Great Experience with My Family
- My Best (or Worst) Experience with an American or Canadian Family
- (Your own topic about your home/family)

When your speeches are ready, form small groups. Take turns speaking to the group for two minutes. When each person finishes his or her speech, another student in the group summarizes the speech. Continue until everyone gives a speech and summarizes someone else's speech.

activity 3

Work in groups of four. Use the verb flash cards you made in Activity 3 on page 126. Each student chooses ten of his or her verbs. Combine your verb cards into one set of forty cards. One student in each group shuffles the cards and gives ten cards to each group member. Each student makes a story with his or her ten verbs. Use the past tense and as many connecting words and adverb clauses as possible.

Take turns telling your stories to the group. When each person finishes his or her story, another student summarizes it. Continue until everyone tells a story and summarizes someone else's story.

CHAPTER six

Emergencies and Strange Experiences

in this chapter

The Past Continous Tense

Setting the Context

Conversation

A policeman is interviewing three witnesses about a bank robbery.

POLICEMAN: Tell me about the robbery. What were you doing? Who did you see?

WITNESS 1: I was standing in line at a teller's window. The robbers entered at exactly 3:00. There were two women and one man.

WITNESS 2: No, there were two men and one woman—and it wasn't 3:00. It was 3:15. I was looking at the clock at the time.

WITNESS 3: Actually, it was almost 3:30.

POLICEMAN: What were the suspects wearing?

WITNESS 2: They were all wearing ski masks!

WITNESS 3: And two of them were wearing big sunglasses.

POLICEMAN: I see. What was the guard doing at the time of the robbery?

WITNESS 1: The guard was sitting on a chair. He was holding his head because he was injured.

WITNESS 2: No, he wasn't. The robbers tied up the guard with a rope, so he was sitting on the floor and couldn't move.

POLICEMAN: Was there anyone helping the guard?

WITNESS 1: No, there wasn't. Everyone was afraid.

POLICEMAN: Were the suspects carrying weapons?

WITNESS 3: Yes, they were all pointing rifles at the customers.

WITNESS 1: No, they weren't. The woman was waving a big knife . . .

exercise Answer these questions about the conversation.

1. Who are the three witnesses talking to? What are they talking about?
2. According to the witnesses, what were the suspects wearing on their faces at the time of the robbery? Were they carrying weapons? What was the bank guard doing?
3. Do the three witnesses remember the same things? According to the picture on page 134, were any of the witnesses correct? Explain.

The Past Continuous Tense

The past continuous tense describes activities in progress (happening) at a specific time or during a period of time in the past. It consists of a past form of the verb *be* before the *-ing* form of a verb. For a review of the rules for spelling *-ing* verbs, see page 40, Chapter Two.

	examples	notes
Statements	I **was standing** in line. The guard **was sitting** in a chair. He **wasn't paying** attention. The tellers **weren't screaming**.	Use contractions with forms of *be* + *not*.
Yes/No Questions	**Was** the child **crying**? **Were** the witnesses **talking**?	In a question, *was* or *were* comes before the subject (except a question-word subject).
Information Questions	Who **was carrying** weapons? What **were** the suspects **wearing**? What **was** the guard **doing**?	With *who* or *what* as the subject, use a singular verb.
there is/are	**There were** two men **holding** guns. **Was there** anyone **helping** the guard?	

Underline the past continuous verb phrases in the conversation about the bank robbery.

example: What <u>were</u> you <u>doing</u>?

Look at pictures 1 to 3 below. Make past continuous statements (affirmative and negative) about them with the phrases next to each witness, as in the examples.

1.

- wear ski masks   <u>The three men were wearing ski masks.</u>
- carry guns   <u>They weren't carrying guns.</u>
- wave knives _____
- hold a sack _____
- stand by the safe _____

2.

- wear ski masks _____
- carry guns _____
- wave knives _____
- hold a sack _____
- stand by the safe _____

3.

- wear masks _____
- carry sacks _____
- wave gun _____
- carry rifles _____
- sit on a chair _____

exercise 3
Work in groups of four. The first student asks yes/no and information questions in the past continuous tense about the situations in Exercise 2. The second student answers according to the information in the first picture; the third student, according to the second picture; and the fourth student, according to the third picture.

example: A: Where was the guard standing?
B: He was standing near the safe.
C: No, he wasn't. He was standing next to the door.
D: He wasn't standing at all. He was sitting.

exercise 4
Work in pairs. Study the picture on page 134. Then one of you closes your book and the other asks questions about the scene in the past continuous tense. The first student tries to answer from memory. Then change roles.

example: A: Were all the suspects carrying guns?
B: The two men were holding guns. One man was pointing a rifle. The woman wasn't carrying a gun.
A: Was there anyone screaming?

Using What You've Learned

activity 1
Work with a new partner. Do <u>not</u> look at your previous partner. Each of you asks and answers these questions.

1. What was your previous partner wearing? Was she or he wearing a watch or any other jewelry?
2. Was she or he holding anything? What was your previous partner doing with her or his hands during the conversation?
3. Was she or he eating or chewing anything?
4. Where was she or he looking? How was she or he sitting?

Variation: Answer the questions above about all the classmates in your group in Exercise 3.

activity 2
Collect magazine pictures or illustrations from children's books in which many activities are going on at the same time. If possible, choose pictures of emergency situations. Then follow these steps:

1. Each person receives a different picture. Study your picture for three minutes. Then turn your picture over. Without looking at it, answer this question: What was happening in the picture? Write as many sentences as you can in the past tense.
2. Now exchange pictures with a partner. Looking at your new picture, answer this question: What is happening right now in the picture? Write as many sentences as you can in the present tense.
3. Compare your lists of sentences. They should be similar, except for the use of the present and past tenses. Make necessary corrections and additions.
4. You can repeat steps 1 to 3 with different pictures.

The Simple Past Tense and the Past Continuous Tense

8:30 p.m.　　　　　9:15 p.m.　　　　　12:15 a.m.

1:00 a.m.　　　　　1:15 a.m.　　　　　1:20 a.m.

Setting the Context
Reading

Yes, officer, I can tell you the whole story. My name is Bill Barker. Until about 1:00 A.M., Jack and Sally Anderson were at a party at our house. Everyone was having a good time, I believe, but I think Jack drank too much. He and Sally were arguing when they left. When they drove away, I got worried, so I followed
5   them in my car. Jack was laughing and singing, I think, while he was driving. It was raining hard, and the streets were wet and dangerous, so I flashed my headlights at Jack. But I couldn't get his attention, and he didn't pull over. He was weaving in and out of the traffic. Suddenly he swerved and hit a fence.

exercise Answer these questions about the story.

1. Who is telling the story? Who is he talking to? Who is he talking about?
2. According to the storyteller, what was Jack Anderson doing when he left the party? What was he doing while he was driving away? Why?
3. Why did the storyteller follow Jack in his car? What did he do? What did Jack do?

A. The Simple Past Tense Versus the Past Continuous Tense

	examples	notes
Simple Past	I **followed** Jack and Sally in my car. Jack **drank** too much. The car **swerved** and **hit** a fence. **Were** the streets wet and dangerous?	Use the simple past tense to talk about events and activities that began and ended at a specific time in the past.
Past Continuous	Jack and Sally **were arguing**. He **was laughing** and **singing**. **Was** it **raining** hard? The car **was weaving** in and out of traffic.	Use the past continuous tense to describe activities that were in progress (happening) at a specific time or during a period of time in the past.

B. Nonaction Verbs

Nonaction verbs express feelings, thoughts, opinions, possession or perceptions. They do not usually appear in a continuous form; they usually appear in a simple form. This chart gives some examples.

	verbs		examples	notes
Feelings, Thoughts, Opinions	want know believe like hate prefer	need think understand love feel be	I **thought** Jack drank too much. Everyone **liked** the party. She **was** tired after the party. We **need** an ambulance! They **felt** sorry about about the accident.	Some nonaction verbs can appear in a continuous form with a different meaning. For example: She **was thinking** about it.
Possession	have own	possess belong to	The car **belonged to** Jack. We **have** a house in the country.	They **were having** fun.
Perceptions	see taste hear	look smell	Jack **looked** drunk. The food **tasted** delicious. We **saw** the accident.	Jack was hurt. He **was seeing** a doctor for a while.

exercise 1   Make sentences about the picture story on page 138. Use the cue words in 1 to 6 below. Use the past continuous tense for action verbs and the simple past tense for nonaction verbs.

example: At 8:30, Jack and Sally Anderson were standing on the porch of Bill Barker's house. They saw the guests inside. The guests were enjoying the party. They were having a good time.

1. 8:30 / Jack and Sally Anderson / stand on the porch of Bill Barker's house.
   They / see / the guests inside.
   The guests / enjoy the party. They / have a good time.
2. 9:15 / the guests / eat the hors d'oeuvres.
   The food / look good / and / taste delicious.
   The punch / contain alcohol. Jack / drink a lot of it.
3. 12:15 / the house / be / a mess.
   Sally / look at her watch. Bill Barker and his wife / seem / worried.
4. 1:00 / the Andersons / get into their car.
   They / argue. Sally / want to drive.
   Jack / appear / intoxicated. It / rain.

5. 1:15 / Jack / drive on the highway. He / speed.
Sally / feel frightened. Jack / laugh and sing.
Bill / follow them in his car. He / flash his headlights.

6. 1:20 / Jack / lie on a blanket. He / be / hurt.
Paramedics / carry him into an ambulance.
Sally / be / very upset. Bill / help her.

 exercise 2   What do you think happened next in the story about Jack and Sally Anderson?
Write six more sentences using the past continuous and simple past tense.

> **examples:**   The ambulance drove away. For about twenty minutes, it was
> speeding through the streets of the city. Paramedics were
> helping Jack inside the ambulance.

When you finish, work with a partner. Read each other's sentences. Are your
sentences similar?

C. *when* and *while* with the Simple Past and Past Continuous Tenses

When and *while* are used to introduce adverb clauses of time. They can connect
two events or activities that happened (simple past) or were happening (past
continuous) at the same time in the past. *When* can also show a sequence of
events—which event happened first, second. The chart below gives some
examples.

	examples	notes
when	Jack and Sally **were arguing when** they **left**. **When** they **drove** away, I **got** worried.	Adverb clauses with *when* are usually in the simple past tense. If both verbs are in the simple past, the action in the *when* clause happened first.
while	Jack **was singing while** he **was driving**. **While** he **was driving**, Jack **was singing**.	Adverb clauses with *while* are usually in the past continuous tense. If both verbs are in the past continuous, it means the two actions were going on at the same time. *While* can appear at the beginning or in the middle of the sentence.
when *or* while	Jack **hit** a fence **while** he **was driving**. Jack **was driving when** he **hit** a fence.	The simple past and the past continuous can appear in the same sentence. One event was in progress when the second event interrupted it.

 Complete these sentences with the past continuous or simple past form of the verbs in parentheses. More than one answer might be correct for some items. The first one is done as an example.

FRED: Hi, Allan. How are you? I _____called_____ you last night about 10:00, but you
1 (call)

_____ home. What
2 (not be)

_____ you _____?
3   4 (do)

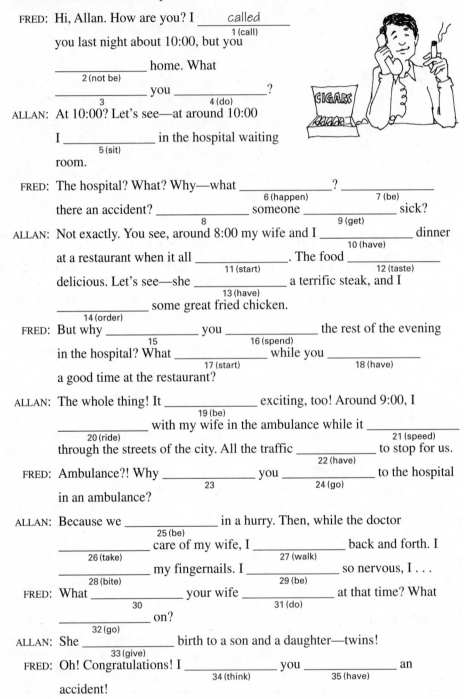

ALLAN: At 10:00? Let's see—at around 10:00

I _____ in the hospital waiting
5 (sit)
room.

FRED: The hospital? What? Why—what _____? _____
6 (happen)   7 (be)

there an accident? _____ someone _____ sick?
8   9 (get)

ALLAN: Not exactly. You see, around 8:00 my wife and I _____ dinner
10 (have)

at a restaurant when it all _____. The food _____
11 (start)   12 (taste)

delicious. Let's see—she _____ a terrific steak, and I
13 (have)

_____ some great fried chicken.
14 (order)

FRED: But why _____ you _____ the rest of the evening
15   16 (spend)

in the hospital? What _____ while you _____
17 (start)   18 (have)

a good time at the restaurant?

ALLAN: The whole thing! It _____ exciting, too! Around 9:00, I
19 (be)

_____ with my wife in the ambulance while it _____
20 (ride)   21 (speed)

through the streets of the city. All the traffic _____ to stop for us.
22 (have)

FRED: Ambulance?! Why _____ you _____ to the hospital
23   24 (go)

in an ambulance?

ALLAN: Because we _____ in a hurry. Then, while the doctor
25 (be)

_____ care of my wife, I _____ back and forth. I
26 (take)   27 (walk)

_____ my fingernails. I _____ so nervous, I . . .
28 (bite)   29 (be)

FRED: What _____ your wife _____ at that time? What
30   31 (do)

_____ on?
32 (go)

ALLAN: She _____ birth to a son and a daughter—twins!
33 (give)

FRED: Oh! Congratulations! I _____ you _____ an
34 (think)   35 (have)

accident!

exercise 4 Make two sentences in the past continuous or simple past about pictures 1 to 4. Use the cue words under each picture. Then combine the two sentences with the time word in parentheses. The first one is done as an example.

1.

Mrs. Brenner / smoke in bed
She / watch TV
(while)

At about 10:30, Mrs. Brenner was smoking in bed.

She was watching TV.

At about 10:30, Mrs. Brenner was

smoking in bed while she was watching TV.

2.

The cigarette / still burn
She / fall asleep
(when)

3.

Mr. Brenner / try to put out the fire
His wife / call the fire department
(while)

4.

The Brenners / leave the house
The firefighters / arrive
(when)

D. Information Questions

examples	possible answers	notes
What time was the party over? **What kind of** car was Jack driving?	About 1:00. A white sports car.	Use *what* or *what kind of* before nouns.
Which hospital did the ambulance go to? **Which friends** were having the party?	It went to New York General. The Barkers.	Use *which* before nouns in questions about choices.
How serious was the accident? **How fast** was he driving?	It was very serious. He was driving too fast.	Use *how* before adjectives and adverbs.

 Make information questions in the past continuous tense or simple past tense from the cue words in 1 to 10. Use *what, what kind of, which,* or *how.*

example: What time did the fire start?

1. time / fire / start?
2. room / the fire / start in?
3. program / Mrs. Brenner / watch on TV?
4. cigarettes / she / smoke?
5. time / Jack and Sally / arrive at the party?
6. late / they / stay?
7. drunk / be / Jack?
8. car / Bill / follow?
9. hard / be / it / rain?
10. fence / Jack / hit?

Using What You've Learned

 Work with a partner. Look at the pictures and reading on pages 138 and 139 again. With your partner, write a conversation between Bill Barker and the police officer. In this conversation, the police officer is asking Bill information questions to find out what happened to Jack and Sally Anderson. To start your conversation, look at the information Bill gives in the reading. Then think of some questions the police officer might ask Bill to get this information. Use the past tense and past continuous tense as much as possible.

	example:	OFFICER:	What's your name?
		BILL:	My name is Bill Barker.
		OFFICER:	What were Jack and Sally Anderson doing at your house?
		BILL:	They were at a party.
		OFFICER:	What time did they leave?
		BILL:	They left about 1:00.
		OFFICER:	Was Jack drinking?
		BILL:	Yes, he was. I think he drank too much.

When you finish, join another pair of students. Role play your conversations. How were your conversations alike and different? Who wrote the longest conversation?

If you like, role play one of your conversations for the class.

activity 2

Write about an emergency or strange experience—for example, a crime, a medical problem, a fire, flood, earthquake, and so on. It can be real or imaginary. Use the simple past tense and past continuous tense to describe the experience. Use *when* and *while* clauses when possible.

When you finish, work in small groups. Take turns. Read your stories to the group. The other group members ask information questions about the details.

When the groups finish, group members can retell other people's stories to the class.

TOPIC **three**

Infinitives After Verbs, Nouns, and Adjectives

Setting the Context
Reading

Shock is a dangerous condition. A serious injury or a heart attack can cause victims to go into shock. You need to consider the possibility of shock in all emergency situations. It's important to recognize the signs of shock: cold, pale skin, weak breathing, and perspiration. Victims have a tendency to feel cold and thirsty. What is the first thing to do? It's essential to keep them warm. You may want to give them a little water, but it is not good to give them alcoholic drinks. They may try to get up, but don't let them. Call for help, and then promise to stay with the victims. They have to remain calm.

exercise Answer these questions about the information above.

1. Who is giving this lecture? Who is he talking to? What is the lecture about?
2. What are two possible causes of shock? What are four signs of shock?
3. What is the first thing to do in case of shock?
4. Is it all right to give shock victims beer? Is it okay to give them water?
5. What else can a person do for a shock victim? What does the victim need to do?

A. Infinitives After Verbs

An infinitive is *to* + the simple form of a verb (for example, *to talk, to listen, to be,* and so on). Infinitives can follow certain verbs. The chart below gives some examples. The verbs with an asterisk (*) have nonaction meanings. They do not usually appear in the continuous form before an infinitive.

verbs		examples	notes
like*	start / begin	You **need to call** an ambulance.	The first verb can be in any tense.
want*	remember*	I **wanted to go** to the hospital.	
prefer*	forget*	He **is starting to go** into shock.	
need*	continue	They **were trying to get** help.	
have*	intend	I **don't know how to give** CPR.	In some negative sentences, *not* comes before the first verb. In other sentences, *not* comes between the infinitive and first verb.
try	know how*	We**'re not planning to drive**.	
plan	ought*	**Try not to make** a mistake.	
expect	learn		

exercise 1 Circle the verb + infinitive phrases in the reading about shock.

example: You need to consider the possibility of shock in all emergency situations.

Complete these sentences with verb + infinitive phrases. Use the two verbs in parentheses in the correct order. The first one is done as an example.

Do you _____know how to take_____ care of an accident victim? Suppose

1 (take, know how)

that a car hits a child and the child is lying in the street. What do you do?

Well, first of all, don't _____ the victim. You

2 (move, try)

_____ with him or her while someone calls for help.

3 (ought, stay)

calls for help. You _____ the child's pulse first. If there

4 (check, need)

is no pulse, _____ CPR immediately. Sometimes there

5 (do, begin)

is a pulse, but the victim is not breathing. In that case, you'll

_____ mouth-to-mouth resuscitation (artificial respiration).

6 (have, perform)

If the child is conscious, he or she may _____ upset.

7 (start, get)

You'll _____ him or her. _____ with

8 (calm, want)   9 (Promise, stay)

the victim. _____ care of the injured child until the

10 (Continue, take)

ambulance arrives.

 **exercise 3**

Make infinitives to complete the following sentences. The first one is done as an example.

1. If you intend *to* help people in emergency situations, you ought *to* take a first aid course.

2. For example, do you know how recognize the symptoms of a heart attack?

3. Suddenly, the victim begins feel pressure in the chest.

4. The pain may continue spread to the neck or arms.

5. Often, the victim starts sweat.

6. He may try stand or walk, but he needs sit or lie down.

7. If his heart is beating, you'll want call for help quickly.

8. If his heart stops, someone has begin CPR immediately.

9. If medical help isn't there yet, you have try keep him alive.

10. Everyone can plan learn the steps for CPR and remember do them correctly.

Add the word *to* as necessary to make infinitives in the four paragraphs below. The first two are done as examples. (*Hint:* You need to add *to* seven more times in paragraph 1, two times in paragraph 2, four times in paragraph 3, and five times in paragraph 4.)

If you want ∧*to* know how ∧*to* save a life, you ought learn cardiopulmonary resuscitation (CPR). However, don't expect learn CPR from a book. For example, the steps in the pictures below may look simple, but you need get special training do them correctly. If you really want learn CPR, plan take a course, perhaps from the Red Cross unit in your area. The information here is only very general. Do not try practice these steps before you take a real first aid course.

First of all, make sure the victim is flat on his back. If he's unconscious, you'll need open the airway. With one hand, you'll have lift the neck. Push back on the forehead with your other hand. (See picture A.)

If the victim isn't breathing, prepare follow the steps for artificial respiration in picture B. Don't forget hold the victim's nose closed with your fingers while you take a deep breath. Quickly, give the victim four full breaths. Remember check for a pulse. If there's a pulse, continue give the victim artificial respiration with one breath every five seconds.

If there is no pulse, try get the victim's heart beating. Kneel next to the victim. Press down on the victim's breastbone and quickly let go. (See picture C.) Continue do this about once a second. After about thirty seconds, remember give the victim artificial respiration (two full breaths). If the victim doesn't start breathe, don't stop! Continue give the victim CPR until help arrives.

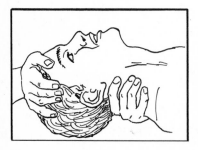

A.

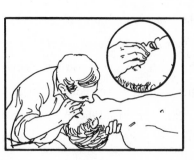

B.

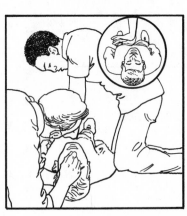

C.

B. Infinitives After Nouns and Adjectives

Infinitives can follow certain nouns and adjectives. This chart gives some examples.

nouns		examples
thing(s)	reason(s)	There were many **things to do.**
time	idea	Do you have **time to help** us?
step(s)	plan(s)	These are the **steps to follow.**

adjectives		examples	notes
able	happy	Be **careful not to hurt** the victim.	
afraid	important	It's **important to act** quickly.	
careful	lucky	It's **essential to stay** calm.	Impersonal *it* often
certain	possible	Was it too **late to call** the doctor?	appears before an
easy	sorry	The ambulance was **ready to go.**	adjective + infinitive.*
essential	sure	We were **lucky to find** this hospital.	
glad	ready		

*In a sentence with impersonal *it,* the infinitive can be the subject; for example:
   It's **essential to act.** = **To act** is **essential.**

C. Infinitives After Noun + *be*

An infinitive can follow the pattern noun + *be*. This chart gives some examples.

nouns		examples
step	purpose	The first **step is to check** the victim's breathing.
goal	idea	The most important **purpose** of first aid **is to save** someone's life.

 Underline the infinitives after nouns, adjectives, and nouns + *be* in the reading on page 146.

   example: It's <u>important to recognize</u> the signs of shock.

Fill in the blanks with *it* or *to* as in the examples.

You may not know all the necessary steps _____ take in an emergency
                                              1

situation. However, if you are in an emergency, _____ is essential not _____
                                                    2   3

panic. _____'s important _____ get help as soon as possible, but you may
         4   5

be able _____ save a life before help arrives. The first step is _____ check
          6   7

the victim's breathing because _____'s vital for the brain and heart _____
                                  8   9

have oxygen. Be careful not _____ injure the victim if you move him or her,
                               10

but don't be afraid _____ perform CPR if necessary. Of course, the best idea
                       11

is _____ take a first aid course. Then you can start _____ learn all the skills
     12   13

you need _____ use in a real emergency.
            14

Rewrite these sentences. Use the word or phrase in parentheses. Make infinitives
and/or other necessary changes as in the examples.

1. In any injury, check the victim's breathing first. (the first step)

In any injury, the first step is to check the victim's breathing.

2. In an emergency, there may not be time for a telephone call. (make)

In an emergency, there may not be time to make a telephone call.

3. Help first and call an ambulance later. (urgent)

4. To learn CPR, attend a course. (important)

5. An instructor will teach you the correct steps. (use)

6. In case of choking, the victim may cough. (try)

7. If the victim is not getting air, you hit him or her on the back. (need)

_____

8. If you know first aid, you will stop the bleeding of a serious wound. (know how)

_____

9. Press a clean cloth on the wound. (useful)

_____

10. Raise the wound above the level of the victim's heart. (another important step)

_____

 *exercise* **8** Correct the underlined grammar mistakes (tenses, infinitives, impersonal *it*) in the story below and on the next page. Write in the correct words as in the example.

A MYSTERY STORY

One night last week, Jack Jordan ~~was calling~~ *called* the famous detective, Edward Grimsley, on the telephone.

"I called <u>tell</u> you about my Uncle Ambrose," he said. "At 8:00 this evening,
      1

I <u>waiting</u> for him at a gourmet restaurant downtown. We were <u>planned</u> <u>meet</u>
  2   3   4

for dinner there. You ought <u>know</u> that he's a very rich man—and famous."
               5

"Yes, I seem <u>remembering</u> his name," answered the detective. In fact, I
            6

<u>reading</u> a newspaper article about him while I was <u>have</u> lunch just a few days
 7   8

ago. <u>Didn't</u> he vacationing on a Caribbean island last week?"
    9

"Yes, he <u>is</u>, and he <u>was</u> brought back a lot of money with him. I'm worried
       10   11

about my uncle because many people <u>were knowing</u> about the money. <u>Is</u> possi-
                            12   13

ble for you to meet me at his apartment?"

Detective Grimsley <u>was</u> agreed to meet Jack, and he <u>is</u> waiting in front of
14 15

the apartment when Jack <u>was arriving</u> by taxi.
16

"Did you <u>trying</u> <u>call</u> him tonight?" he <u>was asking</u> Jack.
17 18 19

"Yes, I did," Jack answered. "When he <u>wasn't coming</u> to dinner, I <u>call</u> his
20 21

number, but I <u>wasn't getting</u> any answer."
22

The two <u>did</u> walked quickly to the door of Ambrose Pennwright's apart-
23

ment. It wasn't locked, so they <u>did open</u> the door and <u>were going</u> into the dark
24 25

room.

"I'll have to <u>turning</u> on the light on the other side of the room," Jack said,
26

and he <u>disappears</u> into the darkness. Soon light <u>was</u> filled the small room. The
27 28

door to the safe behind him was open, and his Uncle Ambrose was <u>lie</u> on the
29

floor in front of him. With a frightened look on his face, Jack <u>steps</u> back over
30

his uncle. "I'm afraid <u>of look</u>," he said to the detective. "Is . . . is he dead?"
31

"He's unconscious," <u>answering</u> Grimsley, "but he's still alive. He's an old
32

man and not very strong. <u>Was</u> easy for someone <u>hit</u> him on the back of the
33 34

head and <u>taking</u> the money from the safe. And that person—I'm sorry <u>saying</u>
35 36

—was you, Jack Jordon. Are you ready <u>for</u> go? You'll have <u>coming</u> with me."
37 38

When you finish, work with a partner. Exchange papers and check each other's
answers. Did you both correct <u>all</u> the mistakes?

Using What You've Learned

 Can you identify some common emergency situations? Match the instructions and
the pictures on page 153. Write the number of each picture in the box next to the
matching instructions. (*Note:* The information here and in Activity 2 is general
and not complete. Do not try to practice these steps before you take a real first aid
course.)

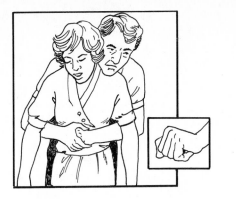

1. Choking

2. Bleeding

3. Poisoning

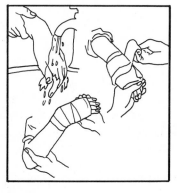

4. Burns

☐
- If the victim is unconscious, do not give him or her anything to drink.
- If possible, find the poison container. Save it for the doctor.
- Call the Poison Control Center and follow instructions.
- Get the victim to a hospital.

☐
- Put the burned part under cold water or put a clean, cold cloth on it. Don't use ice or ice water.
- Cover the burn with clean bandages. Don't put butter or grease on it.
- Raise the burned area.
- A serious burn needs immediate medical attention.

☐
- Put a clean cloth over the wound and press on it with your hand. Add more cloth if necessary.
- Raise the area (arm or leg) above the level of the heart.
- If the bleeding stops, put a bandage over the cloth.
- Get the victim to a hospital.

☐
- Use the Heimlich maneuver: Stand behind the choking victim. Put your arms around the victim's waist. Make a fist with one hand. Close your other hand around your fist. Push your fist inward and upward against the victim's stomach.
- Repeat the maneuver several times if necessary.

activity 2

Work in groups of four. Each person explains some steps for one of the emergencies in Activity 1. Use infinitives when possible. After each person speaks, other group members can add information.

> **example:** A: If someone is choking, it is important to use the Heimlich maneuver immediately. The first step is to stand behind the victim. You need to put your arms around the victim's waist.
> B: You also need to put your arms under the victim's arms.

activity 3

Do you know what to do in other kinds of emergencies? Use a first aid manual or other information (for example, health posters, brochures, and so on). Work in small groups. Discuss what to do in the situations below (and any other emergency situations you may know about).

- drowning
- electric shock
- a broken bone

- an overdose of drugs
- a poisonous snake or insect bite

activity 4

Work in small groups. Each person summarizes part of the mystery story in Exercise 8 on pages 151 to 152. (For example, Student A summarizes the first two paragraphs, student B the next two paragraphs, student C the next four paragraphs, and student D the last two paragraphs.) Use the simple past and past continuous tenses, and infinitives when possible. Be sure to include all the important facts.

When you finish summarizing the story, discuss the answer to this question: How did detective Grimsley know that Jack Jordon hit his uncle and took the money? (The answer is at the bottom of the page.)

activity 5

Do you know a mystery story? Prepare the story (write notes about it), and then tell it to the group or class. Use the simple past and past continuous tenses, and infinitives when possible. Don't tell the ending. Let the group or class figure out the solution from the facts in the story.

How did Detective Grimsley know the truth?
When Jack entered the dark room with the detective, he walked across the room to turn on the light. He didn't fall over his uncle's body; he stepped over it carefully because he knew it was on the floor. Then when the light was on, he stepped back over it. Because Jack already knew about the body, the detective knew that Jack was only pretending to be worried about his uncle. The detective knew that Jack hit his uncle on the head and took the money from the safe.

CHAPTER seven

Health

in this chapter

Topic One:	Verb + Object + Infinitive; Modal Verbs
Topic Two:	Reflexive Pronouns; Tag Questions
Topic Three:	Adjective Clauses

TOPIC one

Verb + Object + Infinitive; Modal Verbs

Setting the Context

Conversation

HUSBAND: How was your day, honey?

WIFE: Well, I woke up with a bad headache this morning, so I thought I should see Dr. Krank. She advised me to take some pills and drink a lot of water.

HUSBAND: Well, that's good advice. Can I get you some water?

WIFE: No, thanks. I didn't want to take all those drugs, so I decided to go to a nutritionist.

HUSBAND: A nutritionist?

WIFE: Yes. He said I'd better change my eating habits, and he persuaded me to buy a lot of health food.

HUSBAND: Oh. That's good.

WIFE: Not really. I tried to eat some, but it tasted terrible. So then I went to a psychologist.

HUSBAND: Oh? And what did he want you to do?

WIFE: He gave me a lot of books to read. And I found out that I have to learn to relax. So I went to a yoga class. The instructor taught me to stand on my head. She said I ought to learn how to breathe correctly.

HUSBAND: Well, how are you feeling now?

WIFE: After all that advice, my headache is worse!

 exercise   Answer these questions about the conversation.

1. Why did the wife go to a doctor, a nutritionist, a psychologist, and a yoga class?
2. What did each expert advise her to do?
3. In your opinion, what should she do?
4. What do you do when you don't feel well?
5. Who do you think are healthier, people in your country or people in the United States? Explain your opinion.

A. Verbs Before Objects and Infinitives

A common sentence pattern is verb + object + infinitive. Certain verbs can appear before objects and infinitives. The chart below gives some examples.

verbs		examples	notes
advise	force	We **expected the ambulance to arrive** quickly.	The object of the verb is the "subject" of the infinitive.
allow	instruct		
ask	order	The doctor **advised the patient to lose** weight.	
convince	remind		
encourage	tell	She did**n't tell her to exercise.**	The word *not* can come before the main verb or before the infinitive, depending on the meaning of the sentence.
expect	want	She **ordered her not to smoke.**	
		She **encouraged her not to buy** junk food.	

 **exercise 1**   Underline the infinitive verb phrases with objects in the conversation between the husband and wife.

example: She <u>advised me to take</u> a lot of medicine.

**exercise 2** Fill in the missing verbs from the verb + noun + infinitive pattern. Use the verbs below. Some sentences might have more than one correct answer.

advise	instruct
expect	convince
ask	remind
force	encourage
beg	tell

1. Many kids don't like vegetables, salads, and other healthy foods. However, most parents try to _____ their children to eat these healthy foods.

2. In supermarkets, kids seldom ask their parents to buy broccoli or carrots. But they often _____ their parents to buy them candy, soda, or ice cream.

3. Lots of adults talk to kids about eating right. Parents, teachers, doctors, and dentists all _____ kids not to eat foods with lots of sugar.

4. Many adults also love sweets. They have to _____ themselves to eat foods low in sugar for better health.

5. Medical research continues to report on the benefits of a low-fat diet. As a result, many doctors _____ their patients to avoid eating foods high in fat.

6. Another thing we hear a lot about in the United States is the importance of regular exercise. However, fitness experts still have to _____ us to exercise daily, in addition to eating healthy foods.

7. Americans often worry about being overweight. Many people _____ their doctors to prescribe diet pills to help them lose weight.

8. However, today many doctors _____ their patients to avoid diet pills because they can be addictive.

9. But people often _____ the doctor to give them pills as the answer to every medical problem.

10. Instead, more doctors now _____ their patients to get in shape by eating well, avoiding foods that are high in fat and sugar, and exercising daily.

 **exercise 3** Write two sentences for each picture here and on page 160. Use the cue words under each picture.

example: • tell / come back / the next day

The doctor told her to come back the next day.

1.

- not allow / park for free
- ask / pay $5 for parking

_____

_____

_____

2.

- order / not, park / fire hydrant
- convince / not, give her a ticket

_____

_____

_____

3.

- ask / take a seat and wait
- remind / not smoke

_____

_____

_____

4.

- tell / step on the scale
- encourage / lose some weight

_____

_____

_____

5.

- want / say "ah"
- tell / breathe deeply

_____

_____

_____

6.

- instruct / take some medicine
- advise / drink a lot of water

_____

_____

_____

B. Modal Verbs: Advice and Obligation

Several modal verbs are used to give advice. *Should* is the most common. *Had better* is used to give strong advice, usually a warning. *Must* expresses necessity or obligation. This chart gives some examples.

	examples	notes
should	You **should** see a doctor. You **shouldn't** eat so much. What **should** I do?	*Should* forms a contraction with *not: shouldn't.*
had better	That woman **had better** get some help right away. I**'d better** call an ambulance. You**'d better** not wait. **Hadn't** we **better** leave?	*Had* forms contractions with subject pronouns: *I (we, you, he, she, they) had = I'd (we'd, you'd, he'd, she'd, they'd).* *Not* comes after *better.* Questions are usually in the negative form.
must	I **must** see a doctor. You **mustn't** forget your doctor's appointment this afternoon.	*Must* is less common than *have to. Must* forms a contraction with *not: mustn't.*

 **exercise 4** Circle the verb phrases with modals in the conversation on pages 156 and 157.

example: So I thought I (should see) Dr. Krank.

exercise 5 Write verb phrases with the modal verbs *should, had better,* or *must* in the blanks. Choose from these simple verb forms. More than one modal might be correct. The first two are done as examples.

do   find   go   spend   eat   get   run   stop

DOCTOR: I hate to say this, Mr. Stone, but you're in terrible shape.

PATIENT: I know that, doctor. What ___should___ I _do_ ?

                                                1   2

DOCTOR: Well, first of all, you're a little overweight. Perhaps you _____

                                                                                         3

       _____ on a diet.

        4

PATIENT: You're right, doctor. I _____ _____ so many desserts.

                                        5 (not)   6

DOCTOR: Right. And you _____ _____ some exercise.

                                   7   8

PATIENT: I know. _____ I _____ every day?

                           9   10

DOCTOR: Yes. But—this is very important—you _____ _____ smoking!

                                                          11   12

PATIENT: You're absolutely right! And cigarettes are expensive too!

    I _____ _____ any more money on them! Well,

             13 (not)   14

    thank you, doctor. I appreciate the advice.

exercise 6 Match the advice below with the "experts" in the picture. Write the letters on the lines, as in the example.

Medical Doctor	A
Nutritionist	B
Psychologist	C
Yoga Teacher	D

1. _A_ take aspirin   **7.** _____ get plenty of rest

2. _____ drink herbal tea   **8.** _____ stand on your head

3. _____ express your feelings   **9.** _____ eat only fruits and vegetables

4. _____ do yoga   **10.** _____ not drink coffee

5. _____ not eat meat   **11.** _____ meditate

6. _____ talk about your childhood   **12.** _____ exercise

Tell the advice each "expert" would give to his or her patients.

    example: The yoga teacher would probably say, "You'd better learn to relax."

Using What You've Learned

activity 1

Work in groups of four. Each of you takes the role of one of the experts in Exercise 6 and gives advice for each of the three situations below. Use modal verbs and verb + object + infinitive.

example: YOGA TEACHER: "The businessman should take a yoga class."

DOCTOR: "I disagree. I would advise him to get a complete physical exam."

1. A teenage girl doesn't want to eat. She is very thin, but she thinks she is still too fat.
2. A successful middle-aged businessman works twelve to sixteen hours every day, seven days a week. He doesn't take time to relax.
3. A college student is tired all the time. He studies a lot, but he's always worried about his grades. He never exercises. He eats a lot of junk food and drinks a lot of coffee.

What advice did each person give for each situation? Each group tells the class, with infinitive phrases after objects.

example: Keiko was the nutritionist. She told the teenager to eat carrots.

activity 2

Work in small groups. Each student describes a health problem (real or imaginary). The group discusses the problem and agrees on a solution. When you finish, one member from each group reports the most interesting problem and solution to the class.

activity 3

Work in small groups. Take turns reading the medical emergencies in situations 1 to 4 below. Guess what happened in each situation. Then explain what the person in each situation should do now. The descriptions include some idioms and cultural information. Work together to guess the meanings of any words or expressions you don't know.

1. Marta was having contractions every few minutes. Her water broke an hour ago. Her sister begged her to stop waiting for her husband and go to the hospital immediately.
2. Benjamin didn't think it was broken, but his wife was trying to convince him to go to the emergency room for an x-ray. He couldn't understand what had happened to the ladder.
3. There was broken glass all over the floor. The child's mother ordered someone to call 911 when she saw him lying there unconscious and bleeding on the floor. The child hadn't noticed that someone had closed the sliding glass door while he was outside.
4. My stomach was killing me. I hardly got any sleep because I was running to the bathroom all night. I was very thirsty so I drank a little water but I couldn't even keep that down.

Reflexive Pronouns;
Tag Questions

Setting the Context

Conversation

Brian and Brenda are exercising on bicycles at a health club.

BRIAN: This health club is great, isn't it?

BRENDA: Oh, it's O.K., but the people are all in love with themselves.

BRIAN: You're right. That man over there with the weights looks very proud of himself, doesn't he?

BRENDA: Did you see all those people watching themselves in the mirror in the aerobics class?

BRIAN: I guess some people here think only of themselves, don't they?

BRENDA: Yeah. Well, I'm finished with this bike. We shouldn't exhaust ourselves.

BRIAN: I'm finished, too. Well, what are you going to do now?

BRENDA: First, I'm going to get myself a massage. Then I'm going to buy myself some new exercise clothes.

BRIAN: I'm going to treat myself to a yogurt shake. Then I'm going to go to the steamroom. Then . . .

exercise Answer these questions about the conversation on page 163.

1. Where are Brian and Brenda? What are they doing? What are they talking about?
2. Why does Brenda say, "People here are in love with themselves"?
3. What are Brian and Brenda going to do next?
4. What do you think about private gyms and health clubs? Do you have something similar in your home country?
5. Do you think many Americans are too concerned with their health and physical appearance? Explain your ideas.

A. Reflexive Pronouns

A reflexive pronoun usually refers to the subject of a sentence or a sentence part. A reflexive pronoun can be the direct or indirect object of a verb, or the object of a preposition. This chart gives some examples.

reflexive pronouns	examples	notes
myself yourself	I don't want to exhaust **myself**. What are **you** going to buy for **yourself**?	Singular reflexive pronouns end in *-self*.
himself herself itself	**He** doesn't like to exercise **by himself**. **She** can lift the weights **by herself**. **The problem** will take care of **itself**.	*By* + reflexive pronoun often means "alone." Sometimes it also means "without any help."
ourselves yourselves themselves	Let's buy **ourselves** a drink. Don't hurt **yourselves** with those weights. **They** think only of **themselves**.	Plural reflexive pronouns end in *-selves*.

exercise 1 Underline the reflexive pronouns in the conversation on page 163 and circle the personal pronouns.

example: That man over there with the weights looks very proud of <u>himself</u>, doesn't (he)?

exercise 2 Fill in the blanks with reflexive pronouns: *myself, yourself, herself, himself, ourselves, themselves,* as in the example.

Myra Meyers looked at _____herself_____ in the mirror and decided that she

wanted to buy _____ a new dress. "But I'll have to lose some

2

weight first," she said to _____. I'm going to get _____

3　　　　　　　　　　　　　　　　　　　4

a membership in the Grunt 'n Groan Health Club. We all have to take care

of _____."

5

The next morning Myra found _____ in a big room with weights
      6
and other exercise equipment. A big sign said, "Do something special for

_____ today." One man was measuring _____ with a
      7   8
tape measure. Two men were watching _____ in the mirror. "I think
                                          9
I'm going to enjoy _____ here," thought Myra.
                       10

B. Tag Questions

A tag question is a statement with a short question attached to the end. The tag
has the same subject as the statement, or a corresponding pronoun. It has the
same verb as, or the auxiliary that corresponds to, the verb of the statement.
People usually use tag questions to ask for clarification or to confirm information they think is true. This chart gives some examples.

	examples	expected answer	notes
Affirmative	You're healthy, **aren't you?**	Yes, I am.	Affirmative statements usually have negative tags.
	He's exercising, **isn't he?**	Yes, he is.	
	I have a fever, **don't I?**	Yes, you do.	For a simple present or past sentence (except with the verb *be*), the tag uses a form of *do*.
	She lifts weights, **doesn't she?**	Yes, she does.	
	You saw a doctor, **didn't you?**	Yes, I did.	
	You'll take medicine, **won't you?**	Yes, I will.	With affirmative statements and negative tags, the speaker expects an affirmative answer.
Negative	You're not getting sick, **are you?**	No, I'm not.	Negative statements have affirmative tags. With negative statements and affirmative tags, the speaker expects a negative answer.
	She doesn't smoke, **does she?**	No, she doesn't	
	They can't lift weights, **can they?**	No, they can't.	

exercise 3 Answer each tag question with the answer the speaker expects to hear.

> **example:** This health club is great, isn't it?
> _Yes, it's the best._ or _Yes, it is._

1. You don't have any aspirin, do you? _____

2. This yoga class is getting really crowded, isn't it? _____

3. Those runners are really moving, aren't they? _____

4. Your father has been a smoker for years, hasn't he? _____

5. We're not too late for beginning aerobics, are we? _____

6. You were out sick for over a week, weren't you? _____

7. I met you at a softball game last summer, didn't I? _____

8. You really like all that healthy food, don't you? _____

9. She lifted 300 pounds, didn't she? _____

10. The president loves to jog, doesn't he? _____

exercise 4 Write the missing subjects in the blanks, as in the example.

It's a beautiful day, isn't __it__ ? You run here every day,
don't _____? It's great exercise, isn't _____? Look at that
          2   3
man! He's running fast, isn't _____? All the people here
                              4
look healthy, don't _____? You don't talk much when you run,
                    5
do _____?
   6

exercise 5 Write the missing verbs in the blanks. Pay attention to tense and number. Make the tag affirmative or negative, as appropriate. The first one is done as an example.

You ran in this race last year, _____ _didn't_ _____ you? The
                                        1
weather was great then too, _____ it? You finished
                                     2
that race, _____ you? But you didn't win, _____
                 3   4
you? We're going to win this year, _____ we?
                                          5
We can do it, _____ we? You're not getting tired,
                     6
_____ you? I'm not boring you, _____ I?
       7   8

 **exercise 6**   Write the missing tag questions in the blanks. The first one is done as an example.

You run this race every year, _____don't you_____? It was
₁

harder last year, _____? You did well last year,
₂

_____? You'll finish this year too, _____?
₃   ₄

We should run faster, _____? We have only a few
₅

more kilometers to run, _____? You could run
₆

faster, _____? But you're not talking much,
₇

_____? You're thinking about other things,
₈

_____? This race is fun, _____?
₉   ₁₀

Using What You've Learned

 **activity 1**   Work with a partner. Describe the pictures at the beginning of Topic Two on page 163. Use reflexive and personal pronouns.

> **example:**   A: The people in the class are looking at themselves in the mirror.
>   B: The instructor is not looking at them.

activity 2   Write tag questions for your classmates, based on the questions below and on page 168.

> **example:**   Who keeps himself or herself in shape?
>   You keep yourself in shape, don't you?

1. Who forced himself or herself to exercise earlier today?

_____

2. Who can lift weights?

_____

3. Who is going to jog today?

_____

4. Who will cook himself or herself health food for dinner tonight?

_____

5. Who isn't going to exercise this week?

_____

6. Who can't stand health food?

_____

7. Who doesn't buy himself or herself vitamins?

_____

8. Who didn't eat dessert yesterday?

_____

9. Who won't ever do yoga?

_____

10. Who is planning to work out later today?

_____

Now play an interview game. All of you walk around the class at the same time and ask the other students your questions. Write down the names of the people who answer yes to each of the first five questions and the names of the people who answer no to the last five. The winner is the first person with ten different names.

What did you learn about your classmates? Each student asks the class three tag questions (different from those above).

example: Juan is a good runner, isn't he?

activity 3

In your notebook, make a list of tag questions for your classmates, based on the following topics.

> academic major
> country of origin
> marital status
> hobbies
> future plans
> living situation
> travel experiences
> sports likes or dislikes
> feelings/opinions about United States or Canada
> feelings/opinions about grammar

example: academic major: You're an engineering major, aren't you?

activity 4

All students walk around the class at the same time and ask other students the tag questions from Activity 3. The winner is the first person with ten different names.

After everyone has finished, take turns sharing what you learned about your classmates.

example: I learned that Marco has been to three World Cup Soccer matches.

Adjective Clauses

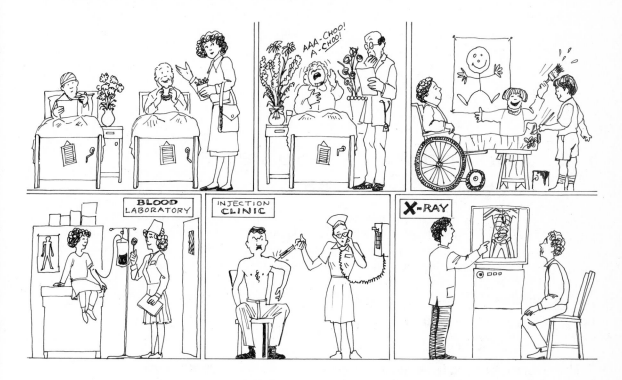

Setting the Context
Reading

Dear Grandmother,

Thank you for the book that you sent me. I'm feeling better today. The doctor who examined me said that I'm doing well.

This hospital is a funny place. All the people who work here are friendly. I especially like the nurse who brings our lunch trays every day.

But the food that she serves us is terrible. The man who is sharing this room can't stand it. The people who visit him bring other food secretly. The food that his family and friends give me tastes much better than hospital food.

Love,
Timmy

**exercise** Answer these questions about the letter on page 169.

1. Who wrote the letter? To whom? Why did he write the letter?

2. Describe the people in the hospital.

3. Describe the food.

4. How is the man sharing Timmy's room getting good food at the hospital?

5. Have you or anyone you know ever been in the hospital? Describe your experience.

A. *who* and *that* as Subjects of Adjective Clauses

An adjective clause modifies a noun. It has a subject and a verb. *Who* or *that* can be the subject of an adverb clause. *Who* is used for people; *that* is used for people or things. Adjective clauses describe, identify, or give more information about the nouns they follow. This chart gives some examples.

examples	notes	
I like the nurse **who (that) brings the food.**	*who*	= the nurse
The doctor **that (who) visits me** is nice.	*that*	= the doctor
We eat the food **that tastes good.**	*that*	= the food

You can use an adjective clause to combine two simple sentences into one more complex sentence.

example: I like the nurse. + **She** brings the food.

↓

= I like the nurse **who** brings the food.

exercise Underline the adjective clauses with *who* or *that* as subjects in the letter on page 169.

example: The doctor <u>who examined me</u> said I was doing well.

exercise 2   Combine the pairs of sentences. Use adjective clauses with *who* or *that* as subjects.

1. The nurse takes blood. + She is nice.

_____

2. The nurse gives shots. + She talks on the phone a lot.

_____

3. The flowers are on the table next to my bed. + They are very beautiful.

_____

4. The doctor examined me. + He told me I was getting better.

_____

5. The patient is allergic to flowers. + She has lots of flowers in her room.

_____

6. The man is sharing my room. + He has a lot of visitors.

_____

7. The boy hurt his head. + He is in the hospital.

_____

8. The man broke his legs. + He is sitting in a wheelchair.

_____

9. The doctor put casts on the man's legs. + He likes to tell jokes.

_____

10. The children are painting the man's casts. + They are having fun.

_____

B. Adjective Phrases

An adjective phrase also modifies a noun. It does not contain a subject and a verb like an adjective clause. You can reduce (shorten) some adjective clauses with *who* or *that* as subjects to adjective phrases. The chart on the next page gives some examples.

	examples	notes
Adjective Clause	The man **who is sharing my room** hates the food.	To make an adjective phrase from an adjective clause in these two examples, leave out *who* or *that*, and the form of the verb *be*.
Adjective Phrase	The man **sharing my room** hates the food.	
Adjective Clause	The flowers **that are on the table** are beautiful.	
Adjective Phrase	The flowers **on the table** are beautiful.	
Adjective Clause	All the people **who work here** are friendly.	Sometimes you can leave out *who* or *that* and add *-ing* to the verb.
Adjective Phrase	All the people **working here** are friendly.	

exercise    Combine the pairs of sentences. Use adjective phrases. Leave out the unnecessary words.

example: The children are funny. + They are staying in this hospital.
The children staying in this hospital are funny.

1. The man gets food from his relatives. + He is in this room.

_____

2. The nurse is nice. + She is carrying the lunch trays.

_____

3. The man has his legs in casts. + He is sitting in a wheelchair.

_____

4. The children draw pictures on the casts. + They are staying in the hospital.

_____

5. The patient is allergic to flowers. + She is in Room 310.

_____

6. The nurse is giving the man a shot. + She is talking on the phone.

_____

7. The man is waiting for the nurse to get off the phone. + He is angry.

_____

8. The boys had their tonsils taken out. + They are eating a lot of ice cream.

_____

C. *who(m)* and *that* as Objects of Adjective Clauses

Who(m) or *that* may also be the object of an adjective clause. This chart gives some examples.

examples	notes
The food **that we ate** in the hospital was terrible.	*That* refers to *food. We* is the subject of the adjective clause.
The nurse $\left.\begin{array}{l}\textbf{who}\\\textbf{whom}\end{array}\right\}$ **she likes** is Ms. Alvarez.	*Whom* is the formal object pronoun.
The injection **that the doctor gave me** was painful. The injection **the doctor gave** me was painful.	*Who(m)* or *that* are often left out of an adjective clause.

You can also use adjective clauses with *who(m)* or *that* as objects to combine two simple sentences into one or more complex sentence.

   examples: The nurse is Ms. Alvarez. + She likes **her**.

= The nurse **whom** she likes is Ms. Alvarez.

The food was terrible. + We ate **it** in the hospital.

= The food **that** we ate in the hospital was terrible.

**exercise 4**   Combine the pairs of sentences. Use adjective clauses with *who(m)* or *that* as objects.

1. The doctors were running to the emergency room. I saw them.

   _____

2. The noises at night were scary. I heard them.

   _____

3. The work was very hard and tiring. The nurses did the work.

   _____

4. The ambulance was red and shiny. The paramedics drove the ambulance.

   _____

5. The patients were in a lot of pain. The nurses checked on them frequently.

   _____

6. The food is terrible. The patients in the hospital have to eat the food.

   _____

7. The flowers were very expensive. The patient's friends sent the flowers.

   _____

8. The children were playing in the elevator. The hospital security guard yelled at them.

   _____

exercise 5   Study the pictures at the beginning of Topic Three on page 169. Then try to complete these sentences about the pictures with adjective clauses or phrases. There are several correct answers.

1. The boy _____ *who is writing a letter* _____ has a bandage on his head.

2. The man _____ is eating a hamburger.

3. The doctor _____ is looking at the chart.

4. The patient _____ has casts on his legs.

5. The woman _____ has flowers in her room.

6. The nurse _____ is trying to take blood

from a child _____ .

7. A man _____ is getting an injection from

a nurse _____ .

8. The doctor _____ is explaining the results

to a patient.

exercise **6**

Dr. Hippocrates writes a health advice column for a newspaper. Here and on page 176 are two letters to him. Fill in the missing words, as in the example. Use the grammar you've learned in this chapter. There might be more than one correct answer for some items.

When you finish, compare your answers with a partner's. Who got the most correct answers?

1.

Dear Dr. Hippocrates,

My problem is that I'm tired all the time. A guy _who_ works with me
1
_____ me _____ sleep more, but I already sleep ten hours every night.
2   3
My girlfriend _____ me _____ get a physical check-up, so I went to
4   5
the clinic. The doctor _____ examined me couldn't find anything wrong. I take
6
good care of _____ . I eat good food and force _____
7   8
_____ exercise regularly. What _____ I do about this problem?
9   10
_____ I see a psychologist? I _____ better _____ something soon
11   12   13
because I _____ n't fall asleep at work anymore.
14

Exhausted

2.

Dear Dr. Hippocrates,

I'm a foreign student at an American university. I can't usually sleep because I worry about my studies all the time. A friend ___1___ uses lots of drugs says that I'd ___2___ take sleeping pills, but I ___3___ take medicine to sleep, should I? The drugs ___4___ my friend takes scare me. The woman ___5___ lives next door ___6___ me ___7___ take a hot bath before bedtime, but it didn't help. She also says that she gets sleepy from the warm milk ___8___ she makes for ___9___. But I don't really think warm milk helps, ___10___ it? You can't stay awake all the time, ___11___ you? I'm so tired, I ___12___ get some sleep! You will give ___13___ some advice, ___14___ you?

Sleepless

Using What You've Learned

activity 1

Look around your classroom. Write eight to ten sentences describing the people in your class using adjective clauses or phrases. When you finish, share your ideas in small groups.

> **examples:** The woman *who is sitting in front of me* is from Romania. The man *on her right* is always kidding around with the teacher. The young woman *closest to the door* is a new student.

activity 2

Work in small groups. Discuss possible solutions to the problems described in the letters to Dr. Hippocrates in Exercise 6 on pages 175 and 176. Agree on one solution for each letter and tell both to the class.

 **activity 3**

Work in pairs. Choose one of the situations below. Prepare a short dialog to perform for the class.

1. Your roommate doesn't eat well, doesn't sleep much, doesn't exercise at all, and smokes too much. Your roommate doesn't like advice, but you are very worried and try to talk to him or her.
2. Your friend hates doctors. He always asks for your advice on health problems and never follows it. You think your friend should see medical professionals.
3. Your friend worries about her appearance all the time. She is always trying new things (diets, exercise programs, vitamins, doctors) to look and feel better. You think your friend looks fine and shouldn't worry about herself constantly.

activity 4

Collect magazine pictures with many things and people in them. Work in groups. One student makes a sentence about a picture. The next student adds an adjective clause or phrase to the sentence and then makes a new sentence. Continue around the group. Repeat the activity with a new picture.

example: A: There is a beautiful woman.
B: There is a beautiful woman who is talking on the phone. Two other women are waiting to use the phone.

focus on testing

Verbs Before Objects and Infinitives; Modals, Tag Questions

Items with verbs before objects and infinitives, and modals and tag questions are often found on standardized English exams such as the TOEFL.

Remember . . .

- A common sentence pattern is **verb + object + infinitive**.
- Certain verbs can appear before objects and infinitives.
- *Should* is the most common modal used to give advice.
- Affirmative statements usually have negative tags; negative statements have affirmative tags.

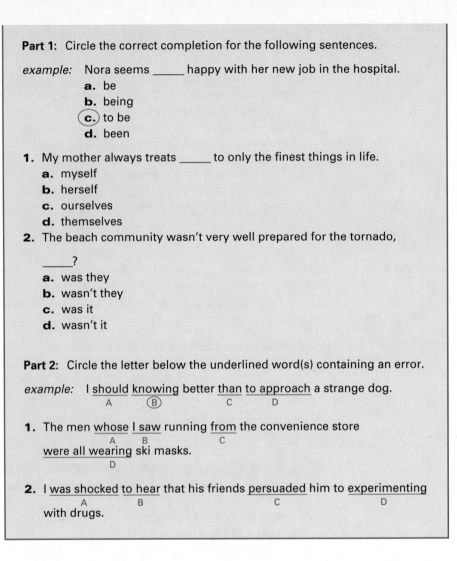

Part 1: Circle the correct completion for the following sentences.

example: Nora seems _____ happy with her new job in the hospital.
- **a.** be
- **b.** being
- **(c.)** to be
- **d.** been

1. My mother always treats _____ to only the finest things in life.
- **a.** myself
- **b.** herself
- **c.** ourselves
- **d.** themselves

2. The beach community wasn't very well prepared for the tornado, _____?
- **a.** was they
- **b.** wasn't they
- **c.** was it
- **d.** wasn't it

Part 2: Circle the letter below the underlined word(s) containing an error.

example: I should knowing better than to approach a strange dog.
  A   (B)   C   D

1. The men whose I saw running from the convenience store
            A   B   C
   were all wearing ski masks.
            D

2. I was shocked to hear that his friends persuaded him to experimenting
     A   B   C   D
   with drugs.

CHAPTER eight

Entertainment and the Media

Review of Tenses: The Past, Present, and Future

Setting the Context

You are going to read about the busy lives of four roommates. Rosa, Nancy, Marilyn, and Ruth. Look at the pictures on page 180. Then do the exercise below.

exercise ▰ Many answers to the following questions are possible.

1. Do the roommates live in a city or out in the country? Explain your answer.
2. Why do they live together?
3. How did they meet each other?
4. What do you like and dislike about their lifestyles?
5. How do you think these women's lives will be different in 10 years?
6. How would this situation be different if it were happening in your country?
7. Did you ever live with a roommate? What did you like and dislike about this living arrangement?
8. Do you think it's better for young adults to live with their parents until they get married or live with roommates? Explain your opinion.

A. The Simple Present Tense, the Simple Past Tense, and the Future: *going to*

	examples	notes	time expressions
Simple Present	A child **comes** to the store every day. The TV **isn't** on. **Do** you **work** in a noisy office? How **are** you? **Do** CDs **cost** a lot in that store? The noise **bothers** you, **doesn't** it?	The simple present tense shows repeated present action. It is also used to give facts and opinions. With non-action verbs, it shows an existing condition.	every day once a week usually sometimes always never
Simple Past	The noise **was** terrible. They **didn't buy** anything. **Did** the phone **ring** a moment ago? What **happened**? Who **did** you **call**? You **had** a hard day, **didn't** you?	The simple past tense shows completed past events and activities.	last week an hour ago in 1994

	examples	notes	time expressions
Future: going to	We**'re going to stay** home. There **isn't going to be** any noise. **Aren't** you **going to see** a movie tomorrow? Where **are** you **going to go** next week? She**'s going to sleep** soon, **isn't** she?	Use *be* + *going to* + *simple form of verb* to talk about future activity, plans, or predictions.	tomorrow next month in a few days a week from now soon later

exercise 1

Complete these sentences with simple past, present, or future verb phrases. Choose from the verbs below. Some verbs will be used more than once.

be   hear   honk   need   shout   take   turn   wake   watch   do

Complete the short answers and tag questions.

Ruth, Marilyn and Rosa have just gotten home from work.

RUTH: Boy, *am* I glad to be home! I'_____ exhausted. My ears really
                                    1
_____ a rest. Every day, I _____ so much noise.
              2   3
At 6:30 this morning, I _____ up to loud music on the clock
                                    4
radio. Then I _____ television during breakfast. Of course I
                        5
_____ on the car radio on my way to work. _____
              6   7
your trip _____ an hour like mine? Then, on the way home,
                    8
a taxi driver in a traffic jam _____ his horn nonstop and
                                          9
_____ at me out his window.
          10

exercise 2

Complete the sentences with simple past, present, or future verb phrases. Choose from the verbs below. Some verbs will be used more than once.

be   do   have   know   listen   play   need   take   turn   watch   make

MARILYN: I _____ what you mean. The teenagers in the record store
                    1
_____ music every afternoon—today at work they
              2
_____ more noise than usual! And there _____ no
              3   4
quiet video games, _____ there? _____ you
                          5   6
_____ a headache all day today too, Rosa? You
              7
_____ some aspirin an hour ago, _____ you?
              8   9 (not)

Interactions I • Grammar

ROSA: Yes, I did, but I still _____ a headache. I really
₁₀
_____ some peace and quiet tonight. I _____
₁₁   ₁₂
off everything—the TV, the CD player, the computer—everything—in

five minutes. During dinner, nobody in this apartment _____

television. And after dinner no one _____ to music. Okay?
₁₃   ₁₄

 Work in pairs. Use one book and pass it back and forth. Take turns reading a time
expression from the chart on pages 181 and 182 out loud. Your partner must make
up a sentence, supplying the correct verb and using the time expression.

example: A: In a few days.
           B: We are going to have a grammar test in a few days.
           A: Excellent. It's your turn. *(gives A the book)*

B. The Continuous Tenses: Past and Present

	examples	**notes**	**time expressions**
Present Continuous	There**'s a horror movie showing** on TV now. She **isn't feeling** good at the moment. **Are** they **relaxing**? What **are** you **doing** right now? You **aren't getting** tired, **are** you?	The present continuous shows action in progress, temporary present action (extended present), or future plans.	right now at this moment tonight next week
Past Continuous	She **was watching** TV an hour ago. They **weren't playing** music. **Were** the children **making** noise? What **were** you **doing** last night around 9:00? He **was working, wasn't** he?	The past continuous describes activities in progress at a specific time or during a period of time in the past.	last Tuesday an hour ago on April 1

Complete the short answers and tag questions with the appropriate tense form of each verb. You will use past and present continuous and simple past and present. The first two are done as examples.

NANCY: You're eating _____ dinner here, aren't _____ you? Where _____
          1 (eat)   2   3 (be)
Rosa?

RUTH: Oh, she _____ home to dinner tonight. She _____
          4 (not come)   5

still _____. She often _____ to work evenings.
    6 (work)   7 (have)

NANCY: But she _____ her work, _____ she? There
         8 (love)   9

_____ always something exciting _____.
    10   11 (happen)

MARILYN: Yes, there really _____. For example, right now she
            12 (be)

_____ probably _____ around the newsroom,
    13   14 (rush)

_____ information from the teletype machine, and
    15 (get)

_____ a story. I _____ her at work one day last
    16 (write)   17 (visit)

week around this time of the evening: there _____ seven
                       18

reporters _____ back and forth, three editors _____
        19 (run)   20 (shout)

at them, and several photographers _____ questions.
            21 (ask)

RUTH: But when you _____ home from that visit, _____
        22 (get)   23

you exhausted, Marilyn?

MARILYN: Yes, I _____ so. I wonder how Rosa does it!
        24 (guess)

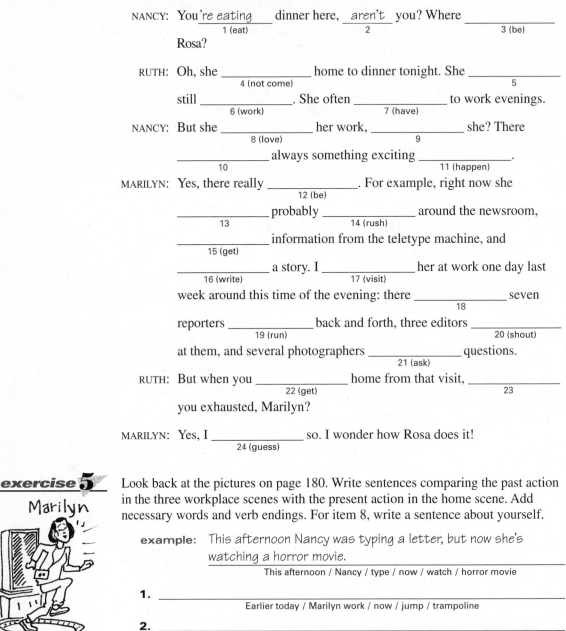

Marilyn

Look back at the pictures on page 180. Write sentences comparing the past action in the three workplace scenes with the present action in the home scene. Add necessary words and verb endings. For item 8, write a sentence about yourself.

example: This afternoon Nancy was typing a letter, but now she's watching a horror movie.
      This afternoon / Nancy / type / now / watch / horror movie

1. _____
      Earlier today / Marilyn work / now / jump / trampoline

2. _____
      All day / Ruth / listen / now / read / newspaper

3. <u>   </u>

This morning / Ruth / work / very hard / now / relax

4. <u>   </u>

This afternoon / Marilyn / listen / loud rock music / now / listen classical music

5. <u>   </u>

Earlier today / Rosa / get / information / important / story / now / finish / final / draft

6. <u>   </u>

All day / Nancy / sit / desk / now / sit / couch

7. <u>   </u>

This afternoon / Marilyn's head / kill / her / now / knees / hurt / because / she /
jump / trampoline

8. <u>   </u>

All morning / I / now / . . .

Using What You've Learned

activity 1

Work in pairs. Discuss your answers to the questions in the exercise on page 181. When you've finished, join another student pair and compare opinions.

> **example:** A: I think they are living together because they're old friends from childhood and they like being together.
>
> B: That's an interesting idea. I don't think many American adults are still in contact with their childhood friends. I think they live together to save money.

activity 2

Work in groups of four. Each person makes up a personal history for one of the roommates in the pictures on page 180. Include answers to the following questions in your history. When everyone has finished, each person reads his or her history to the group.

1. How old is she?
2. How many brothers and sisters does she have? Is she the oldest, the youngest, or in the middle?
3. Where is she from?
4. What's her educational background? Did she graduate from high school or was she a dropout? Did she go to college? Which one? What was her major?
5. Where did she go to on summer vacations when she was a student?
6. What are her future career plans?
7. What are her hobbies? Favorite sports? Favorite kinds of food?
8. What is she frustrated about?
9. How's her love life?
10. Would you like to be her? Why or why not?

Work in pairs. Ask and answer questions with these cue words, in the appropriate tense form. Make necessary additions and changes.

1. How / be / your day / yesterday / ?
2. What / you / do / all day / ?
3. What / you / do / at 4:00 yesterday afternoon / ?
4. you / watch TV / last night / ? (If so) What / you / watch / at 9:00 / ?
5. What / you / listen to on the radio / yesterday (last week) / ?
6. You / watch TV (listen to the radio) / every day / ?
7. you / read a daily newspaper / ? (If so) What / you / read / ?
8. What magazines / you read / every month / ?
9. What / you / watch (listen to, read) tomorrow / ?
10. How / the media / affect your life / ?

Summarize for the class what you learned about your partner.

TOPIC two

Summary of Modal Verbs;
Summary of Pronouns

Setting the Context
Brainstorm

As a whole class or in small groups, list all the different kinds of movies you can name. Discuss which kinds you like and dislike. Explain your opinions.

Work in pairs. Use one book and pass it back and forth. Take turns reading out loud a sentence from the following chart. Omit the modal. Your partner must repeat the sentence, supplying a correct modal. Most boxes have two or more sentences, but choose just one at a time. In some cases, there is more than one correct modal.

> example: A: _____ you help me?
> B: *Can* you help me?
> A: That's right. Your turn. Here's the book.

A. Summary of Modal Verbs

meaning	modal	examples
Present Ability	can	TV violence **can be** harmful to children.
	can't	I **can't watch** violent movies.
Past Ability	could	We **couldn't see** that new horror movie last night because it was sold out.
	couldn't	
Future Possibility	may (not)	There **may be** a romantic movie on tonight.
	might (not)	We **might be** too late.
Future Plans, Predictions	will/won't	What **will happen** next?
		Will he **die**? (No, he **won't**).
Requests	can('t)	**Can** you **help** me?
	could(n't)	**Could** he **change** places with me?
	will/won't	**Will** you please **be** quiet?
	would	**Would** you **hand** me the TV guide?
Present/ Future Permission	may (not)	**May** I **have** some ice cream?
	can('t)	**Can** I **watch** another program?
Advice	should(n't)	We **should be** careful.
	had better (not)	We'**d better not talk** during the movie.
		Hadn't we **better get out** of here?
Obligation	must(n't)	We **must do** something.

exercise 1

Fill in the missing modals in the three movie dialogues. In some cases, there is more than one correct answer. Then, for each dialogue, identify the movie genre from the list below, and write the letter of the genre in the box next to each number.

westerns (W)   romances (R)   horror movies (H)

1. A: You'd _____ not go in there. People say that old house is
   1
haunted. If you do, you _____ not come out alive.
   2

B: You _____ scare me with your silly old ghost stories. I
   3
_____ go in that house, with you or without you.
   4

2. A: Oh, no. Don't go. Not yet.

B: Darling, I _____ go. The taxi's waiting.
   5

A: How _____ you do this to me? You're my reason for
   6
living. I _____ die without you.
   7

B: We _____ be strong, my love. I _____ never forget you.
   8   9

A: I _____ believe we _____ never see each
   10   11
other again.

3. A: _____ I help you, ma'am?
   12

B: Yes. I _____ find the sheriff immediately. _____
   13   14
you kindly tell me where he is?

A: My pleasure. Sheriff Jackson _____ be down at the dry
   15
goods store, or he _____ be over at the stables. Then again,
   16
he _____ be in his office.
   17

B: Thank you kindly. I'm sure I _____ find him myself.
   18

A: Please allow me to accompany you, ma'am. A young lady
_____ be walking around by herself in this town at night.
   19

B: If you insist. But I'm warning you. If you touch me, I
_____ kill you.
   20

exercise 2

Match each of the sentences to the appropriate speaker or thinker: write the letter of the balloon in the parentheses. Then complete the sentences with the missing modal verbs (there are several correct answers). The first two are done as examples.

1. _____May_____ I ask a favor? _____Would_____ you please turn down the
   1   2
volume? (*b*)

2. Do you have a date less than once a year? Well, then you _____
   3
buy Glisten Toothpaste right away! (   )

3. And now our reporter in the traffic helicopter _____ tell you
   4
   freeway drivers about present conditions. ( )

4. I _____ think with all that noise! _____ you turn
   5 (not)   6
   it down? ( )

5. The president of the United States _____ leave on a tour of Asia
   7
   next month. His plans are not yet certain, but he _____ visit
   8
   China and Japan. ( )

6. Because of an accident on Highway 405, traffic _____ be very
   9
   slow. You _____ arrive home for another hour. ( )
   10 (not)

7. You _____ take another route if possible. ( )
   11

8. _____ I give you some advice? If you want to be popular,
   12
   you _____ have a bright smile! And only this week, I
   13
   _____ make you a special offer. ( )
   14

9. Tension is increasing on the border. Negotiators _____ be able
   15 (not)
   to come to an agreement. ( )

10. You _____ watch so much TV, anyway! You _____
    16 (not)   17
    turn off the set. ( )

B. Summary of Pronouns

Personal pronouns replace nouns (people or things). Possessive adjectives come
before nouns; possessive pronouns do not come before nouns. Reflexive pronouns refer to the subject of a sentence or sentence part.

personal pronouns

	Singular	**Plural**
Subject Pronouns	I	we
	you	you
	he, she, it	they
Object Pronouns	me	us
	you	you
	him, her, it	them

possessive adjectives and pronouns

	Singular	**Plural**
Possessive Adjectives	my your his, her, its	our your their
Possessive Pronouns	mine his hers	ours yours theirs

reflexive pronouns

Singular	**Plural**
myself yourself himself herself itself	ourselves yourselves themselves

C. Indefinite Pronouns

Indefinite pronouns refer to people or things the speaker or writer doesn't identify. They begin with *some-, any-, no-,* or *every-* and end with *-body, -one,* or *-thing.*

examples	notes
Someone is making noise. I want to tell you **something**. Are you looking for **somebody**?	A pronoun with *some-* usually appears in an affirmative statement or in a question.
Nobody liked the movie. Who left early? **No one**. I didn't see **anything**.	A pronoun with *no-* usually appears as the subject. *Not + any-* is more common as the object. *No one* is two words.
Everybody likes movies. We can't see **everything**.	A pronoun with *every-* means "all the people" or "all the things."

exercise 3   Circle the correct pronoun.

Look at these movies. [They / Them / Their]
are all about sex and violence! [I / me / myself]
don't want my family to see [they / them / theirs].
[Anybody / Something / No one] should see garbage
like this. When [I / me / myself] was a kid, I used to
enjoy [me / mine / myself] at good movies. The kids
today don't enjoy [anyone / them / themselves] at
these movies. But [everyone / any / no one] knows that
violence isn't only in the movies. Did [some / anyone /
nobody] read the newspaper last night? One crazy man
shot [he / him / his] wife and [they / them / their]
baby, and then [he / him / anyone] killed [he / himself / herself]. A couple tried to poison [theirs / them /
themselves] after [somebody / anybody / nobody] set
their home on fire.

exercise 4   Complete these sentences with pronouns from the Summary of Pronouns charts on
pages 189 and 190. There might be more than one correct answer. The first one is
done as an example.

    __I__ 'm a football widow and _____ hate TV! During the football
season, _____ don't have a husband because _____'s married
to the set. When _____ 'm in the room with _____, _____
doesn't say a word to me; I have to talk to _____.
For months _____ children forget that
_____ have a father. _____ can hardly
remember _____ names, anyway. _____ talked
to _____ neighbors about _____ and _____ all
have the same problem with _____ husbands.
Does _____ have a solution? _____ need advice!
_____ 'm not sure _____ family can survive
another football season.

Using What You've Learned

activity 1

Work in groups of four. Each group chooses a different one of these five statements. One pair of students prepares arguments for the statement; the other pair prepares arguments against it. Use modal verbs and pronouns when appropriate. Then each group of four has a "debate" about the topic for the class; each student speaks for one minute. The class decides on the "winner" of the debate (the pair with the more convincing arguments). Then the class continues the discussion.

1. Television is hurting our young people.
2. The violence on TV and in movies creates violence in real life.
3. There should be government censorship (control) of TV programs and movies.
4. Sports heroes and movie and television stars are of no value to society.
5. Public television has better programs than the other networks.

activity 2

Work in small groups. Discuss how the topics addressed in Activity 1 are different in your country. What do you think the United States should do to correct the problem of violence in this society? When you've finished, share your ideas with the class.

activity 3

Work in pairs or small groups. Using the pronoun charts on pages 189 and 190, make up sentences using as many pronouns as possible. You earn one point for each pronoun used correctly. Take turns making up and saying sentences. Play for five minutes. The winner is the person with the most points.

example: You should see yourself in that outfit. It's you! (4 points)

activity 4

In small groups, discuss and defend your favorite kinds of movies. Here are a few types we have not discussed already: animated, suspense, thrillers, psychodramas, adventures, comedies, and documentaries. When your group is finished, one person will summarize each member's favorite kinds of movies and the reasons.

example: A: I love adventure films. When I go to the movies, I want to see action; car chases, bombs blowing up, people getting killed. Movies should have all that stuff.
B: Oh, I can't stand those kinds of movies. They shouldn't even make those movies. All that violence can have a bad effect on kids. I like comedies. When I go to the movies, I want to laugh and forget about my worries.

Summary of Infinitives

Setting the Context
Discussion Questions

1. Look at the pictures below. Do you like to watch these kinds of TV programs and commercials?
2. How do these TV programs and commercials compare with those in your home country?
3. What kinds of TV programs do you prefer to watch? Why?
4. Do you use TV to improve your English? If so, how?
5. Do you advise your classmates to watch more or less TV? Why?

a.

b.

c.

d.

exercise ▼ Work with a partner. List many possible endings to the sentence stems below. When you finish, compare your sentences with another student pair.

1. I'm ready to _____

2. It's rude to _____

3. It's too hot to _____

4. Do you want to _____

5. Remind me to _____

A. Infinitive Patterns

Infinitives can appear in different positions in a sentence.

	examples	notes
After Nouns/ Pronouns	There are no good **programs to watch.** You need **something to do.**	The noun is usually the "object" of the infinitive.
After Adjectives and with the Impersonal it	I'm **ready to change** the channel. **It's rude to shout.** **It's** too **hot to go** outside.	The impersonal *it* has no real meaning; the infinitive is the subject of the sentence.
After Verbs	Do you **want to go** out? **Remind** me **to check** it.	The "subject" of the infinitive can be the subject or the object of the main verb.
In a Purpose Phrase	Let's go outside **to get** some fresh air.	In a purpose phrase, *to = in order to.*

 **exercise 1**   Write *to* or X (no word) in each blank.

WOMAN: Oh, darling, you must _____ believe me! I could never _____ love
                                    1   2
anyone else but you.

MAN: Linda, I'm sorry _____ have _____ say this, but I can't _____ believe you
                              3   4   5
anymore. You used _____ be here—in my arms—every night. Now I'm
                              6
lucky _____ see you once a week. I drove around all night _____ find
              7   8
you. I must _____ know the truth! I'll _____ do anything _____ know.
                    9   10   11

WOMAN: What are you trying _____ say? You don't really _____ think that I'm
                                    12   13
seeing another man, do you?

MAN: I don't _____ know anymore. I'm too confused _____ think. I just need
               14   15

_____ know . . .
 16

WOMAN: It . . . it's hard _____ tell you this, but . . . Are you ready _____ hear
                     17   18

everything? You'd better _____ sit down. There's so much _____ say . . .
                                 19   20

exercise 2

Arrange the words under the lines into sentences. Add *it* and *to* as necessary.

1. It isn't easy to be honest.

easy / be honest / isn't

2. _____

I / begin / don't / know how

3. _____

don't want / hurt you / I

4. _____

afraid / say this / I'm

5. _____

tell you / is / wrong

6. _____

not / better / know / is

7. But _____

impossible / go on this way / is

8. _____

any longer / wait / refuse / I

9. _____

expect / you / everything / tell / me

10. _____

find out / intend / I

B. Infinitives After Verbs

Some verbs take infinitives; some take infinitives after objects. Some verbs fit into both patterns. Here are some common examples:

verb + *to* + verb		verb + object + *to* + verb	
example: He intends to win.		*example:* We expect you to win.	
like	start	like	expect
would like	begin	would like	remind
want	remember	want	teach (how)
prefer	forget	need	tell
need	continue	advise	urge
have	intend	allow	warn
try	know how	encourage	persuade
plan	ought	force	promise
decide	learn	order	
expect	manage		
fail	pretend		
hope	seem		
refuse			

exercise 3  Complete the sentences with the appropriate forms of the verbs in parentheses, in the correct order. Add *to* and an object, if necessary. The first two are done as examples.

HOST: And now it's time for the popular game show, "All or Nothing"!

Let's welcome our current champion, John Martinez! John

<u>started to play</u> our game just three days ago, and
1 (start, play)

now he has $29,553 in prizes! I just found out that John's

wife, Gloria, <u>persuaded him to come</u> to our show, so he
2 (persuade, come)

_____ some great prizes for her too! And
3 (intend, win)

now please welcome today's challenger, Nancy Johnson! Nancy

is a schoolteacher who _____ married next
4 (plan, get)

month. Her fiancé _____ "All or
5 (urge, play)

Nothing" to win some money for their honeymoon. Now, you

folks in the audience, please _____
6 (remember, not shout)

out the answers. We _____ an equal
7 (want, have)

chance. All right, then, Nancy and John, do you both

_____ our game?
8 (know how, play)

CONTESTANTS: Yes, Bob!

HOST: Very good. May I _____ carefully
9 (urge, think)

before you _____ any questions, but
10 (try, answer)

_____ fast. As always, I
11 (not forget, think)

_____ your intuition.
12 (encourage, trust)

Your first answer is usually right on the money on "All or

Nothing"!

Using What You've Learned

activity 1

Talk about television. First, complete these sentences for yourself. Include an infinitive. Add one statement of your own.

1. When I watched TV in my country, I used _____

_____

2. In this country, I bought a TV _____

_____

3. I think it's a good idea _____

_____

4. The people who make TV programs need _____

_____

5. The movies on TV are too _____ for me _____

_____

6. When I see commercials, I usually want _____

_____

7. I'm usually eager _____

8. _____

Now work in small groups. Each of you in turn reads aloud one of your sentences. The other group members ask questions and discuss the ideas. Then summarize your group's discussion for the whole class.

activity **2**

Complete these questions about television. Include an infinitive. Add questions of your own.

1. In your opinion, should parents allow their children _____

   _____?

2. Does TV prepare people _____?

3. Why do you like _____?

4. Do commercials persuade you _____?

5. What might you advise people _____?

6. _____?

7. _____?

Work in pairs. Ask and answer the questions. Then tell the class one of your partner's opinions.

TOPIC **four**

Summary of Comparisons with Adjectives and Adverbs

Setting the Context
Reading

Read the advertisements on the following page.

exercise 1 Answer these questions about the advertisements.

1. What kinds of products are the ads trying to sell?
2. What adjectives commonly describe each of these products? For example, what adjectives commonly describe movies?
3. What kinds of ads do you like? Which don't you like? Why?
4. How do ads in the United States or Canada compare with those in your home country?

exercise 2 Write the nouns from column B after the adjectives in column A that best describe them. There might be more than one correct answer.

A

1. cleaner <u>floors</u>
2. brighter _____
3. more popular _____
4. louder _____
5. less expensive _____
6. lower _____
7. more helpful _____
8. bigger _____
9. more convenient _____
10. sweeter _____

B

floors
lemonade
locations
newspapers
people
prices
salesclerks
servings
smile
stereo speakers

Summary of Comparisons with Adjectives and Adverbs

comparisons	examples	notes
as + *Adjective/* *Adverb* **(+ as)**	These tapes are **as cheap as** those. This toothpaste tastes **as good as** that one. This newspaper **isn't as** expensive.	The *as* comparison may not appear if the sentence is clear without it.
Adjective/ *Adverb* **+ -er** **(than)**	Our prices are **lower than** in other stores. *The Whom* play **louder than** other rock bands. *Monster Madness III* is **scarier than** *Monster Madness II.* CDs sound **better than** records. *Monster Madness III* is **worse than** *Love Tales.*	Add *-er* to most one-syllable adjectives and adverbs. If a word ends in *-y,* change the *y* to *i* and add *-er.* *Good* and *bad* have irregular comparative forms: *good/better; bad/worse.*
more/less + *Adjective/* *Adverb* **(+ than)**	Our music is **more popular**. The *Daily News* is **less expensive than** other newspapers.	Use *more/less* with most adjectives that have more than one syllable.

 **exercise 3** Study the pictures below. Fill in each blank with a word or words from the list. Some words may be used more than once. The first two are done as examples.

bigger	newer	good	cheaper
smaller	older	better	more/less expensive

Ron thinks his electronic equipment is __better__ than Pete's because it is
__more expensive__ . Pete's black-and-white TV is _____ than Ron's
2   3
big-screen color one. Of course, it's _____ too. Pete's speakers are
4
_____ than Ron's, but they sound as _____ as Ron's.
5   6
Pete's VCR was _____ than Ron's because Pete bought a used one.
7
However, Ron's VCR is _____ than Pete's. Pete believes that just
8
because Ron's equipment is _____ doesn't mean that it is
9
_____.
10

exercise 4

Make questions using comparisons with adjectives or adverbs. Use the cue words.
More than one question might be possible. The first one is done as an example.

1. Is advertising / important / in your country / in the United States?

   Is advertising as important in your country as in the United States?

   Is advertising more (less) important in your country than in the
   United States?

2. Is advertising / expensive / in your country / in the United States?

   _____

   _____

3. Are billboards / common / in your country / in the United States?

   _____

   _____

4. Are they / colorful?

   _____

   _____

5. Are newspapers in your language / interesting / newspapers in English?

   _____

   _____

6. Are American TV commercials / good or bad / those in your country?

   _____

   _____

7. Do you think movies in your country are / good / those in the United States?

   _____

   _____

8. Is the variety of music in the United States / great / in your country?

   _____

   _____

9. Do young people in your country play music / loud / young people in the United States?

   _____

   _____

10. Is the media / powerful / in your country / in the United States?

   _____

   _____

 **exercise 5** In this exercise, you will review all the grammar from this chapter. Choose the correct word and write it in each blank.

The headlines in today's paper _____ often the top stories on last
                                                         1 (can / were / are)

night's TV news broadcast. _____ may reappear again next weekend
                                       2 (they / them / their)

as twenty-minute segments on a news magazine show. At times, the media

covers a story so closely that we _____ more about
                                    3 (heard / hear / hearing)

_____ than we want _____.
 4 (them / they / it)   5 (know / knew / to know)

Today we _____ in the Information Age, a time in which our
          6 (are living / will live)

world _____ _____ than ever before. The
    7 (changed / is changing) 8 (faster / more fast / more faster)

rapid exchange of information _____ just one of the changes. The
                         9 (was / is / did)

job market of the future _____ also experience dramatic changes.
                  10 (might / do / are)

For example, it is predicted that over 80 percent of today's kindergarten

students one day _____ jobs which _____ not
         11 (had / have / will have)   12 (do / did / doing)

even exist yet.

Using What You've Learned

activity 1

Work in small groups. Ask and answer the questions in Exercise 4 on pages 201 and 202. Tell the reasons for your answers. Then summarize your discussion for the class.

activity 2

Work in pairs or small groups. Choose one situation below and prepare a short conversation. Perform your conversation for the class.

1. You and your friends just saw a movie together. Now you are discussing the film. You all have different opinions.
2. Your roommate likes TV and watches it all the time. You think that television is a waste of time. You want to play music in the apartment, but you can't when the TV is on.
3. You like to see plays for entertainment. One of your friends prefers movies. Another prefers concerts. You are trying to make plans together for the weekend.

focus on testing

Past and Present Continuous Tenses, Pronouns, Modals, Infinitives, and Comparisons

Problems with the past and present continuous tenses, pronouns, infinitives, and comparisons are often found on standardized English tests.

Remember . . .

- The past continuous tense describes activities in progress during a period of time in the past.
- *Can/can't* are used to express present ability/inability.
- A possessive adjective comes before a noun.
- Use ***more/less*** + **adjective** (+ ***than***) with most adjectives that have more than one syllable.

Part 1: Circle the correct completion for the following sentences.

example: I'm afraid she's very worried about _____ teenage son.
     a. she
     b. herself
     c. hers
     d. her

1. Sorry I couldn't call you sooner. The phone _____ off the hook all morning.
   a. was ringing
   b. rang
   c. were ringing
   d. rung

2. I _____ usually get through the first time I try calling my family overseas. The lines are all busy.
   a. had better not
   b. can't
   c. wasn't
   d. haven't

Part 2: Circle the letter below the underlined word(s) containing an error.

example: Living <u>in</u> a foreign country <u>is</u> more <u>difficulter</u> <u>than</u> living in
                    A   B   Ⓒ   D
one's own country.

1. My parents <u>were getting</u> married just <u>six months</u> <u>after</u> <u>they met</u>.
                         A   B   C   D

2. He said he <u>wanted</u> <u>to go</u> outside <u>to getting</u> <u>some</u> fresh air.
                       A   B   C   D

CHAPTER nine

Social Life

STUDENT ACTIVITIES & NOTICES

TOPIC **one**

The Present Perfect Continuous Tense

Setting the Context
Conversation

A group of friends are in a noisy restaurant.

CARLOS: Nicolae, I'm glad we have this chance to talk. What have you been doing all semester?

SALLY: I don't think he heard you.

CARLOS: *(shouting)* Nicolae! It's great to see you again! What's been happening with you?

NICOLAE: *(shouting)* I've been studying in the library a lot this semester. I'm still working on my thesis.

CARLOS: How long have you been doing it?

NICOLAE: What? I can't hear you.

SALLY: The band has been playing for a long time, hasn't it? When are they going to take a break?

DEAN: What did you say? Is something going to break? I didn't hear you. I've been listening to the band.

CARLOS: *(shouting)* Nicolae, how long have you been writing your thesis so far?

NICOLAE: Writing? Oh, I've been writing for years. In fact, I've been working on a new book since last month.

DEAN: What did you say? Do you have a job? Where have you been working?

NICOLAE: No, I . . .

CARLOS: We've been waiting for service for over a half-hour, haven't we? What has the waiter been doing all evening?

SALLY: What? What have I been doing? Well, I've been . . .

CARLOS: No, I said . . . The waiter hasn't been paying attention to us.

DEAN: I don't understand. Who's been paying? For what?

CARLOS: I've been complaining about the waiter.

NICOLAE: What did you say?

SALLY: What was that?

DEAN: I'm sorry, I can't hear you.

---

exercise Answer these questions.

1. Who is talking? Where are they? What are they talking about? What problem are they having?
2. What has Nicolae been doing this semester?
3. What has been happening at the restaurant?
4. What have Sally and Carlos been complaining about?
5. What have you been doing this semester?

A. The Present Perfect Continuous Tense: Patterns

The present perfect continuous tense consists of *have/has been* before the *-ing* form of a verb.

	examples	notes
Affirmative Statements	I**'ve been writing** a term paper. She**'s been babysitting.**	Here are contractions with subject pronouns: *I (we, you, they) + have =* *I've, we've, you've, they've* *he (she, it) + has = he's, she's, it's*
Negative Statements	I **haven't been sleeping** enough. She **hasn't been working.**	Here are contractions with *not*: *have + not = haven't* *has + not = hasn't*

exercise 1 Underline the present perfect continuous verb phrases in the statements in the conversation on pages 206 and 207.

  example: I've been studying in the library a lot this semester.

exercise 2 Complete these statements with the present perfect continuous form of each verb in parentheses. The first one is done as an example.

DIANE: I've been studying _____ a lot this semester too. This week I
                    1 (study)

_____ a term paper. My roommate
           2 (write)

_____ me. But we _____
           3 (help)   4 (not work)

all the time. We _____ a good time, too. We
                            5 (have)

_____ tennis and _____.
           6 (play)   7 (relax)

JIM: So you _____ yourselves these days. I
                       8 (enjoy)

_____ much. I _____
              9 (not relax)   10 (think)

about a vacation for a while. My wife _____ really
                                                11 (work)

hard these days, too. She _____ time for herself.
                                     12 (not take)

She _____ for extra money and she
                 13 (type)

_____ too.
              14 (babysit)

DIANE: Wow, it sounds like you both _____ much too hard.
                                                15 (work)

Why _____ you _____ about taking
         16   17 (think)

a vacation? Just take one!

B. The Present Perfect Continuous Tense: Forms and Patterns

	examples	**notes**
Yes/No Questions	**Have** you **been studying** a lot? **Has** she **been living** here long?	Here are possible short answers: *Yes, I (we, you, they) have.* *Yes, he (she, it) has. No, I (we, you, they) haven't. No, he (she, it) hasn't.*

	examples	notes
Tag Questions	You**'ve been working** a lot, **haven't** you? He **hasn't been studying, has** he?	A form of *have* appears in the tag: with a negative tag, the speaker or writer expects an affirmative answer; with an affirmative tag, a negative answer.
Information Questions	Where **have** you **been living**? Who**'s been playing** music? What**'s been happening**?	With *who* or *what* as the subject, the verb is singular.

 **exercise 3** Circle the present perfect continuous verb phrases in the questions in the conversation at the beginning of the chapter.

> **example:** What (have) you (been doing) all semester?

 **exercise 4** Fill in the blanks with the present perfect continuous form of each verb in parentheses. Complete the tag questions and the short answers. The first two have been done as examples.

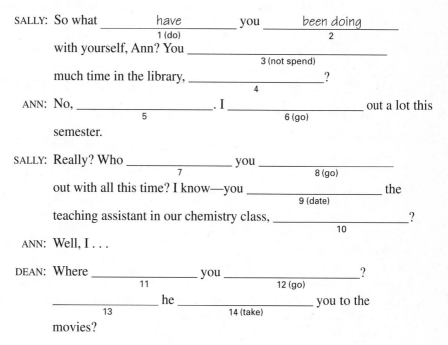

SALLY: So what _____*have*_____ you _____*been doing*_____
 1 (do)   2
 with yourself, Ann? You _____
 3 (not spend)
 much time in the library, _____?
 4

ANN: No, _____. I _____ out a lot this
 5   6 (go)
 semester.

SALLY: Really? Who _____ you _____
 7   8 (go)
 out with all this time? I know—you _____ the
 9 (date)
 teaching assistant in our chemistry class, _____?
 10

ANN: Well, I . . .

DEAN: Where _____ you _____?
 11   12 (go)
 _____ he _____ you to the
 13   14 (take)
 movies?

CARLOS: You _____ him out to dinner,
15 (invite)

_____? Where _____ you
16   17

_____?
18 (eat)

ANN: Well, we . . .

JANET: You _____ home much, _____?
19 (not stay)   20

I know—because I _____ to call you.
21 (try)

SALLY: Your life sounds so romantic. Married life is completely different. We

_____ out at all, _____, Carlos?
22 (not go)   23

CARLOS: Of course, _____. Why, just three months ago we
24

went out for a pizza!

SALLY: But what _____ we _____ for the
25   26 (do)

last three months?

CARLOS: We _____ lots of time alone. What could
27 (spend)

be more romantic than that?

SALLY: Oh, Carlos. Watching old horror movies on late night TV isn't exactly

what I had in mind.

C. The Present Perfect Continuous Tense: Time Expressions

Time expressions for the present perfect continuous tense refer to a time period
that began in the past and continues to the present.

examples		notes
until now up to now before now so far	all day (long) all year (long) all my life	These expressions mean "past time up to the present moment."
today this week	these days nowadays	These expressions are also common with the present continuous.

examples	notes
since last September since 1981	A sentence with *since* is always in a perfect tense. It means "from (*time period*) until now."
for a while (now) for two days	*For* can appear with any tense; with the present perfect continuous, it refers to an amont of time before the present moment.
How long?	This expression is for questions. It means "for what period or amount of time?".

 **exercise 5** Fill in the blanks with any time expression from the chart on pages 210 and 211 that makes sense. Compare your answers with another student. Several answers may be correct.

1. Linda has been lonely _____ when her best friend

   transferred to another school.

2. I was homesick all last year. But _____ I'm feeling much

   better because I've been making some friends.

3. My roommate has been worrying about that test _____.

4. He has wanted to get married and have kids _____.

5. The student government has been planning this dance _____.

6. The weather has been very strange _____, hasn't it?

7. Those two have been going together _____.

8. She's been working full-time and going to school _____.

   She's completely stressed out.

9. Usually I feel fine, but I've been having headaches everyday _____

   _____.

10. My relationship with my boss has been going great _____.

exercise 6   Arrange these groups of words into sentences. Use the present perfect continuous form of each verb (except in short answers). Add tag questions and short answers if necessary. Part of the first item is done as an example.

1. A: You haven't been attending many parties this summer, have you?
not attend many parties / this summer / You / (tag) / ?

     B: No, I haven't.
No, (short answer) / .

the same thing about you / wonder / I / .

2. A: _____
these days / someone special / date / you / ?

     B: _____
not date / up to now / I / anyone special / .

3. A: _____
this delicious food / Why / you / not / eat / all evening / ?

not diet / you / this month / (tag) / ?

     B: _____
No, (short answer) / .

But / stomach trouble / for a while / I have / .

4. A: _____
Oh, really? that / go on / How long / ?

     B: _____
ever since I can remember / trouble with my stomach / have / I / .

5. A: _____
get along with your boyfriend / you / these days / ?

B: _____
No, (short answer) / .

_____
do strange things / He / for weeks / .

6. A: _____
treat you well / so far / he / (tag) / ?

B: _____
We / since last week / to each other / not speak / .

D. *all, since, for:* Time Expressions

A phrase with *since, for,* or *all* can answer the questions "how long?" or "since when?"

examples	notes
How long (since when) have you been eating? I've been eating **since 8:00.**	*Since* appears with a point in time (*since 4:00, this morning, last week*).
I've been eating **for hours.**	*For* appears with an amount of time (*for five minutes, two days, several weeks*).
I've been eating **all evening long.**	*All* appears before a word for a time period.

exercise 7 Fill in the blanks in the letter with the words *since, for,* or *all.* The first one has been done as an example.

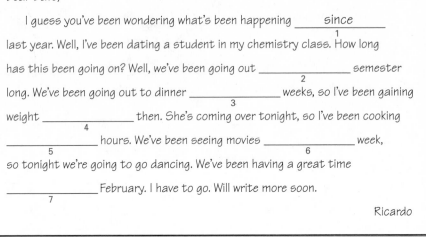

Dear Dave,

I guess you've been wondering what's been happening ___since___ ₁
last year. Well, I've been dating a student in my chemistry class. How long

has this been going on? Well, we've been going out _____ semester ₂

long. We've been going out to dinner _____ weeks, so I've been gaining ₃

weight _____ then. She's coming over tonight, so I've been cooking ₄

_____ hours. We've been seeing movies _____ week, ₅ ₆

so tonight we're going to go dancing. We've been having a great time

_____ February. I have to go. Will write more soon. ₇

Ricardo

exercise 8 In small groups, restate each sentence in Exercise 7 with a different time expression that has the same meaning. Record your answers in your notebook. Compare them with the other groups' answers when everyone has finished.

example: I guess you've been wondering what's been happening since last year.

I guess you've been wondering what's been happening all year.

Using What You've Learned

activity 1 Suggest time expressions for the present perfect continuous tense. Begin with a very recent time and add expressions for times further and further in the past. Your teacher will write the expressions on the board.

examples: for the last few minutes, since this morning, since last night, for three days, all week long

Work in small groups. Each of you makes a sentence about yourself with one of the time expressions on the board.

examples: A: I've been thinking about this activity for the last few minutes.
B: I've been feeling sick since this morning.

Then ask and answer questions with "how long?" or "since when?".

examples: A: How long have you been studying English?
B: Since the beginning of the year.

Each of you tells the class something you learned about one other student in your group.

 **activity 2**

Work in pairs. Use one book and pass it back and forth. Take turns reading out loud one of the time expressions from the chart on pages 210 and 211. Your partner must make up a sentence, supplying the correct verb and using the time expression. There are enough sentences for six turns each.

> **example:** A: until now
> B: Hmmm . . . I have understood all the grammar we've studied until now.
> A: Good. It's your turn. Here's the book.

activity 3

Write three to five true statements describing a classmate. Do not say the student's name. After each student reads his or her paragraph to the class, the class will guess the identity of the mystery student.

> **example:** The mystery student works at the Hyatt Hotel after class every day. She's been studying English for four years. She's been married since she was 21 and has three children.

activity 4

Follow the directions for Activity 3, but write about famous people your class-mates should know.

> **example:** The mystery celebrity is a very famous singer and dancer. He has been singing and dancing professionally since he was a child. He may be most famous for his moon walk dance step.

The Present Perfect Tense

Setting the Context
Conversation

ESTELLA: We haven't gone out in a month.

JULIE: I know. There hasn't been a good movie in town for weeks.

KATHLEEN: And I've been sitting by this phone for hours, but no one has called.

ESTELLA: We've been living in this apartment since January and we haven't gotten to know our neighbors yet.

JULIE: How long has the lesbian couple next door been living here?

KATHLEEN: I don't know. The old couple upstairs has been here for years, but I haven't seen them since last week.

JULIE: I've heard the family with three kids every day for a month. They've been playing a lot of music.

ESTELLA: Have the three guys in Apartment 2-G been here long?

JULIE: Hmmm . . . I think they've been around since April.

KATHLEEN: I've got an idea! Let's have a party next weekend. We'll invite all the neighbors.

 Answer these questions.

1. Who lives in the apartment building? How long have they been there?
2. Why are the three women going to have a party next weekend?
3. Have you gotten to know your neighbors since your last move? Why or why not?
4. Have you ever had neighbors who became good friends? What happened?
5. Have you ever felt lonely and bored? When? What did you do about it?

A. The Present Perfect Tense

The present perfect tense consists of *have/has* before the past participle form of a verb.

	examples	notes
Affirmative Statements	We**'ve been** here a year. She**'s worked** a long time.	Here are some past participles: *worked (work), been (be), seen (see).*
Negative Statements	I **haven't seen** them since last week.	Contractions, short answers, and tag questions with *have/has* are the same in the present perfect tense as in the present perfect continuous.
Yes/No Questions	**Have** you **lived** here since January?	
Tag Questions	We **haven't gone** out for a while, **have** we?	
Information Questions	Who **have** you **met** in the last few weeks?	
there + be	There **haven't been** any parties in weeks, **have there**? (No, **there haven't**.)	A time expression with *in* is common in negative sentences.

exercise 1 Underline the present perfect verb phrases in the conversation.

   example: We <u>haven't gone</u> out in a month.

**exercise 2**   Arrange these words into sentences.

SERGIO: _____
1 (been living / How long / have / we / here so far / ?)

DICK: _____
2 (here / since April, / We've / been / haven't we / ?)

SERGIO: _____
3 (Yes, / have / we.)

_____
4 (have / And what / done / we / in all these months / ?)

BOB: _____
5 (a lot of television / We've / watched / .)

DICK: _____
6 (read / up until now / every newspaper / And we've / .)

SERGIO: _____
7 (Right! / any restaurants in the neighborhood / we / But have / gone out to / ?)

DICK: _____
8 (haven't / No, we / .)

SERGIO: _____
9 (any good movies / There / haven't / this month, / been / have there / ?)

_____
10 (attended / haven't / any sports events / And we / .)

_____
11 (any fun / had / Have / we / ?)

_____
12 (Where / gone / have / we / ?)

B. Past Participles

You can learn past participles in groups.

	examples			notes
Simple Form	put	cost	run	The participle is the same as the simple form of the verb.
Participle	put	cost	run	
Simple Form	meet	buy	spend	The participle is the same as the simple past tense.
Participle	met	bought	spent	
Simple Form	call	watch	invite	In all regular verbs, the participle is the same as the simple past tense.
Participle	called	watched	invited	
Simple Form	drink	ring		The simple form has *i;* the participle has *u.*
Participle	drunk	rung		

exercise 3   Fill in the blanks with past participle forms. Choose from the verbs in the table on page 218. The first one is done as an example.

PAULA: Let's go out to the movies tonight!

LESLIE: We'd better not. We've _____*spent*_____ too much money already this
₁
month. We've _____ new furniture—remember? It's
₂
_____ us several hundred dollars.
₃

PAULA: You're right. Well, has anyone _____ on the phone this week
₄
so far? Has anyone _____ us to dinner?
₅

LESLIE: No, the phone hasn't _____ once.
₆

PAULA: Well, there's a good program on TV. Should we turn it on?

LESLIE: No, we've _____ TV every night this week.
₇

PAULA: Well, I've _____ some soda in the refrigerator. Do you want
₈
some?

LESLIE: No, thanks. I've _____ two cans already today.
₉

PAULA: Well, then, what should we do? I've _____ out of ideas.
₁₀

LESLIE: You know, we haven't _____ all the neighbors in this
₁₁
apartment building. Why don't we have a party next weekend?

exercise 4

Work in pairs or small groups. Using the past participle chart on page 218, make up sentences using participles. You earn one point for each participle used correctly. Take turns making up and saying sentences. Play for five minutes. The winner is the person with the most points.

example: I have never drunk so much coffee in my life.

C. More Past Participle Forms

	examples			notes
Simple Form	draw	eat	fall	The participle consists of the simple
Participle	drawn	eaten	fallen	form with an -n or -en ending.
Simple Form	give	know	see	
Participle	given	known	seen	
Simple Form	break	choose	get	The simple form consists of the past
Participle	broken	chosen	gotten	tense with an -n or -en ending.
Simple Form	speak	tear		
Participle	spoken	torn		
Simple Form	drive	write		The /ay/ sound of the simple form
Participle	driven	written		changes to /I/ in the participle, which ends in -n or -en.
Simple Form	be	do	fly	These are irregular.
Participle	been	done	flown	

 **exercise 5**   Complete these sentences with the present perfect form of the verbs in parentheses. The first one is done as an example.

ESTELLA: How many party invitations __have__ you __written__ so far, Kathleen?
            1 (write)   2

KATHLEEN: Oh, I _____ about five. And I _____ out a few to
                    3 (do)   4 (give)
some neighbors downstairs.

JULIE: And I _____ to the family with the three teenagers.
                5 (speak)

* * * * *

SERGIO: What are we going to buy for the party on Friday?

DICK: We _____ everything in the refrigerator, _____
              6 (eat)   7
we? We'll have to buy a lot of things.

BOB: I _____ some ads out of the newspaper—they're for special
            8 (tear)
sales. We _____ already _____ most of our
              9 (spend)   10

grocery money for this month. I thought we could save some money by comparing prices.

* * * * *

PAULA: _____ you _____ CDs for the party on Friday?
　　　　　　　　　11　　　　　　12 (choose)

LESLIE: No, I _____ too busy. But I _____ some
　　　　　　　　　13 (be)　　　　　　　　　　14 (get)
decorations. And my little sister _____ us a great picture
　　　　　　　　　　　　　　　　　　　15 (draw)
to use on our invitations.

PAULA: Wonderful! You know, we _____ a party
　　　　　　　　　　　　　　　　　16 (not give)
in ages. I forgot how much fun it was.

exercise 6 Answer these questions about the conversations in Exercise 5.

1. What have the three women done to get ready for their party?
2. What have the three men done for their party?
3. What have Paula and Leslie done for their party?
4. Have you ever done any of these things? Which ones?
5. What do you think is going to happen on Friday?

Using What You've Learned

activity 1 Working in pairs, ask and answer questions in the present perfect with these cue words. Add questions of your own.

1. you / see your friends often / this semester / ?
2. Where / you / go / ?
3. What / you do / ?
4. Who / you meet / ?
5. What / you like / ?

Summarize your conversation for the class.

activity 2 Work in small groups. Make a list of difficult situations or problems, real or imaginary, that involve friends, dating, and other social relationships.

examples: My girlfriend hasn't called me in a month.

My roommate and I have been arguing about the housework.

My best friend is white and she wants to marry a black man.

Students in the group take roles and act out the situation. The group gives suggestions and then discusses possible solutions to the problem.

Each group presents one situation to the class. The class discusses it.

since clauses; *The Present Perfect Continuous Tense Versus the Present Perfect Tense*

Setting the Context

Conversation

A talk-show host is interviewing two couples on his TV program.

HOST: Good afternoon, and welcome again to "Intimate Interviews."
Today we have two gay couples with us to discuss their relationships.
Let's start with Hanna and Kathy. Hanna, how long have you known that you were a lesbian?"

HANNA: I've known since I was a young girl, probably six or seven. I knew that one day I would fall in love with a woman and spend my life with her.

HOST: Kathy, have you and Hanna experienced much discrimination as a lesbian couple?

KATHY: No, we haven't. We've always been honest about our relationship with our families, friends, coworkers, and neighbors. We've been surprised at all the love and support we've received.

HOST: Has that been your experience, Robert?

ROBERT: No, it hasn't. When I told my best friend in high school I was gay, he never spoke to me again. My parents told me to move out of the house when they found a love letter from my first boyfriend. Fortunately, however, my life has improved since that time.

HOST: How has it improved?

ROBERT: Well, my parents have joined P-FLAG—that's Parents, Families, and Friends of Lesbians and Gays.

HOST: It's an international organization that's working to stop discrimination against gays and lesbians.

ROBERT: Right. Since they joined P-FLAG, my parents have changed their ideas about gays and lesbians. Now we are all one family again, and they love Young.

HOST: What about your family, Young?

YOUNG: My family has had a difficult time. It is hard for them to understand or accept our relationship. But Robert's family has changed their way of thinking, so I hope my family can too.

exercise Answer these questions.

1. Who is the host interviewing today? What have they been talking about?
2. How have the experiences of the lesbian couple differed from those of the gay couple? What are some possible reasons for their different experiences?
3. What difficulties do you think lesbian and gay couples experience that most heterosexual couples do not?
4. Have you known any lesbian or gay people or couples? How has knowing or not knowing lesbians and gays affected your opinion of this minority group?

A. Clauses with *since*

A sentence in the present perfect or present perfect continuous tense often has a clause with *since*.

examples	notes
They've been in love **since the first time they met.**	The verb in the *since* clause is usually in the simple past tense.
Since I started my new job, I've been traveling more.	A *since* clause can come at the beginning or at the end of a sentence. Use a comma after the clause when it comes at the beginning of the sentence.

 **exercise 1** Combine the two sentences into one sentence using *since*. Use correct punctuation.

> example: Young has been studying hard. He was accepted to study at a college in the United States.
>
> *Since he was accepted to study at a college in the United*
>
> *States, Young has been studying hard.*

1. Hanna and Kathy bought a house. Both their families have come to visit them.

_____

_____

2. He has been staying at the office very late. Alfonso got a new job.

_____

_____

3. Robert's parents have changed their ideas about gays and lesbians. They joined P-FLAG.

_____

_____

4. They moved to an apartment off campus. I haven't seen Maria and Yoko.

_____

_____

5. Hanna's mother broke her leg. She has been living with Hanna and Kathy.

_____

_____

6. Young's parents found out he was gay. They haven't been able to accept him as their son.

_____

_____

7. We haven't been going to the movies very often. We had children.

_____

_____

8. The Gay Civil Rights Movement began. Many gay, lesbian, and straight (heterosexual) people have been working for equal rights for all.

_____

_____

B. The Present Perfect Continuous Tense versus the Present Perfect Tense

The present perfect continuous and present perfect tenses express activity that has taken place in a time period that began in the past and extends to the present.

	examples	notes
Present Perfect Continuous	How long **have** you **been living** here? We**'ve been talking** for hours.	Expresses duration of or repetition of action from a past time up to the present.
Present Perfect	How long **have** you **been** here? I**'ve known** him all my life.	Expresses duration of a nonaction verb from a past time up to the present.
Present Perfect Continuous	Who**'s been drinking** my soda? (The glass is half empty.)	Emphasizes continuation (noncompletion) of action.
Present Perfect	Who**'s drunk** my soda? (The glass is empty.)	Emphasizes completion of action.
Present Perfect Continuous	**Have** you **been working** here long? = **Have** you **worked** here long?	Sometimes there is little difference in meaning between the present perfect continuous and the present perfect.

exercise 2 Fill in the blanks in the letter with an appropriate form (present perfect continuous, present perfect, or simple past) of each verb in parentheses. More than one answer may be correct. The first one is done as an example.

Dear Yukiko,

I __'ve been living__ in New York for two months now, and I _____
  1 (live)   2 (learn)
a lot. In general, I _____ very happy up until now, but I _____
                          3 (be)   4 (feel)
a little lonely too.

Since I _____ this apartment, I _____ some of the
              5 (rent)   6 (meet)
people in the building. There are some interesting couples. In the past few weeks,

I _____ a lot to an American woman who is married to a Vietnamese
    7 (talk)
man. A Peruvian man and his American wife _____ to invite me to
                                                              8 (promise)
dinner sometime, but they _____ it yet. Actually, I _____
                                    9 (not do)   10 (not see)
the inside of an American family's apartment since I _____ here.
                                                                    11 (move)
    A very nice Arab woman _____ me a few times. She _____
                                  12 (visit)   13 (be)
married to an American for several years. She says she _____
                                                              14 (have)
problems with the customs of the United States since she _____
                                                                      15 (move)
here, and there _____ some cultural conflicts in her marriage.
                      16 (be)
    I'm surprised at the number of cross-cultural couples that I _____
                                                                        17 (get)
to know since last month. And now an American student _____ me
                                                                  18 (ask)
out. I _____ on a date since I _____ my country. And I
          19 (not go)   20 (leave)
_____ never _____ a boyfriend, as you know. What do
    21   22 (have)
you think? Should I go?

                                                  Your friend,

                                                  Monique

1. A: You look depressed. Is there anything wrong?

   B: Well . . . it's just that I ~~didn't have~~ *haven't* had a date since last summer.

   A: Yeah, I know . . . but why do you stay home all the time? You don't

       go to a party for months. You've have to get out more to meet

       people.

   B: I guess so. I have met some nice women in my classes, but they

       haven't been liking me. I haven't been had much fun for the begin-

       ning of the semester.

2. A: Hey, you guys, it's time to get ready for the party. We've got to

       clean up this apartment.

   B: I've cleaning up all morning, and I've haven't finished yet. Why

       you haven't been helping me?

   C: I've been thinking about the refreshments and the music since

       hours. Someone has to make the plans.

3. A: Have you heard the news about Margie?

   B: No, I didn't. What happened?

   A: She been going out with her boss!

   B: Really? How long this been going on?

   A: They've dating since he has been getting a divorce a few

       months ago.

Using What You've Learned

activity **1** Complete these sentences in your own words. Use the present perfect or present perfect continuous tense.

I _____ in this country since

_____. Since I arrived here, _____

_____. I _____

_____ for _____,

but I _____n't _____ in the

last _____.

Work in groups. Each of you reads your paragraph aloud. The group asks questions and then summarizes and discusses the ideas.

activity **2** Work in groups. Discuss the answers to these questions. Use the present perfect or present perfect continuous tense, when possible.

1. What experiences have you had with cross-cultural relationships?
2. Are you, or do you know people, in a cross-cultural marriage?
3. What problems have they had?
4. How have they solved problems?
5. What advantages might a cross-cultural couple have in today's world?
6. What advantages and disadvantages might their children have?

Summarize your discussion for the class.

activity **3** Work in pairs or small groups. Choose one situation below and prepare a short conversation. Perform your conversation for the class.

1. You're at a party and you don't know many people. You begin a conversation with a compliment.
2. You're at a party. The music is terrible, the room is too warm, and there isn't enough food. Complain to another guest.
3. Your husband, wife, girlfriend, boyfriend, best friend, or someone else has been doing several things that bother you. You can't stand it anymore. Criticize him or her as gently as possible.

Present Perfect and Present Perfect Continuous Tenses, Using *for* and *since*

Problems with the use of the present perfect and present perfect continuous tenses, and *for* and *since* are usually found on standardized tests of English proficiency.

Remember . . .

*   The present perfect continuous tense expresses continuation or repetition of an activity from the past time up to the present.
*   A sentence in the present perfect or present perfect continuous tense often has a clause with *since.*
*   Sometimes there is little difference in meaning between these two tenses.
*   *For* usually refers to a specific amount of time; *since* means from a past time period until now.

Part 1: Circle the correct completion for the following sentences.

example: You've been sick a lot this semester, _____ you?
>   **a.** have
>   **b.** haven't
>   **c.** were
>   **d.** weren't

1. Who _____ my soda? It's only half full now and I've only had one sip!
    a. drank
    b. has been drinking
    c. has drunk
    d. drunk
2. How long have you _____ here?
    a. worked
    b. been working
    c. working
    d. a and b
3. I have always _____ to be a famous movie star.
    a. want
    b. been wanted
    c. been wanting
    d. wanted

Part 2: Circle the letter below the underlined word(s) containing an error.

example: My cousin <u>has</u> <u>been living</u> <u>in</u> New York <u>since</u> three months.
                          A   B   C   Ⓓ

1. I <u>have</u> <u>been going</u> to Disneyland four times <u>since</u> I <u>came</u> to the
    A   B   C   D
United States.

2. He <u>has</u> <u>been going</u> to graduate school <u>since</u> <u>over</u> ten years.
    A   B   C   D

Customs, Celebrations, and Holidays

Gerunds and Infinitives as Subjects

Setting the Context
Conversation

A family is celebrating two birthdays at the same time. The grandfather is sixty-five years old. Jenny is five years old today.

MOTHER: Isn't this fun, Dad? It's so nice to celebrate your birthdays together.

GRANDFATHER: Well, maybe it's fun to celebrate Jenny's birthday, but I'm too old to like birthdays.

JENNY: But, Grandpa, having a birthday is very special. You *have* to enjoy yourself.

JIMMY: Grandpa, hurry up. It's time to make a wish and blow out the candles.

GRANDFATHER: Blowing out sixty-five candles is too hard.

FATHER: Then it will be Grandpa's job to cut the cake.

GRANDFATHER: Eating cake and ice cream is bad for an old man.

JENNY: Opening the presents is more fun. It's hard to wait.

GRANDFATHER: It's silly to give presents on birthdays.

JIMMY: Grandpa, shhh . . .

(The family sings "Happy Birthday." Then Jenny and the grand-father blow out all the candles.)

JENNY: Hooray! Now all our wishes will come true! *(She hugs her grandfather.)*

GRANDFATHER: *(smiles)* Well, maybe having a birthday isn't so bad after all.

exercise  Answer these questions about the conversation.

1. What does Jenny think about birthdays? What does the grandfather think? Why?
2. What are some American birthday customs?
3. What are some birthday customs in your culture?
4. Do you like celebrating birthdays? Why or why not?

Gerunds and Infinitives as Subjects

Gerunds and infinitives appear as subjects of sentences. Their meaning is identical.

examples	**notes**
Getting presents is fun. It's fun **to get** presents. Is **celebrating** birthdays universal? Is is universal **to celebrate** birthdays?	A sentence with an infinitive subject begins with the impersonal *it;* the infinitive follows the adjective or noun.

exercise 1 Circle the gerund subjects and underline the infinitive subjects after the impersonal *it* in the conversation.

example: It's so nice to celebrate your birthdays together. Having a birthday is very special.

In two different ways, tell the opinions of these people about celebrating birthdays. Use the words in the balloons with gerunds and with *it* and infinitives.

example: Celebrating birthdays is wonderful.
= It's wonderful to celebrate birthdays.

1.
a. _____
= _____
b. _____
= _____

2.
a. _____
= _____
b. _____
= _____

3.
a. _____
= _____
b. _____
= _____

4.
a. _____
= _____
b. _____
= _____

Make an equivalent sentence, with a gerund or an infinitive, for each of these sentences.

example: Guessing what's in the box is hard.

It's hard to guess what's in the box.

1. Decorating the house with balloons and colored streamers takes time.

_____

2. It's hard to blow up balloons.

_____

3. Making a wish before you blow out the candles is very important.

_____

4. It's not easy to blow out all the candles.

_____

5. Hearing my family and friends sing "Happy Birthday to You" always makes me cry.

_____

6. Opening the presents is exciting.

_____

7. But washing the dishes after the party is no fun.

_____

8. It's sad to have to wait a whole year for your next birthday.

_____

TOPIC **two**

Gerunds and Prepositions

1.

2.

3.

4.

5.

6.

Setting the Context

Brainstorm

Number off by sixes. Join the other students with your number. Identify the holiday with your number. Make a group list of all the words and phrases you can think of associated with your holiday. Share your list with the class.

Read the information below. Then match each description with one of the holiday pictures on page 236. Write the number of the picture on the line.

  4   No one needs to apologize for eating a lot on this holiday. The next day, people recover from having too much turkey, sweet potatoes, stuffing, cranberry sauce, and pumpkin pie.

_____ On this holiday, people look forward to getting cards, chocolates, and flowers from their sweethearts.

_____ On this holiday, many people give gifts to relatives and friends. The night before, excited children dream about opening their presents.

_____ There's usually champagne for toasting this holiday. Many people plan on watching football games on TV the next day.

_____ Children don't usually worry about burning themselves with fireworks, but their parents do. Instead of heating up the house by cooking, many families have a barbecue in the backyard.

_____ Children rarely get tired of saying "Trick or Treat" on this holiday. Then their parents have to stop them from eating too much candy.

A. Gerunds After Prepositions

Sometimes the *-ing* form of a verb is a gerund. A gerund functions as a noun and can be the object of a preposition.

examples	notes
Instead **of celebrating** at home, they went out to dinner.	A gerund can be part of a phrase.
She made a wish **before blowing out** the candles.	A gerund can have an object.

Answer these questions about the information on holidays at the top of this page.

1. What do people often have to recover from on the day after Thanksgiving?
2. What do people look forward to on St. Valentine's Day?
3. What are children excited about before Christmas?
4. What do many people plan on doing on New Year's Day?
5. What happens on Halloween?
6. What do parents worry about on the Fourth of July?

Underline the gerunds after prepositions in your answers to Exercise 1.

example: People often have to recover from <u>eating</u> too much on the day after Thanksgiving.

exercise  Complete each sentence with a gerund. The first one is done as an example. Choose from these verbs:

add	dry	serve
bake	eat	sit
buy	get	stand
carve	look	start
clear	put	stuff
cut	save	take

Making Thanksgiving dinner is no easy job. Only by _____*starting*_____
                                                            1
very early can the cook finish everything. Some cooks save time by

_____ the rolls and pies instead of _____
          2   3
them themselves.

Before _____ the turkey into the oven, the cook usually
                    4
fills it with a bread or rice mixture. By _____ the turkey, he
                                                    5
or she prevents it from _____ out. Three to six hours later,
                                6
the turkey is ready. After _____ it with a sharp knife and
                                        7
_____ it to family and guests, the cook can finally sit down
          8
and enjoy the meal.

It seems that only a short time after _____ down at the
                                                    9
table, everyone has finished. After _____ all that food, no
                                                10
one feels much like _____ up. Especially because they
                                11
know, without even _____ , that the kitchen is a complete
                                12
mess. Finally, one brave family member starts by _____
                                                                13
up and beginning to clear off the plates. After _____
                                                            14
everything off the table, the family has to put away the leftover food. Many

cooks plan for turkey soup or turkey sandwiches by _____
                                                                15
all the leftover turkey. After _____ all the meat off the
                                        16

bones, some cooks even save the carcass. By _____ the

17

bones to the soup, cooks make a rich, flavorful broth their families will enjoy

for days.

B. Gerunds After Adjectives with Prepositions

A gerund can follow an adjective-preposition combination. Here are some common phrases:

afraid of	good at
committed to	happy about
content with	interested in
disappointed in (with)	tired of
excited about	worried about

Complete the sentences with the missing prepositions and gerunds. Use the verb in parentheses. The first one is done as an example.

Children are always happy ___about celebrating___ holidays, but most
1(celebrate)

American children get especially excited _____ ready
2(get)

for Halloween. Every year in October, children who usually hate to go to

the market begin to get interested _____. They are eager to pick
3(shop)

out a costume and a pumpkin.

Adults who are good _____ pumpkins cut happy or sad faces in
4(carve)

them. With lighted candles in them, the pumpkins become jack-o'-lanterns,

symbols of Halloween.

On October 31, children go trick-or-treating. They never seem to get tired

_____ from house to house to fill their bags with candy. Little
5(run)

children are sometimes afraid _____ out on Halloween because
6(go)

of the ghosts and monsters on the streets. Their parents are often worried

_____ their children's teeth from all those sweets.
7(save)

Unfortunately, modern parents must also be committed _____
8(protect)

their children's safety. Some parents are afraid _____ their
9(let)

kids go trick-or-treating at all. They worry _____ poisoned
10(find)

candy or razor blades hidden in apples. Their children have to be content

_____ at private parties or shopping malls.
11(trick-or-treat)

exercise 5

Choose five adjective-preposition combinations from the list on page 239. Write five true statements about yourself.

example: I'm afraid of walking alone at night.

exercise 6

Take turns sharing your true statements from Exercise 5 with a partner. Practice finding similarities and differences.

examples: A: I'm afraid of walking alone at night.
B: I am too. I always ask someone to go with me.

B: I'm excited about going to the Valentine's Day Dance.
A: You are? Boy, not me. I'm not too good at dancing.

C. Gerunds and Phrasal Verbs

A gerund can follow a phrasal verb or verb-preposition combination. The preposition can have an object in addition to the gerund.

examples	notes
I **believe in sending** flowers.	The person or thing who performs the action of the gerund can be the same as the subject of the sentence (for example, *I believe* + *I send flowers*).
He doesn't **approve of women sending** flowers.	The person or thing who performs the action of the gerund can be different from the subject of the sentence (for example, *He doesn't approve* + *Women send flowers*).

Here are some common phrasal verbs and verb-preposition combinations:

admit to	give up
believe in	object to
count on	thank (someone) for
dream of	think of

 **exercise 7** Complete the sentences here and on page 242 with the missing particles or prepositions and gerund. Use the verb in parentheses. The first one is done as an example.

(It is February 14. Michael has received flowers. The card says "From a Secret Admirer.")

MICHAEL: *(to himself)* Red roses! They're beautiful! I bet they're from Janet. It's

so nice of her to think ___of buying___ flowers on Valentine's Day.
                          1 (buy)
I'll call her.

(He dials Janet's number. The phone rings.)

JANET: Hello.

MICHAEL: Hi, Janet. It's Mike. I just wanted to thank you _____ so
                                                              2 (be)
romantic. I've often dreamed _____ roses from a woman.
                              3 (get)
I can always count _____ your _____ something
                   4   5 (do)
nice.

JANET: Roses? I . . . uh . . . don't believe _____ men gifts. I also
                                    6 (give)

object _____ women _____ the first step in a
               7   8 (take)

relationship.

MICHAEL: *(to himself)* Hmmm . . . she doesn't admit _____ the flowers.
                                                     9 (send)

Then who sent them? I can't give _____ to find out.
                                        10 (try)

(He dials the phone. A woman answers it.)

MICHAEL: Hello, Betty. It's Mike. Have you ever thought _____
                                                      11 (send)

flowers to a man?

Using What You've Learned

activity 1

Work with other students from your country or culture. Choose a holiday and prepare a description of it for the class, using gerunds when possible. Tell the class about it and answer questions.

    example: In our country, Germany, we look forward to **celebrating Fasching** (*Carnival*) every spring. Dancing and parades are common activities, and it's customary to wear costumes. People look forward to **having a great time** at Fasching all during the long, cold winter.

activity 2

Work in pairs. Write a role-play that takes place during a holiday. Use the phrasal verbs listed below to create as many verb + preposition + gerund phrases as you can. Perform your role-play for the class. These are some common verb-particle combinations:

approve of	feel like	put off
believe in	forget about	rule out
care about	get out of	succeed in
count on	hear of	talk about
decide against	look forward to	work at
dream about	object to	worry about
dream of	plan on	

activity 3

Work in pairs. How many verb + preposition + gerund combinations can you remember from the different role-plays in Activity 2? The pair with the longest list reads it to the class.

Verbs and Gerunds; Verbs Before Objects and Simple Forms of Verbs

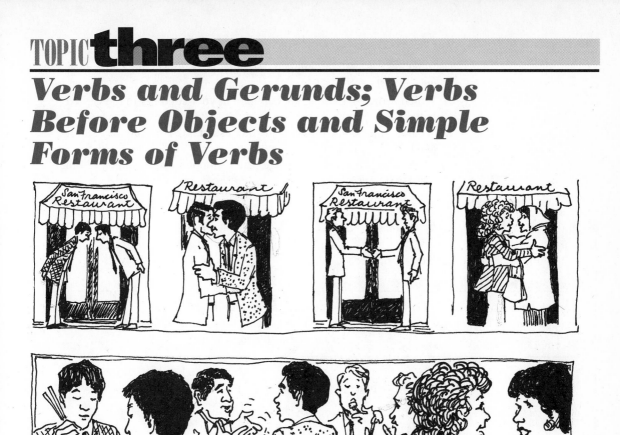

Setting the Context
Reading

Body Language

Many body movements and gestures, sometimes called body language, are specific to a given culture. For example, in some cultures, when two friends greet each other, they usually kiss each other on the cheek or hug each other. In other societies, women may hug or kiss each other, but men commonly shake

5   hands. In some countries, such as Italy, people generally use their hands to gesture while speaking, often loudly. In most Asian countries, however, people are taught to speak quietly while keeping their hands still.

1. What are the pairs of people doing outside the restaurant? How does each pair differ?
2. Which forms of greeting are common in your country? In the United States?
3. What are the people doing inside the restaurant? How are they sitting? How are they moving? How are they eating?
4. Which forms of "body language" are common in your country? In the United States?

A. Verbs Before Gerunds

Certain verbs can precede gerunds.

examples	notes
Stop doing that! I **like eating** with chopsticks.	The gerund can include an object or a phrase. Some verbs can also come before an infinitive (for example, *I like to eat with chopsticks*).

Here are some common main verbs for the pattern **verb + verb-*ing:***

advise	hate	stop
avoid	like	suggest
begin	prefer	try
continue	risk	
enjoy	start	

 Fill in the missing verbs from the conversations at the restaurant.

1. _____ snapping your fingers. Waiters don't like people doing that.

2. I _____ waiting for service in a restaurant.

3. But I don't _____ hissing at him.

4. I actually _____ eating at home. Restaurant food is never as good as my own cooking.

5. I think I'd better _____ looking for a new job.

6. Have you ever _____ waiting on tables? It's not as easy as it looks.

 Write a verb phrase in the appropriate tense from the two verbs in parentheses. Include a gerund. The first one is done as an example.

THE DINNER PARTY (PART 1)

Martin was pleased when his American friend, Keith, invited him to a dinner party on Friday night. Immediately, he ___began planning___ for

1 (begin / plan)

the party. He _____ gifts to people, so he asked his room-

2 (like / bring)

mate, Kevin, for suggestions. Kevin _____ a bottle of

3 (suggest / take)

wine. But Martin didn't drink wine, so he bought Keith a new CD player for

his car. Kevin _____ casual clothes to the party, but Martin

4 (advise / wear)

_____ his best suit and tie. Kevin _____

5 (prefer / wear)　　　　　　　　　　　　6 (hate / see)

Martin buy such an expensive gift and wear fancy clothes. But Martin ignored

his advice.

B. Verbs Before Objects and Gerunds

Certain verbs that take objects can precede gerunds.

examples	notes
The waiter **heard the man hissing.** Didn't you **notice them waving?**	The object of the main verb performs the action of the *-ing* verb. The word *while* does not appear but it *could* appear: *Didn't you notice them while they were waving?*

Here are some common main verbs for the pattern **verb + object + verb-*ing*.**

find　　hear　　notice　　see　　watch

Certain verbs that can take the pattern **verb + verb-*ing*** can also appear in the pattern **verb + object + verb-*ing*.**

examples	notes
I don't **remember eating** in that restaurant.	When the main verb has no object, the "subject" of the gerund (the person or thing that performs the action) is the same as the subject of the sentence. (The example on the left means "I don't remember" + "I ate in that restaurant".)
I don't **remember John eating** in that restaurant.	This sentence means "I don't remember" + "John ate in that restaurant."

Here are some common verbs for the patterns **verb + verb-*ing*** and **verb + object + verb-*ing*:**

appreciate　　can't stand　　(don't) mind　　hate　　like　　remember

exercise 3 Write a verb phrase in the appropriate tense from the two verbs and the object in parentheses, if any. Include a gerund. The first one is done as an example.

THE DINNER PARTY (PART 2)

When Friday night arrived, Martin _____*started getting*_____
　　　　　　　　　　　　　　　　　　　　　　　　1 (start / get)
ready several hours in advance. The invitation said that the party was going

to begin at 7:30. Martin always _____ late, so he
　　　　　　　　　　　　　　　　　　　2 (avoid / be)
arrived at Keith's house at 7:15. He _____
　　　　　　　　　　　　　　　　　　　　　3 (find / Keith's girfriend / work)
in the kitchen, and he _____ a shower. After Keith
　　　　　　　　　　　4 (hear / Keith / take)
got dressed, he came to talk to Martin.

"Martin, I don't _____ me that you were

                            5 (remember / your / tell)

coming to the party early. Would you _____ me

                            6 (mind / help)

with the cooking?"

    Martin didn't want to _____ mistakes in Keith's

                            7 (risk / make)

kitchen so he _____ to his friend while Keith

                            8 (continue / talk)

worked. Martin also gave him his present.

    "Martin, I really _____ me

                            9 (appreciate / your / give)

this lovely gift, but I can't accept it. It's too much," said Keith.

    Martin felt insulted. "Please take it. I _____

                            10 (can't stand / your / refuse)

it."

    Keith _____ tears from

                            11 (notice / Martin / wipe)

his eyes with the back of his hand.

---

exercise 4   Combine each pair of ideas into one sentence with a gerund.

    example: Keith couldn't stand + Martin was talking to him in the kitchen.
                 = Keith couldn't stand Martin talking to him in the kitchen.

1. Keith couldn't stand + Martin was talking to him in the kitchen.
2. Martin saw + Keith's sister was sitting in front of the TV.
3. He enjoyed + He was watching the show with her.
4. Finally Martin heard + Other guests were arriving.
5. He noticed + They were wearing casual clothes.
6. Martin continued + He was watching TV.
7. Keith saw + Martin was watching TV.
8. Keith hated + Keith saw his friend be impolite to other guests.

---

exercise 5   Complete each sentence stem. Compare sentences with one or two classmates.

1. I can't stand people _____ .
2. Did you notice that man _____ ?
3. I don't remember _____ .
4. Her parents don't mind _____ .
5. Have you seen anyone _____ ?
6. Everyone heard the baby _____ .
7. I really appreciate you _____ .
8. I don't mind _____ .

C. Verbs Before Objects and Simple Forms of Verbs

Certain verbs with objects precede simple verb forms.

example: I'll **let** him watch TV.

Here are the most common verbs for the pattern **verb + object + verb:**

have   let   make

In general, verbs of perception that can take the pattern **verb + object + verb-*ing*** can also appear in the pattern **verb + object + verb.**

examples	notes
May I **watch** you **cook?** I **watched** them **cooking.**	The *-ing* form of the verb emphasizes the continuation of the action.

Here are the most common verbs for the patterns: **verb + object + verb** and **verb + object + verb-*ing*:**

see   watch   notice   hear

exercise 6  Write a verb phrase in the appropriate tense from the two verbs and the object in parentheses. Include the simple form of a verb or a gerund. The first one is done as an example.

THE DINNER PARTY (PART 3)

From his chair in front of the TV set, Martin <u>watched the guests socialize</u>.

1 (watch / the guests / socialize)
He waited for Keith to introduce him to his friends, but Keith was busy.

Finally a woman who _____ there spoke to him.

2 (see / Martin / sit)
"Hi _____ myself. I'm Susan. I'm Keith's cousin.

3 (let / me / introduce)
Don't you have anything to drink? I'll _____ you

4 (have / Keith / fix)
something."

Martin was very thirsty, but he wanted to be polite. "No, Susan. I don't

want to _____ me," he answered.

5 (make / Keith / serve)
"Okay," said Susan. "Anyway, it's time for dinner. Come on. I'll

_____ next to me."

6 (have / you / sit)
"Thank you," said Martin. "_____ you with your

7 (let / me / help)
chair."

"Oh, Martin, you are so old fashioned. I never _____
8 (let / men / do)
things for me that I can do myself." Martin _____ out her
9 (watch / Susan / pull)
chair in amazement. "I have a lot to learn about this culture," Martin thought.

 Reread all three parts of "The Dinner Party." Then complete these sentences with information from the story. The first one is done as an example.

Martin began _____getting ready_____ for Keith's dinner party several
1
days in advance. His roommate advised _____
2
_____ , but Martin preferred _____
3
_____. Martin was feeling nervous about the party, and he
wanted to avoid _____.
4
When he arrived at the party, he saw _____
5
and he heard _____. When he gave Keith
6
his gift, Keith said that he appreciated _____ ,
7
but that he couldn't take it.

While he was waiting for the other guests, Martin noticed _____
8
_____ , so he sat down with her. When the party started, he
noticed _____. He was feeling shy, so he
9
continued _____.
10
Finally Martin let _____. Susan had
11
_____.
12
Martin insisted on _____.
13
He was very surprised that she didn't accept his offer.

Using What You've Learned

Work in small groups. Discuss the story "The Dinner Party." Use gerunds when possible. Answer these questions.

1. What social mistakes did Martin make?
2. What mistakes might he make next?
3. What social rules do you know for dinner parties in the United States or Canada?
4. Compare these rules with customs in your countries.

example: Martin insisted on wearing his best suit. When he noticed the other guests wearing casual clothes, he felt uncomfortable.

Summarize your discussion for the class.

activity **2**

Work in pairs. Take turns reading out loud an example of an adjective-preposition and verb-particle combination from the lists below. Your partner must make up a sentence, supplying a logical gerund and completing the sentence.

example: A: good at. Hmmm. My roommate is very **good at avoiding** his turn to do the dishes.
B: famous for: George Burns is famous for smoking cigars and living to be 100.

COMMON ADJECTIVE-PREPOSITION COMBINATIONS

good at	successful in	guilty of
adequate for	content with	innocent of
enough for	careful about	jealous of
famous for	happy about	proud of
good for	afraid of	tired of
necessary for	aware of	preferable to
sorry for	capable of	similar to
suitable for	conscious of	

COMMON VERB-PARTICLE COMBINATIONS

believe in	dream about	object to
succeed in	forget about	look forward to
approve of	talk about	decide against
dream of	worry about	put off
hear of	count on	feel like
get out of	plan on	rule out
care about	work at	

Comparison and Contrast

Setting the Context
Conversation

MIRIAM: I'm so excited to be here. I love going to weddings.

SU LING: I do too. In fact, I cry at most weddings.

MIRIAM: So do I. My husband has never been able to understand that.

SU LING: Neither has mine. Sometimes I think men are from a different planet.

MIRIAM: Me too. I guess the only thing I don't really like about weddings is the champagne.

SU LING: Really? I don't either. It always gives me a headache.

MIRIAM: You know, I never realized we had so much in common.

SU LING: Neither did I.

Answer these questions about the conversation on page 251.

1. Are these people old friends or did they just meet? How do you know?
2. What do they have in common?
3. List six ways of expressing similarities.

Comparison and Contrast

There are many different ways to express similarities and differences.

	examples	notes
Similarities	Miriam is **the same as** Su Ling. Miriam is **like** Su Ling. Miriam is **similar to** Su Ling. Jenny likes weddings. + Jimmy likes weddings. = Jenny likes weddings, **and so** does Jimmy. = Jenny likes weddings, **and** Jimmy does **too**.	*And* joins two affirmative sentences. *So* comes before an auxiliary verb (*be, do, can, have,* and so on); *too* comes after the auxiliary verb. In informal conversation, similarities can be expressed like this: A: I always cry at weddings. B: **So do I.** A: I usually get a headache from drinking champagne. B: **I do too.**
	She doesn't like champagne. + They don't like champagne. = She doesn't like champagne, **and neither** do they. = She doesn't like champagne, **and** they **don't either.**	*And* joins two negative sentences. *Neither* comes before the auxiliary verb; *either* comes after the auxiliary verb. In informal conversation, similarities can be expressed like this: A: I haven't been to a party in ages. B: **Neither have I.** A: In my family, we never celebrate birthdays. B: **We don't either.**
Differences	Mary is **different from** Fred. Mary likes Birthday celebrations, **but** Fred doesn't.	*But* joins one affirmative and one negative sentence or shows a contrast.

exercise 1   Practice expressing similarities in informal converations.

example: I have always loved holidays. I have too.

1. My sister loves parties. _____

2. They have always loved cake and ice cream. _____

3. She never eats the icing. _____

4. I hate washing dishes. _____

5. I didn't go to the party last night. _____

6. He loves getting presents. _____

7. I don't really like surprise parties. _____

8. I couldn't go to my high school reunion. _____

9. He has never liked New Year's Eve parties. _____

10. I don't know how to dance. _____

11. I can't remember her name. _____

12. We really should be going. _____

13. We had a fabulous time. _____

14. I thought the food was terrific. _____

15. I didn't really have a very good time. _____

exercise 2    Work with a partner (from another country or culture if possible). Ask each other the following questions and write down your partner's answers.

1. When is your birthday?

_____

2. What is your favorite American holiday?

_____

3. What's your least favorite American holiday?

_____

4. How do you celebrate the New Year in your country?

_____

5. Do you like holidays? Why or why not?

_____

_____

6. In your family, who likes celebrating holidays the most?

_____

7. What is the most important holiday in your country?

_____

8. Do you think celebrating holidays is important? Why or why not?

_____

Now compare your information using the forms of comparison and contrast listed on page 252.

examples: Maria's birthday is in October, but mine is in April.

Maria's favorite holiday is Christmas, and so is mine.

The New Year's celebration in Maria's culture is different from New Year's in my culture.

exercise 3 This exercise reviews the grammar in this chapter. Correct the errors in these stories. Some sentences are correct.

1. A classmate invited Aziz to a bachelor party for a guy in their chemistry

class. It was a surprise party, so everyone avoided ~~to talk~~ _talking_ about it. Aziz

pictured many single men have a party with many single women, and he

worried about to go to the party alone, so he invited his sister. She wasn't

interested in go. She said she didn't enjoy meeting new people because

her English wasn't very good. Aziz knew he couldn't make her to go, but

he kept urging her, and finally she agreed. When they arrived at the party,

Aziz's sister couldn't stop stare. All the guests were men! The host laughed

and laughed.

2. Thanh was really worried about to take his final exam in economics. But

he did well on the exam, and afterward he didn't feel like go home. He

preferred to celebrate. His friend, Frank, suggested go out for some beer.

Thanh accepted and thanked Frank for inviting him. They went with three

other classmates, drank a lot, and ordered food, too. When Thanh saw everyone to contribute money to pay the check, he began worry. He didn't have a dime. He was expecting Frank to pay for everything because Frank invited everyone. So he asked Frank to let him borrowing some money. He appreciated Frank lend him the money.

3. Go to dinner parties was one of Miguel's favorite activities. In his country, Miguel used to going out every night of the week. After to be in the United States for a few months, he got tired of stay home all the time. He began going out to discotheques. One night, two women at a disco invited Miguel to dinner that weekend. He didn't wait long before accept. When the evening of the dinner arrived, Miguel was with a few friends. They left his apartment at 8:30, so Miguel went to the women's place at 9:00. They were upset. They said they were planning on starting dinner at 7:30, and now the food was ruined. Miguel apologized for that he followed the customs in his country, but he was still very embarrassed.

Using What You've Learned

activity 1 Work in small groups. Act out the situations in Exercise 3 and then discuss them. What cultural rules are important in each? Summarize your discussion for the class.

activity 2 Work in small groups with students from different cultures. Describe typical celebrations in your cultures. Discuss the similarities and differences in other cultures. Possible topics: weddings, funerals, births, birthdays, or becoming adult rituals.

example: A: In China, the bride always wears red or pink.
B: In Vietnam too.
C: In my country, brides almost always wear white.
A: Really? I was very surprised when I first saw an American bride all in white. You see, in my country, people only wear all white to a funeral.
C: We wear black to funerals, like they do in this country.
D: So do we.

activity 3 Work in pairs or small groups. Choose one situation below and prepare a short conversation. Use as many of the grammar patterns in this chapter as possible. Perform your conversation for the class.

1. It's a year later and Martin has learned all the important cultural rules for correct party behavior. He's at another party at Keith's house.
2. You are at a bachelor party or a bridal shower for your roommate. He or she has just graduated from college and is going to get married. Make toasts and congratulate your roommate.
3. At a party or holiday celebration, you have had a cultural misunderstanding with an American or person from another culture. Solve the problem.

focus on testing

Gerunds

Problems with gerunds are often found on standardized English tests.

Remember . . .

- Sometimes the *-ing* form of a verb is a gerund.
- A gerund functions as a noun and can be the object of a preposition.
- A gerund can follow a phrasal verb, or an adjective-preposition, or verb-preposition combination.

Part 1: Circle the correct completion for the following sentences.

example: People rarely get tired of _____ the congratulations and good wishes of their friends and relatives on their wedding day.
    a. hearing
    b. hear
    c. to hear
    d. heard

1. As a feminist, I believe in women _____ equal pay for equal work.
    a. earned
    b. have been earning
    c. earning
    d. earn

2. Although the children are very young, their parents let them _____ up as late as they want.
    a. staying
    b. stay
    c. stayed
    d. to stay

Part 2: Circle the letter below the underlined word(s) containing an error.

example: Many children are afraid of to sleep in the dark.
              A   B Ⓒ D

1. Get married is one of the biggest events of a person's life.
   A   B   C   D

2. A: I have never liked the taste of alcohol.
         A   B
   B: Neither do I.
        C   D

CHAPTER **eleven**

Science and Technology

The Present Perfect Tense

Setting the Context

Conversation

JULIE: Mom, I've been so worried about Kyle. All he does is play computer games.

MOM: He hasn't stopped eating and sleeping, has he?

JULIE: Very funny, Mom. This is serious. What should I do?

MOM: Okay, I'm sorry. Have you ever tried getting him interested in team sports?

JULIE: Yes, but he prefers playing computer sports games.

MOM: How about hobbies? Doesn't he collect coins from around the world?

JULIE: Well, he used to. He hasn't touched that stuff since Armando bought him his first Nintendo game.

MOM: So, what does Armando say about all this?

JULIE: How should I know? He hasn't spoken more than two words to me since he got on line!

exercise Answer these questions about the conversation.

1. Why is Julie asking her mother for advice?
2. Why does Julie's mother ask her if her son has stopped eating and sleeping?
3. Who is Armando?
4. What do Julie's husband and son have in common?
5. What do you think Julie should do?

A. Present Perfect Tense: Unspecified Past Time

The present perfect tense is used to express an unspecific past time that extends to the present. There are often no specific time markers in these sentences.

statements	examples	notes
Affirmative	I**'ve learned** a lot about computers.	The action took place in the past, but the specific past time does not appear.
Negative	We **haven't** even **had** time to set up the new system.	

questions	examples
Affirmative	**Have you seen** the new Mac 875?
Negative	**Haven't you started** balancing your checkbook electronically?

exercise 1 Underline all examples of the present perfect to express unspecified past time in the conversation.

example: Mom, <u>I've been</u> so worried about Kyle.

 **exercise 2** Write a present perfect verb in each blank. Decide which verbs should be affirmative and which should be negative. Choose from these verbs:

have give up go notice see stop try work

Today's parents _____ many changes in their children who frequently play video or computer games. Many parents say they don't like the changes they see. "He _____ outside to play in
₂
months." "My daughter _____ reading completely. She
₃
always used to have her nose in a book." "I _____ any
₄
of my son's friends in weeks. I'm not sure he still has any friends." Parents

_____ always _____ many challenges in raising their children,
₅
however—perhaps never more than today. "We _____
₆
yet, but we are frustrated," one parent told us. "Sometimes it seems like we

_____ everything. But nothing _____
₇   ₈
so we'll just keep on trying. We may just throw the darn thing away someday."

B. Unspecified Past: Time Expressions

A present perfect or present perfect continuous sentence in the unspecified past often includes a number or a frequency expression. Some time expressions appear between *have/has* and the past participle; others appear at the end of the sentence.

examples	notes
I've been on hold **for 10 minutes.**	From 10 minutes ago until now.
She's **always** loved to read.	*always* = all her life
We haven't seen him **today.**	*today* = from this morning until now
Have you **ever** played those computer games?	*ever* = at any time until now
The lab has **just** ordered new electron microscopes.	*Just* indicates the immediate past. It appears between an auxiliary and a past participle.

Interactions I • Grammar

examples	notes
Lately, we haven't been using them much. They've had a lot of bad luck **recently.**	*Recently* and *lately* indicate the past. They can appear at the beginning or end of the sentence.
She's **already** found several chromosome pairs. I haven't seen your new computer **yet.**	*Already* and *yet* mean "by this time." *Already* suggests "earlier than expected." *Already* and *yet* appear in the verb phrase or at the end of the sentence.
Haven't I told you to finish your homework before playing with the computer?	Sometimes no time frame is stated.

exercise 3 Work in pairs. Ask each other questions with these cue words. Answer with numbers or expressions of frequency.

> example: You / ever / use / a computer / ?
>
> Q: Have you ever used a computer?
> A: Sure, I've used a computer lots of times.

1. How many different kinds of computers / you / use / ?
2. You / ever / be / to a computer training class / ?
3. Which word processing programs / you / learn / ?
4. You / have / more experience with IBMs or Macs / ?
5. You / use / a computer / today / ?
6. You / ever / use / a laser printer / ?
7. How many times / you / want / to hit your computer / ?
8. How many of your friends / work / with computers / ?

exercise 4 Arrange these words into present perfect or present perfect continuous sentences, as in the example.

example: <u>I've just bought a new CD-ROM for my computer.</u>

(just / CD-ROM / a new / I buy / for my computer / .)

1. _____

(just / the professor / the grades / announce / for the last lab / .)

2. _____

(never / I / be / in a class / so frustrated / .)

3. _____

(be / a lot of / recently / There / in the lab / explosions / .)

4. _____

(already / Most of the students / the experiment / finish / .)

5. _____

(fail / lately / All of my experiments / .)

6. _____

(ask / the lab tech / yet / you / for help / ?)

7. _____

(never / to ask for help / I / in a science class / have / .)

8. _____

(never / either / have / so many disasters / You / .)

Using What You've Learned

 **activity 1** Work in pairs. Write a conversation between two parents or a parent and a child. The parents are concerned that the child has been spending too much time playing computer video games. Perform your role-play for the class.

 **activity 2** Work in small groups. Choose topics from the natural sciences and technology. Take turns talking about successes and failures (real or imagined) in that area, using the present perfect (continuous) tense and time expressions. After each round, the group votes on the "best claim." The winner tells if the claim was real or imagined. Then repeat the activity with another topic.

example: Our lab group in chemistry has made several correct hypotheses already this semester.

Each group tells the class its "best claim."

The Present Perfect (Continuous) Tense Versus the Simple Past Tense

Setting the Context

Conversation

JULIE: All right, you two. I've about had it with all the time you're spending on your computers. Our family is falling apart!

ARMANDO: Falling apart? Honey, don't you think you're exaggerating things a bit?

KYLE: Ah, Mom, come on.

JULIE: Tell me, Kyle, when was the last time you made your bed and cleaned your room?

KYLE: Ummm . . . , let's see. Last week?

JULIE: Nice try. In fact, you haven't done any of your chores all month. And you, dear, have you done the laundry lately or cooked a meal in recent memory?

ARMANDO: Okay, Julie. You're right. You have been doing all the work around the house lately. So, what's your solution?

JULIE: A two-hour time limit on computers each day, beginning after all chores are finished.

ARMANDO
AND KYLE: Two hours!!!

1. How is Julie probably feeling?
2. Why does she say their family is falling apart?
3. Who is supposed to clean Kyle's room and make his bed?
4. In fact, who has been doing those chores for the last month?
5. What do Armando and Kyle think of Julie's solution?

The Present Perfect Tense, the Present Perfect Continuous Tense, and the Simple Past Tense

The present perfect tense expresses activity at unspecified times in the past. The present perfect and present perfect continuous tenses express activity in the time period up to the present moment. The simple past tense expresses activity completed at specified past times.

	examples	notes
Present Perfect	I've **never** been there. Have you **ever** used this software? Where have you been hiding **lately**?	No time expression is necessary with the present perfect tense, but these expressions are common: *just, recently, lately, already, yet, never.*
Present Perfect Continuous	He**'s been playing** Nintendo since he was six. She**'s wanted** to be a scientist since she was little. I**'ve been studying** English for years.	Here are examples of time expressions for past time up to the present moment: *so far, up to now, for years, in a long time, this year.* A *since*-clause is common with the present perfect continuous.
Simple Past	I saw her **last week**. Did you go to class **yesterday**? I played real baseball **when I was a kid**.	Here are examples of specific past times: *last night, two hours ago, in 1983.* A *when*-clause is also common with the simple past.

exercise ▮ ▾   Complete the sentences with the present perfect, present perfect continuous, or simple past form of each verb in parentheses. The first one is done as an example.

SAL: Chris, how are you? I _____haven't seen_____ you in ages! What
    1 (not see)
_____ you _____ this semester?
    2   3 (do)

CHRIS: Well, I _____ a lot of time in the science labs.
                4 (spend)

SAL: Labs? Are you taking more than one science class?

CHRIS: Oh, of course. I'm a pre-med student.

SAL: Really? How long _____ you _____
                        5   6 (be)
interested in medicine?

CHRIS: Oh, for ages. I _____ to be a doctor ever since I
                        7 (want)
_____ a kid. My parents never _____ a girl
    8 (be)   9 (say)
_____ be a doctor. In fact, they _____ always
    10 (can't)   11
_____ me to follow my passion. So, here I am.
    12 (encourage)

SAL: That's great. I _____ always _____ pre-med
                        13   14 (admired)
students. That's a rough program.

CHRIS: It really is. Last semester I _____ human anatomy, biology, and
                                    15 (take)
genetics. This semester is even worse!

SAL: Wow, I bet you _____ really hard all year. That's prob-
                        16 (work)
ably why I _____ you at any parties or football games.
            17 (not see)

CHRIS: Gosh, I _____ to a party since last year. I really
                18 (not be)
_____ too hard. Let me ask you something. When
    19 (work)
_____ the last time a girl _____ you out for
    20 (be)   21 (ask)
a date?

SAL: I don't think a girl _____ ever _____ me out.
                            22   23   (ask)

CHRIS: Well, good. That puts us in the same boat because I

_____ never _____ a guy out. But
    24   25 (ask)
I _____ just _____ to change that.
    26   27 (decide)
By the way, you and Denise _____ last Christmas,
                                28 (break up)
didn't you?

SAL: Yes.

CHRIS: So, will you go out dancing with me next Friday?

SAL: You bet I will. Wait until I tell my mom I'm going out with a doctor!

 Complete each sentence with true information about yourself.

1. My family has never _____.

2. I haven't _____ in ages.

3. When I first came to this school, I _____.

4. My friends have just _____.

5. I've always_____.

6. I have been _____ ever since I _____.

7. I haven't _____ for a long time.

8. One of my teachers has been _____ recently.

9. Have you ever _____?

10. When I was _____, I _____.

11. My roommates have already _____.

12. Has she _____ yet?

Using What You've Learned

activity 1

Work in small groups. Choose one sentence above and say it to your group. The next student repeats the first sentence and adds her or his example of that sentence. The last person says all other sentences before adding her or his own. Start again with another sentence.

examples: A: I haven't been to the movies in a long time.

B: Gina hasn't been to the movies in a long time. I haven't done my laundry for a long time.

C: Gina hasn't been to the movies in a long time. Fred hasn't done his laundry for a long time. I haven't called my parents in a long time.

activity 2

Work in pairs. Write a conversation between two school friends. In the conversation, the friends first make small talk and find out what each has been doing lately. Then one asks the other out for a date. Practice your role-play and perform it for the class.

Superlative Forms

Setting the Context

Conversation

JULIE: Hey, guys, come here. I've got the greatest surprise for you.

ARMANDO: I hope it's nothing like your last surprise.

KYLE: What is it, Mom?

JULIE: It's a book about the most important scientific inventions and technological advances in history.

KYLE: Can I see it?

JULIE: Sure. Look in the beginning and tell us what some of the most interesting inventions were.

KYLE: Okay. Well, one of the oldest listed is the flush toilet. It was invented
in 1589. I wonder what people used before that . . . Wow, listen to this.
The word processor was invented in 1965 by IBM. That was before I
was born! Hey, check this out . . .

ARMANDO: *(whispering to Julie)* You are the most amazing woman I've ever met.
You've got him reading for fun!

exercise Answer these questions about the conversation.

1. Why do you think Julie bought the book?
2. Why do you think Armando tells Julie she's the most amazing woman he's
   ever met?
3. What did Armando mean when he said he hoped this surprise was nothing
   like Julie's last one?

Superlative Forms

The superlative form of an adjective or adverb expresses the difference between a noun and a group of nouns (two or more).

examples	notes
It's **the latest** personal computer from IBM. Which word processing program is **the easiest**?	A superlative form usually ends in *-est* or follows the words *the most*. It always has the marker *the.* For spelling rules for superlative forms, see below.
What is **the most popular** video game of all? Who finished **most quickly**? She's **the most intelligent** person I've ever met.	Most words with more than one syllable form the superlative with ***most* + adjective** or **adverb.** Do not use *-est* endings with *most.*
Which company has sold **the most PCs**? Which program takes **the least time** to learn?	*Most* and *least* indicate amounts. These words usually appear before nouns.
That was **the best** meal I've ever eaten. That was one of **the worst** movies I've ever seen.	Irregular superlative forms include: good/best, well, bad(ly)/worst, far/farthest, little/least, much/most.

Spelling Rules for Adjective/Adverb + *-est*

1. For most one-syllable words, add *-est.*

   examples: fast / fastest   tall / tallest   long / longest

   When the last letter is *-e,* add only *-st.*

   examples: nice / nicest   large / largest

2. For two-syllable words ending in *-y,* change the *-y* to *i* and add *-est.*

   examples: crazy / craziest   easy / easiest

3. If the word ends in a single consonant after a single vowel, double the last consonant and add *-est.*

   examples: big / biggest   thin / thinnest

example: I've got <u>the greatest</u> surprise for you.

exercise 2 Fill in the blanks with your opinions about the information in the box below.

YEAR	INVENTION OR ADVANCE	INVENTOR OR ORIGIN
1285	eyeglasses	Alessandra de Spina
1589	flush toilet	Sir John Harington
1718	machine gun	James Puckle
1798	mass production	Eli Whitney
1827	microphone	Charles Wheatstone
1837	electric motor	Thomas Davenport
1850	refrigerator	James Harrison / Alex Twining
1890	motion pictures	William Friese-Greene
1902	air conditioning	Willis H. Carriet
1923	frozen food	Clarence Birdseye
1928	color television	Jon Logie Baird
1940	radar	Robert M. Page
1958	laser	Charles A. Townes
1960	weather satellite	NASA, United States
1973	microcomputer	Trong Troung

example: The most important invention listed is _____ *the laser* _____.

1. The most recent invention listed is _____.

2. The oldest invention listed is _____.

3. The most unusual invention listed is _____.

4. The silliest invention listed is _____.

5. The best invention listed is _____.

6. The worst invention listed is _____.

7. The invention of most service to humankind is _____.

8. The invention of least service to humankind is _____.

9. The most important invention for women listed is _____.

10. The most important invention for men listed is _____.

11. The most important invention for children listed is _____.

12. The most surprising invention for its day is _____.

exercise 3 Describe the information in the box on page 271 using superlatives. You can use the following adjectives and adverbs or use your own ideas:

amazing	ordinary
dangerous	ridiculous
expensive	significant
important	strange
interesting	tiny

example: The most amazing invention listed is the weather satellite.

1. _____

2. _____

3. _____

4. _____

5. _____

6. _____

7. _____

8. _____

9. _____

10. _____

Using What You've Learned

activity 1

Work in small groups. Take turns sharing your opinions from Exercises 2 and 3. Support your opinion with logical arguments. Practice disagreeing politely with others' opinions.

example: A: In my opinion, the most important invention of all those listed is the laser.

B: Why do you say that?

A: The advances made in medical science with laser surgery, laser skin treatments, and laser X rays for diagnosis have improved people's lives directly.

C: I see your point, but I don't agree. To me, the most significant invention on the list is the . . .

Summarize your discussion for the class.

The biggest memory in a computer can hold over 5 billion bytes of information.

The earliest computers were extremely expensive and huge.

The longest surgery ever performed lasted 37 hours.

The most famous scientist in history is Albert Einstein.

One of the most expensive medical procedures frequently performed is open heart surgery.

activity 2

Work in small groups. If possible, use reference books for this activity. List ten superlative facts about scientific discoveries or technological advancements, real and imaginary.

example: The longest surgery ever performed lasted 37 hours.

Each group in turn reads aloud one of their sentences. The class tries to guess whether the information is true or false.

Variation: Each group prepares ten questions about superlative facts or opinions.

example: Who is the most famous scientist alive today?

Each group in turn reads aloud a question. The class tries to answer it.

activity 3

Cross out the errors in the reading and write the corrections above them. Some sentences are correct. No sentence has more than one error.

In the history of inventions list included in this chapter, the ~~most~~ earliest inventions were the simplest. For example, in 1285, Alessandra de Spina has invented eyeglasses. Another simple but very important invention was the flush toilet. It has been invented in 1589 by Sir John Harington.

In 1850, two men have been working together to invent a machine that changed the way modern families ate, the refrigerator. Approximately 75 years later, Clarence Birdseye revolutionized cooking again when he has introduced frozen food to the modern world. Since the early 20s, food manufacturers have been worked hard to find new foods to offer in frozen form.

The entertainment industry has also seeing great changes in technology. First, back in 1827, Charles Wheatstone invented the microphone. Ever since, singers have been sung to audiences of hundreds and thousands in enormous stadiums. However, microphones were no longer new when motion pictures have arrived in 1890. The movies made it possible for people all over the world to see the popularest stars at affordable prices. In the United States, going to the movies on Saturday afternoon or evening with your sweetheart has been becoming a tradition. More recently, videogames and compact disk players have become essential parts of many families' home entertainment equipment.

Other more recent inventions include some of the most complex and useful objects humans have inventing, such as weather satellites, the artificial heart, and the laser. Naturally, not all inventions can be extremely significant. Years from now, we may not remember that someone has created the pet rock, lamps that turn on when you clap, and misting systems for patio cooling. However, from the most significant to the most silly, there seems to be no limit to the creative genius that drives inventors to create something absolutely new.

Present Perfect Continuous Tense and Superlatives

Problems with the present perfect continuous tense and superlative forms are often found on standardized English tests.

Remember . . .

- The present perfect continuous tense expresses activity in the time period up to and including the present moment.
- To form the superlative, use **the** + **adjective** + **-est** for one-syllable words; use **the most** + **adjective** for words of more than one syllable.
- Do not use *-est* endings with *most*.

Part 1: Circle the correct completion for the following sentences.

example: I've _____ so hard lately that I haven't even had time to complain.
- **a.** work
- **b.** working
- **c.** been work
- **d.** been working ⟵circled

1. He _____ soccer ever since he could walk.
- **a.** has play
- **b.** has been played
- **c.** has been playing
- **d.** has playing

2. My grandmother is one of the _____ people I've ever met.
- **a.** most interesting
- **b.** most interestingest
- **c.** interestingest
- **d.** interesting

Part 2: Circle the letter below the underlined word(s) containing an error.

example: He's been teaching at this university since twenty years.
   A   B   C   D⟵circled

1. Recently, all my friends have been gotten married.
   A   B   C   D

2. My sister's high school basketball team played very well lately.
   A   B   C   D

You, the Consumer

in this chapter

Review of Tenses

Setting the Context
Predictions

Work with a partner. Together make up some predictions about the picture above.

1. What is the problem?
2. Who did the young man call?
3. What are they saying to each other?
4. Why is the young man holding a guarantee?
5. What will he do when he gets off the phone?
6. What does his apartment smell like?
7. How does the young man feel?
8. Has something like this ever happened to you? Tell your partner about it.

exercise

Join another pair of students. Share and compare your predictions. Report the most interesting similarities and differences to the class.

> **example:** We all thought that the young man's refrigerator broke down. But two of us thought he made it worse while trying to fix it.

A. Simple Forms

Most verb phrases appear in the time frame of the past, the present, the present perfect, or the future. Here are the simple forms of each tense.

	examples	notes
Past	I **bought** a refrigerator a few months ago. **Did** you **do** anything to it?	The simple past tense expresses activity completed in the past.
Imperative	**Come** quickly! **Don't wait** any longer.	Orders and directions use the simple forms of verbs.
Present	I **have** a problem. Repairs **are** expensive, **aren't** they? The fridge **smells** terrible. We often **get** calls like this, **don't** we?	The simple present tense expresses facts, habits, repeated action, or emotions, perceptions, and conditions (nonaction verbs).
Present Perfect	I've **called** them twice. The fridge **has broken down**. It's **been** out of order for a week. You **haven't had** any food all this time, have you?	The present perfect tense expresses activity completed at unspecified past times or situations (usually with nonaction verbs) in the time period up to the present.
Future: going to, will	What **are** they **going to do**? What **will** they **do**? The food **is going to spoil, isn't** it? The food **will spoil, won't** it?	The future expresses activity that will begin after the present time.
Modal Verbs	They **couldn't go** yesterday. We **can't come** out now, **can** we? I'll **tell** the manager right away. He **may come** next week.	A simple modal verb phrase (**modal** + **verb**) may refer to past, present, or future activity.

exercise 1 Study the chart on page 279. Create an example sentence of your own similar to the twenty examples in the chart.

    example: My roommate got a job a couple of weeks ago.

exercise 2 Complete these sentences with the correct form (simple, simple present, simple past, future, or present perfect) of the verb in parentheses. There might be more than one correct answer. Complete the short answers and the tag questions. The first two are done as examples.

MELISSA: Ugh! Something _____smells_____ terrible in here! What
                                1 (smell)
    _____happened_____ ?
        2 (happen)

ANDY: The refrigerator _____ down last night, and all the food
                        3 (break)
    _____ .
       4 (spoil)

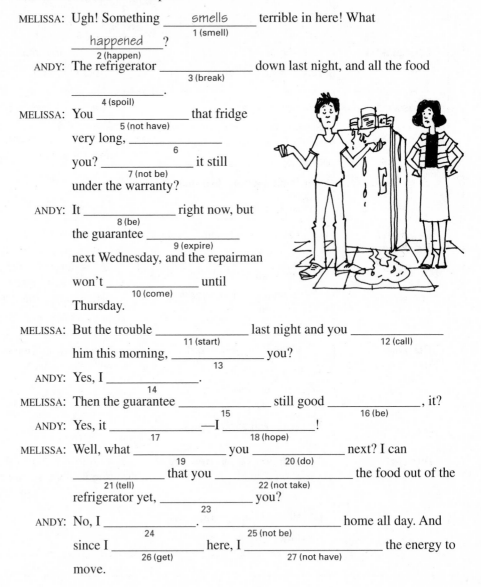

MELISSA: You _____ that fridge
           5 (not have)
    very long, _____
                6
    you? _____ it still
          7 (not be)
    under the warranty?

ANDY: It _____ right now, but
          8 (be)
    the guarantee _____
               9 (expire)
    next Wednesday, and the repairman
    won't _____ until
          10 (come)
    Thursday.

MELISSA: But the trouble _____ last night and you _____
                  11 (start)   12 (call)
    him this morning, _____ you?
                      13

ANDY: Yes, I _____ .
          14

MELISSA: Then the guarantee _____ still good _____ , it?
                      15   16 (be)

ANDY: Yes, it _____ —I _____ !
              17   18 (hope)

MELISSA: Well, what _____ you _____ next? I can
                  19   20 (do)
    _____ that you _____ the food out of the
       21 (tell)   22 (not take)
    refrigerator yet, _____ you?
                    23

ANDY: No, I _____ . _____ home all day. And
          24   25 (not be)
    since I _____ here, I _____ the energy to
        26 (get)   27 (not have)
    move.

MELISSA: Why? Where _____ you _____ all this time?
28   29 (be)

ANDY: Well, first I _____ to a supermarket, then I _____
30 (go)   31 (try)

a department store, then . . .

MELISSA: You _____, when the refrigerator _____, you
32 (mean)   33 (break)

_____ shopping? Why? What _____ you
34 (go)   35

_____?
36 (buy)

ANDY: Nothing! The clerk at the appliance store _____ me to buy
37 (advise)

an ice chest, but I couldn't _____ one in the middle of
38 (find)

January!

MELISSA: Poor boy! You _____ some help now, _____
39 (need)   40

you?

ANDY: Yes!

B. Continuous Forms

Continuous verb forms emphasize duration (continuation) of action. Only action verbs can appear in continuous verb phrases.

	examples	notes
Present Continuous	The food **is rotting.** What **are** you **doing** now? It **isn't working,** is it? He**'s coming** next week.	The present continuous expresses action at the present time and future plans.
Past Continuous	It **was working** fine yesterday, wasn't it? What **were** you **doing** at the time?	The past continuous expresses past action, usually around a specific past time.
Present Perfect Continuous	I**'ve been having** problems with it for a long time. How long **have** you **been using** it?	The present perfect continuous expresses duration of action from a past time up to the present.

Complete these sentences with the appropriate continuous verb forms (past, present, or present perfect). There may be more than one correct answer. Complete the short answers and tag questions. The first two are done as examples.

(Andy's mother calls him on the phone.)

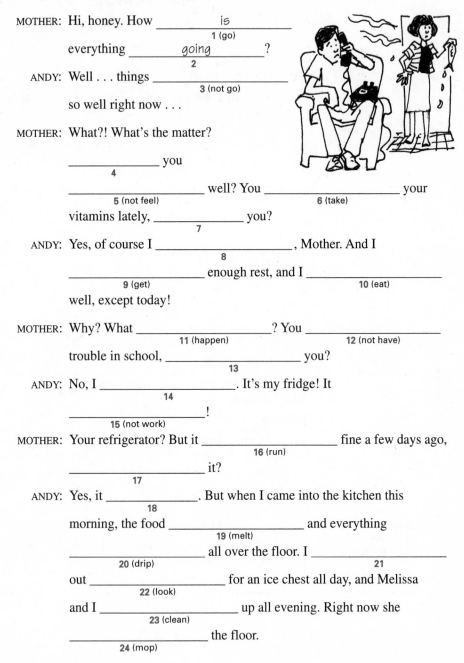

MOTHER: Hi, honey. How _____is_____ everything _____going_____?
1 (go)   2

ANDY: Well . . . things _____ so well right now . . .
3 (not go)

MOTHER: What?! What's the matter?

_____ you
4

_____ well? You _____ your
5 (not feel)   6 (take)

vitamins lately, _____ you?
7

ANDY: Yes, of course I _____ , Mother. And I
8

_____ enough rest, and I _____
9 (get)   10 (eat)

well, except today!

MOTHER: Why? What _____? You _____
11 (happen)   12 (not have)

trouble in school, _____ you?
13

ANDY: No, I _____. It's my fridge! It
14

_____!
15 (not work)

MOTHER: Your refrigerator? But it _____ fine a few days ago,
16 (run)

_____ it?
17

ANDY: Yes, it _____. But when I came into the kitchen this
18

morning, the food _____ and everything
19 (melt)

_____ all over the floor. I _____
20 (drip)   21

out _____ for an ice chest all day, and Melissa
22 (look)

and I _____ up all evening. Right now she
23 (clean)

_____ the floor.
24 (mop)

MOTHER: Melissa? _____ you still _____ out with her?
₂₅   _{26 (go)}

You two _____ serious, _____ you?
_{27 (not get)}   ₂₈

_____ you _____ anyone else?
₂₉   _{30 (not date)}

ANDY: Mother, I thought we _____ about the refrigerator!
_{31 (talk)}

MOTHER: So, you _____ serious!
_{32 (get)}

C. Time Expressions

Here are examples of time expressions common for present, past, future, and general time (time that is unspecified or nonspecific).

	examples	**notes**
Past	yesterday, the day before yesterday, an hour ago, last week, in 1967	Past time expressions with *last* do not include *the*.
Present	(right) now, at this moment, at present, this week, nowadays, these days	Present time expressions refer to the present moment or the temporary time period around it.
Future	tomorrow, the day after tomorrow, next week, in a few days, a year from now	Future time expressions with *next* do not include *the*. *In* has the same meaning as *from now*.
Past to Present (Present Perfect)	up until now, so far, in the last week, since Wednesday, since I got up	The word *since* may begin a phrase or a clause.
General (Unspecified)	every day, once a week, now and then, often, sometimes, never, for a long time, then, next, after that	Time expressions of frequency, duration, sequencing, and so on can appear with different tense forms.

exercise 4 Complete the sentences with the appropriate tense form (simple, past, present, present perfect, or future tense, simple or continuous) of the verbs in parentheses. Several answers may be correct. Complete the short answers and tag questions. The first one is done as an example.

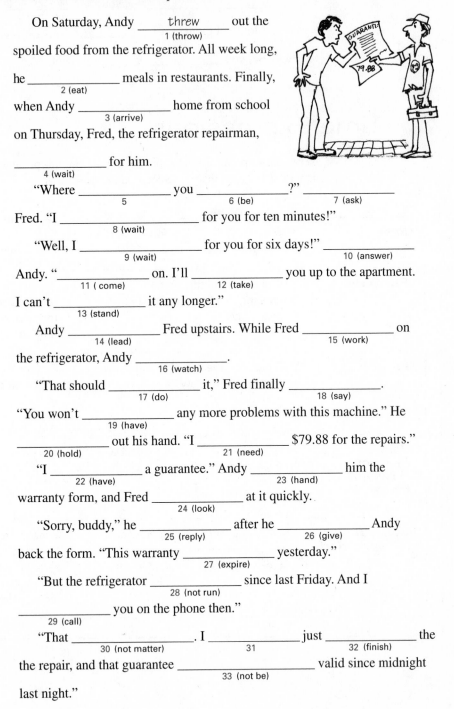

On Saturday, Andy ___*threw*___ out the
        1 (throw)

spoiled food from the refrigerator. All week long,

he _____ meals in restaurants. Finally,
    2 (eat)

when Andy _____ home from school
      3 (arrive)

on Thursday, Fred, the refrigerator repairman,

_____ for him.
   4 (wait)

"Where _____ you _____?" _____
        5   6 (be)   7 (ask)

Fred. "I _____ for you for ten minutes!"
     8 (wait)

"Well, I _____ for you for six days!" _____
      9 (wait)   10 (answer)

Andy. "_____ on. I'll _____ you up to the apartment.
    11 (come)   12 (take)

I can't _____ it any longer."
     13 (stand)

Andy _____ Fred upstairs. While Fred _____ on
      14 (lead)   15 (work)

the refrigerator, Andy _____.
        16 (watch)

"That should _____ it," Fred finally _____.
       17 (do)   18 (say)

"You won't _____ any more problems with this machine." He
      19 (have)

_____ out his hand. "I _____ $79.88 for the repairs."
   20 (hold)   21 (need)

"I _____ a guarantee." Andy _____ him the
      22 (have)   23 (hand)

warranty form, and Fred _____ at it quickly.
        24 (look)

"Sorry, buddy," he _____ after he _____ Andy
       25 (reply)   26 (give)

back the form. "This warranty _____ yesterday."
        27 (expire)

"But the refrigerator _____ since last Friday. And I
        28 (not run)

_____ you on the phone then."
   29 (call)

"That _____. I _____ just _____ the
      30 (not matter)   31   32 (finish)

the repair, and that guarantee _____ valid since midnight
        33 (not be)

last night."

Andy _____ to get angry. "I _____ a refrigerator
      34 (begin)   35 (not have)

for the last six days. I _____ out all week because I couldn't
                              36 (eat)

_____ any food in the house. And now you _____ me
      37 (keep)   38 (tell)

that the guarantee _____ good any more. I _____ a
                          39 (not be)   40 (have)

guarantee, and I _____!"
                      41 (not pay)

      "Well, then, I _____ to the store manager. We'll _____
                          42 (talk)   43 (see)

about this . . ." _____ Fred as he _____ the apartment.
                        44 (shout)   45 (leave)

      "You _____ darn right we _____ about this!", Andy
                  46 (be)   47 (see)

_____. "We _____ that I _____."
      48 (reply)   49 (see)   50 (not pay)

"_____ you in court!"
      51 (see)

Using What You've Learned

activity 1   Work in pairs. Take turns reading out loud examples of time expressions from the
chart on page 283. Your partner must make up a sentence, supplying the correct
verb and using the time expression. There are enough sentences for twelve turns
each.

> **example:**   A: for a long time
>   B: Hmmm. I have been studying English grammar *for a long time*.
>   A: Good. Now you pick one for me.

activity 2   Work in pairs. Imagine a conversation between Fred and the store manager, and
then a telephone conversation between Andy and the manager. Role-play the conversation from Exercise 4 between Andy and Fred and your imaginary conversations. Use as many different verb tenses as possible. Try to solve the problem.
Then tell your solution, or summarize your conversations, for the class.

activity 3   Work in small groups. Discuss the answers to these questions, using as many verb
tenses as possible.

   1. Have you had any problems with products that broke drown?
   2. What happened?
   3. What did you do about the problems?
   4. Were you satisfied with the results? Why or why not?
   5. Are you having any consumer trouble now? What are you going to do?

Choose the most interesting problem and prepare a role-play for the class. The
class discusses it.

Summary of Phrasal Verbs

FRED   ANDY

Setting the Context

Class Discussion

Answer these questions about the picture.

1. What is this place?
2. Who showed up here?
3. Why aren't they getting along?
4. Who is the judge listening to?
5. What is he trying to find out?
6. What is the judge looking over?
7. What is he going to decide? Do you agree with that decision? Why or why not?
8. How would this situation be different if it were happening in your country?

exercise   Work in pairs. Write a story or a dialogue. Use as many verbs from the phrasal verbs chart on page 287 as possible. Present your story or dialogue to the class.

> **example:**   A: Thanks for stopping, mister.
> B: Looks like your car *broke down*. What seems to be the trouble?
> A: To tell you the truth I can't quite *figure it out*. I've *listened to* the engine, checked the battery and *looked over* all the hoses. Everything seems to be fine.

A. Phrasal Verbs

Phrasal verbs consist of a verb with at least one other short word. Some combinations take an object, and some do not.

	examples	notes
No Object	He **hasn't come** back. When **will** you **move out** (of your house)?	A phrasal verb can appear before a prepositional phrase.
Object: Inseparable	A driver **ran into** my car. This doesn't **look like** my furniture.	In inseparable phrases, the preposition always appears right after the verb and before the object.
Separable	I **picked out** furniture. = I **picked** furniture **out**. Don't **give up** the fight. = Don't **give** it **up**.	In separable phrases, the particle can come before or after the object. If the object is a pronoun, the particle must come after it.

Here are common examples of phrasal verbs. Some phrases belong in more than one list. A phrase with the preposition in parentheses may follow some items.

take no object	take an object	
Inseparable	**Inseparable**	**Separable**
break down	decide on	call back look up
come back	listen to	call up move out
come over	look into	check out pick out
come up	look for	drop off pick up
get along (with)	look like	figure out put off
get together	run into	fill out take out
give up		find out throw out
look out (for)		get together turn down
move out		give back turn in
run out (of)		give up write down
show up		leave out write out
		look over

exercise 1 Fill in the missing verbs in the correct tenses, as in the example, using the words in the list. Some of the words will be used more than once. The first one has been done as an example.

break	clean	look	show
call	come	put	take
check	find	run	wake

Andy has been having a terrible week. One morning, he ___woke___ up to
                1

a real mess in his kitchen. During the night the refrigerator _____
                          2

down. By the next morning, all the food was starting to rot and melt. Andy

_____ up the repairman immediately only to _____
   3   4

out that he couldn't _____ out the refrigerator until the following
            5

Thursday. To make matters worse, the refrigerator's guarantee was supposed to

_____ out that Wednesday. That morning, Andy _____
   6   7

off _____ out all the rotting food until he _____ back
     8   9

from _____ for an ice chest. Unfortunately, in the middle of January
     10

there were no ice chests for sale anywhere. But Andy did have some good

luck that day. Shortly after he _____ back from the unsuccessful
            11

shopping trip, his good friend Melissa _____ up to help him
                12

_____ up the smelly mess.
  13

B. Meanings

Some phrasal verbs have literal meanings; you can figure out the meaning from the words. Others, however, are idioms; the combinations have special meanings.

	examples	notes
Literal Meaning	When are you going to **come back**? I'm **looking for** a good lawyer.	come back = return look for = want to find
Idioms	Why don't you **come over**? We don't **get along** very well. Don't **bring up** that subject. Did they **call** the trial **off**? No, but they **put** it **off**.	come over = visit get along = have a good relationship bring up = mention call off = cancel put off = postpone

Do you know the meanings of the phrasal verbs in the lists on pages 287 and 288? If not, look them up. Use them in sentences and discuss the meanings of the idioms.

 Fill in the blanks with the words below, as in the example. Some of the words appear several times.

along   down   into   out   over   up

It is always best to get ____along____ with the people you do business
                              1

with and to look _____ for bad deals or fraud. If you do run
                      2

_____ a problem, however, you might want to look _____
        3   4

the possibility of taking the case to Small Claims Court.

Filing a suit in Small Claims Court is easy. First, look _____ the
                                                                5

address and telephone number of the municipal court in your area. When

you call them _____, ask for the Small Claims Office and find
                    6

_____ the office hours.
        7

When you go to the Small Claims Office, you fill _____
                                                            8

a simple application. Be sure that you don't leave any information

_____. When you finish, you will probably have to wait in line to
        9

turn your application _____ to one of the clerks. He will look it
                            10

_____ and give you a court date. Be sure to write it _____
        11   12

so that you don't forget it or show _____ on the wrong day. Good
                                          13

luck in court!

Answer these questions about the paragraphs in Exercise 3. Use a phrasal verb in each sentence of your answer.

1. In what situation might you want to go to Small Claims Court?
2. How do you locate the Small Claims Office in your area?
3. What will you have to do in the office?
4. What will the clerk do?
5. What should you do before you leave? Why?

exercise 5   Fill in the blanks with the phrasal verbs below, as in the example. Include the object in parentheses, if there is one.

call up	get together	show up
decide on	leave out	talk over
drop off	listen to	write down
fill out	look into	

After you ___fill out the appropriate forms___ in the Small Claims
                    1 (the appropriate forms)
Office, the court will serve the papers; in other words an official will

_____ at the home or workplace of the
                2 (them)
defendant. Perhaps the defendant will _____
                                              3 (you)
on the telephone or ask to _____ with you to
                                        4

_____. Then perhaps you can settle
            5 (the problem)
the case out of court. If this does not happen, however, you should

_____ of the case. Your list of facts
            6 (the important facts)
should be complete; be sure not to _____.
                                            7 (anything)

If the defendant does not _____ for the trial,
                                      8

you will win the case automatically. If he or she does appear, however, the

judge will _____. After you, the defendant, and
                  9 (your stories)
witnesses have presented your evidence and told your points of view, the judge

will _____. If you are unhappy with the verdict,
          10 (a verdict)
you can look into the possibility of hiring a lawyer to sue for damages.

Using What You've Learned

activity 1   Work in small groups. Create a story with the phrasal verbs in the lists on pages 287 and 288. The first student begins the story. As soon as he or she uses one phrase correctly, the second student continues the story, and so on. End the story after about five minutes. Then summarize it for the class.

example: Jack woke up suddenly to the sound of loud music.
"Turn the music down!" he shouted to his son.
"We should throw out that CD player," his wife said.

 Work in groups of three. Take the roles of the people in the picture at the beginning of Topic Two (the plaintiff, Andy; the witness, Melissa; and the defendant, Fred). Prepare your cases. Then choose a judge from the class and act out a trial. The class discusses the verdict.

Variation: Prepare and act out a case on a real or imaginary problem.

TOPIC **three**

Review of Infinitives and Gerunds; Verb Complements

Setting the Context
Class Discussion

Discuss the following ideas.

1. What are the advantages and disadvantages of buying on credit?
2. How do people buy things who don't like or don't have credit? What are the advantages and disadvantages of buying this way?
3. Middle-aged Americans have more personal debt and less personal savings than any generation before them. What are some of the possible causes of this change? What are some of the possible results?
4. How do people buy things in your country? How does this compare to the way people buy things in this country?
5. What personal experiences have you, your family, or friends had in the area of saving money, buying things, and credit?

Answer these questions about the picture on page 291.

1. What kind of store is this? What do they sell?
2. Name and describe the items in the store.
3. What do the signs mean? Do you believe them? Why or why not?
4. Describe the people. How do they look, and how are they probably feeling?
5. Would you like to shop here? Why or why not?

A. Infinitives and Gerunds

Infinitives (*to* + **verb**) and gerunds (**verb**-*ing*) can appear in various positions in a sentence.

examples		notes
Infinitives We agreed **to buy** a dining room set. The salesclerks advised us **to buy** on credit.	**Gerunds** I suggest **buying** on credit. They saw the children **playing**.	Both infinitives and gerunds can appear after verbs; sometimes the main verb takes an object.
It's not difficult **to qualify** for credit.	**Qualifying** for credit isn't difficult.	Both infinitives and gerunds can be subjects; a sentence with an infinitive subject usually includes the impersonal *it*.
The salesclerks are eager **to sell** furniture. Which is the best couch **to buy**?	You can save money by **paying** cash. Think about **buying** on time. We're interested in **choosing** a mattress.	Infinitives can appear after adjectives or nouns. Gerunds can appear after prepositions, which often appear in phrases with verbs or adjectives.
You can use your credit card **to make** a purchase.		An infinitive phrase can express purpose.

exercise Complete these sentences with the infinitive or gerund form of each verb in parentheses. The first one is done as an example.

(Leo, Marie, and their son Scott are on their way home after a dinner party at the home of Dan and Ruth.)

Interactions I • Grammar

LEO: Well, I certainly enjoyed ___seeing___
1 (see)
Dan and Ruth again. The food was delicious,
and they were really excited about

_____ that new dining room set.
2 (get)

MARIE: Well, at least Ruth was. I think that Dan only
agreed _____ the set because he
3 (take)
was tired of _____.
4 (shop)

LEO: Maybe. But Ruth said the deal was too good _____. The
5 (resist)
salesclerk suggested _____ a credit agreement, so they need
6 (sign)
_____ only $35 a month.
7 (pay)

MARIE: I know that Ruth was eager _____ his advice, but I'm afraid
8 (take)
that Dan wasn't.

SCOTT: Why? _____ on credit is a good idea, isn't it? You can get more
9 (buy)
things by _____ monthly payments, can't you?
10 (make)

MARIE: Yes, but _____ finance plans costs a lot more than
11 (use)
_____ cash.
12 (pay)

LEO: Right. Stores want customers _____ on _____
13 (agree)   14 (finance)
because it's easier for them _____ more money that way.
15 (make)
There's a monthly finance charge _____.
16 (pay)

SCOTT: Oh. But you like _____ credit cards, don't you? Isn't it more
17 (use)
convenient and safer _____ cards than money?
18 (carry)

LEO: Yes, it is. But you ought _____ your bills as soon as possible.
19 (pay)
That way, the bank doesn't keep _____ interest.
20 (charge)

MARIE: Exactly. It's dangerous _____ too many purchases on a credit
21 (put)
card if you can't afford _____ for everything right away. I don't
22 (pay)
like to see people _____ into debt that way.
23 (get)

LEO: Me neither. I'm glad we've decided _____ our money before
24 (save)
_____ expensive things instead of _____ on credit.
25 (purchase)   26 (buy)

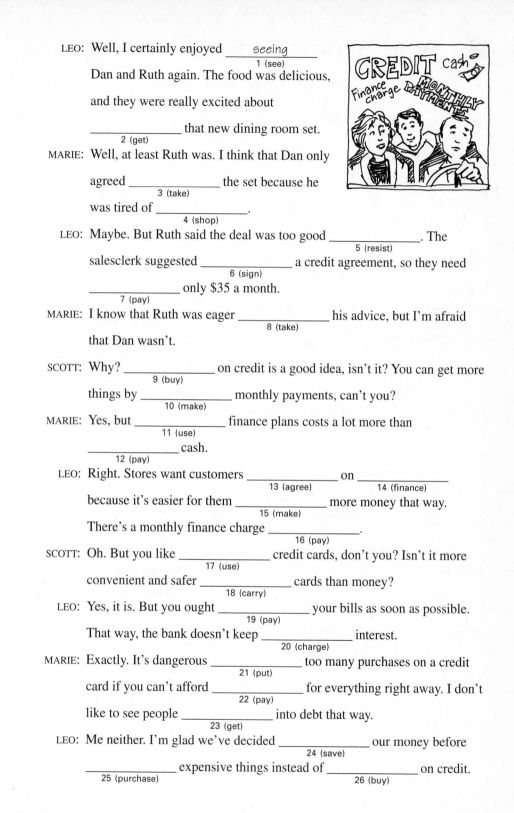

B. Verb Complements

Certain verbs can appear in various patterns with complements.

	examples	notes
Verb + to + Verb	What have you **decided to buy?**	
Verb + Object + to + Verb	The clerk **advised us to charge** our purchases.	Most verbs for this pattern are verbs indicating speech (*tell, warn,* and so on).
Verb + Verb-ing	I **suggest paying** cash as often as possible.	
Verb + Object + Verb-ing	We **appreciated his giving** us advice. He **saw us discussing** our decisions.	A possessive form often comes before a gerund. Many verbs for this pattern are verbs of perception (*hear, see, smell,* and so on).
Verb + Object + Verb	I won't **let you get** into debt. What did you **hear them say?**	The verbs *have, let,* and *make* follow this pattern. Other verbs for this pattern refer to perception.

Here are examples of common verbs for patterns with complements. (More complete lists are on pages 196, 244, 246 and 248.)

verb + to + verb

like	have	decide	continue
want	try	begin	ought
need	plan	remember	

verb + object + to + verb

like	advise	order	persuade
want	allow	teach	promise
need	force	tell	

verb + verb-*ing*

like	hate	suggest	try
enjoy	begin	advise	remember
prefer	stop	continue	

verb + object + verb-*ing*

see	hear	hate	(don't) mind
watch	find	remember	can't stand
notice	like	appreciate	

verb + object + verb

have	make	watch	hear
let	see	notice	

exercise  What experiences have you had with money, credit, and consumerism? What are your habits and opinions? Complete these sentences with verb complements, adding objects if necessary. (There are many possible answers.)

examples: I've always *tried to pay my bills right away* _____.

I don't let my *children use my credit cards* _____.

1. I've always tried _____.

2. I usually advise my _____.

3. I've often suggested _____.

4. I don't let my _____.

5. I've decided _____.

6. I often promise _____,

but then I can't stop _____.

7. I don't like to see _____.

8. My _____ sometimes tell(s) me _____

_____.

9. He / She / They hate _____.

10. My _____ likes _____ but I prefer _____

_____.

11. More people ought _____.

12. If I have children, I'll teach them _____.

13. I plan to continue _____.

14. My parents (never) forced me _____.

15. Most people prefer _____.

16. Some people can't stand _____.

17. More people need _____.

18. Too many parents let _____.

19. I hate _____.

20. We must begin _____.

Using What You've Learned

activity 1

Work in small groups. The first student reads aloud his or her first sentence from Exercise 1. The next student repeats the sentence and then adds a new sentence. The next student repeats the second sentence, adds a new one, and so on.

examples: I've always tried to pay my bills on time.

Luisa has always tried to pay her bills on time.

I've always tried to postpone payment as long as possible.

Repeat the activity with the other sentences. Then continue the discussion about money, credit, and consumerism. Try to use a different verb, with a complement, in each sentence.

Summarize your discussion for the class.

activity 2

Work in pairs. Write a 30-second radio or TV commercial. Underline each verb complement you use and use as many as possible. Perform your commercial for the class.

example: A: Tired of <u>letting people take</u> advantage of you? Sick of <u>watching others get</u> promoted while you stay in a dead-end job? Of course you are!

B: Well, folks, today is your lucky day. Our new videotape training session is all you <u>need to buy</u> to change your life for the better forever!

Review of Comparisons with Adjectives and Adverbs

Setting the Context
Pair Interviews

Work in pairs. Take turns interviewing each other. Take notes on the information you learn to help you repeat it to another pair.

1. Do you like to go shopping for food? Why or why not?
2. Do you prefer shopping at a large supermarket or a small neighborhood market? Explain the reasons for your preference.
3. Does your town or city have any ethnic markets, such as Italian, Asian, or Mexican markets? Have you ever been to one? Describe your experience.
4. Do you ever use discount coupons from newspapers or magazines? What are the advantages and disadvantages of using coupons?
5. How do you and the people you live with divide the cost of food? What do you like and/or dislike about the way the cost of food is managed?
6. How does shopping for food in your country differ from shopping for food in this country?

exercise

With your partner from the pair interviews activity, join another pair of students. Take turns sharing information about each other. Notice similarities and differences. Share the most interesting similarities and differences with the class.

Comparisons with Adjectives and Adverbs

comparisons	examples	notes
Simple Form	Generic products aren't **expensive.** We have to decide **quickly.**	Most adjectives come before nouns or after certain verbs. Adverbs can appear in various positions.
as + adjective/ adverb (+ as)	Store brands aren't **as attractive as** name brands, but they may be just **as good.**	
Adjective/ Adverb + -er (than)	Prices are **higher** this year **than** last year, and they're going up **faster.**	
more/less + Adjective/ Adverb (+ than)	Generic brands are **more economical than** name brands. Processed food is usually **less nutritious.**	
Superlative Form	The **largest** package may not be the **wisest** or **most appropriate** choice for your family.	For spelling rules and irregular superlative forms, see page 270.

exercise
Complete these sentences with the correct form of each word in parentheses. The first one is done as an example.

Prices this year are _____ higher _____ than prices were last year.

                                1 (high)

Every year things get _____. To save money, you need to

                                    2 (expensive)

pay the _____ possible prices for the items that you need.

                 3 (low)

Here are some suggestions:

- Compare prices of _____ products. Some brands
  4 (similar)
  of products are _____ than other brands, and the
  5 (expensive)
  quality may not be much _____. The quality of
  6 (good)
  _____ brands, which come in _____
  7 (generic)   8 (plain)
  packages than the _____ "brand names," may be just as
  9 (famous)
  _____ as the quality of the _____ items.
  10 (good)   11 (high-priced)

- When you buy an item on sale, check that the "bargain" price is really

  _____ than the _____ price. If
  12 (low)   13 (regular)
  possible, compare the sale price of the item in _____
  14 (different)
  stores to make sure you are getting the _____ price.
  15 (good)

- Before you go shopping, make a list of the items that are the

  _____ and buy only those things. Don't buy things that
  16 (important)
  you don't need just because they are _____ than usual,
  17 (cheap)
  and don't buy items just to "keep up" with your friends.

- It's not a _____ idea to go food shopping when you are
  18 (good)
  hungry: You will probably be _____ than usual and make
  19 (careful)
  the _____ choices about what you really *need* to buy.
  20 (bad)

Using What You've Learned

activity 1

Work in pairs. Tell your partner about an unwise purchase or deal you made. When you have both finished, join another pair and listen to all four stories. Choose the most interesting story to share with the class.

example: Once I got a letter in the mail saying that I had won a brand new car, a new color TV, a diamond ring, or a remote control phone. All I had to do to collect my prize was visit a housing development and listen to their sales pitch for an hour. It sounded like a super deal to me so I went. It turned out the place was over an hour's drive from my house, the sales pitch was a lot longer than one hour, and they really pressured you to buy a lot or a home. The final insult was watching them pull out these cheap phones out of a big box to give us all our prizes as we left. That was the day I learned there's no free lunch. Now when I get those "You have won . . ." letters in the mail, I throw them right in the trash.

activity 2

Work in small groups. Discuss the meanings of the expressions below. Decide if you agree or disagree with them and explain why. Tell your group about similar sayings in your home country.

1. There's no free lunch.
2. If it seems too good to be true, it probably is.
3. Money talks.
4. Lo barato sale caro. (= What is cheap ends up being expensive.)
5. A bird in the hand is worth two in the bush.

activity 3

Work in pairs. Choose one situation and prepare a dialogue. Then perform your best conversation for the class.

1. You want to buy a used car from a dealer, but you don't know a lot about cars. You want to pay the lowest price possible; the dealer wants you to pay the highest.
2. You picked up your car from a repair shop and paid for the repairs. The next day, it broke down. You call the shop and ask the mechanic to tow your car and to repair it correctly or to give you your money back.
3. You are sitting in a park in a big city. You have heard that there are many shopping bargains in the city, and you want to take advantage of them. Have a conversation with the person on the bench next to you.
4. Think of a consumer situation of your own.

focus on testing

Past Continuous Tense, Infinitives, and Gerunds

Items about the past continuous tense, infinitives, and gerunds are often found on standardized English tests.

Remember . . .

- The past continuous tense expresses past action, usually around a specific past time.
- Infinitives can appear after verbs, adjectives, or nouns.
- Use a gerund following a verb or adjective + preposition.

Part 1: Circle the correct completion for the following sentences.

example: When Mr. Anderson arrived home from work, his wife _____ for him with a loaded gun.
  a. wait
  b. was waiting
  c. waiting
  d. have waited

1. Where _____? I've been waiting for you for over an hour!
  a. were you being
  b. did you are
  c. are you been
  d. have you been
2. They've finally decided _____ a baby after being married for ten years.
  a. having
  b. have
  c. to have
  d. had

Part 2: Circle the letter below the underlined word(s) containing an error.

example: I've been study for our next exam all week.
  A   B   C   D

1. My family often talks about to buy a restaurant together.
       A   B   C   D

2. I don't mind people to wear hats in the theater if they take them off
       A   B   C
  before the show starts.
              D

Index